Dissecting
Hannibal Lecter

Dissecting Hannibal Lecter

Essays on the Novels of Thomas Harris

Edited by Benjamin Szumskyj

with a foreword by Daniel O'Brien

McFarland & Company, Inc., Publishers
Jefferson, North Carolina, and London

LIBRARY OF CONGRESS CATALOGUING-IN-PUBLICATION DATA

Dissecting Hannibal Lecter : essays on the novels of Thomas
    Harris / edited by Benjamin Szumskyj ; with a foreword by
    Daniel O'Brien.
        p.   cm.
    Includes bibliographical references and index.

    ISBN-13: 978-0-7864-3275-2
    softcover : 50# alkaline paper ∞

    1. Harris, Thomas, 1940–   — Criticism and interpretation.
    2. Lecter, Hannibal (Fictitious character)   I. Szumskyj, Benjamin,
    1982–
    PS3558.A6558Z63 2008
    813'.54–dc22   2007041494

British Library cataloguing data are available

Cover photograph: Tom Noonan in *Manhunter* (1986),
Anchor Bay Entertainment/Photofest

Manufactured in the United States of America

*McFarland & Company, Inc., Publishers
    Box 611, Jefferson, North Carolina 28640
    www.mcfarlandpub.com*

To Thomas Harris and Anthony Hopkins

Acknowledgments

This book was supported by many like-minded individuals, for whom I am very grateful. I would first like to thank David Sexton and Dorothy Maguire for their engaging correspondence. I'd like to thank Daniel O'Brien, Peter Messent, Tony Magistrale, Robert H. Waugh, Tony Williams, Davide Mana, S.T. Joshi, Ali S. Karim, Phillip A. Ellis, John Goodrich, Scott D. Briggs, Charles Gramlich and Philip L. Simpson for submitting some of the finest essays on Harris's literature ever to be assembled in one place. I'd also like to mention the late John Brosnan, whose study of Harris's works will one day be published. God bless.

Contents

Foreword

DANIEL O'BRIEN

Thomas Harris has never craved the limelight. The world of book signings, print interviews and talk show appearances is not for him. He shares Hannibal Lecter's love of elusiveness and game-playing. In late 2000, I was asked to write *The Hannibal Files* (2001), a study of the Lecter phenomenon. The original writer had dropped out, for reasons I never fully understood. Writing *The Hannibal Files*—timed to coincide with the release of *Hannibal* (2001)—presented something of a challenge. While I was familiar with the two existing films, this was the first time I read the books, which proved a revelation. Following a tight schedule, I read the novels in quick succession. Perhaps for this reason, Harris's dark universe made an indelible impression on my mind.

I was introduced to Harris's work—albeit indirectly—years before I knew his name. Michael and Harry Medved's *The Golden Turkey Awards* (1980) mentioned the thriller *Black Sunday* (1977), based on Harris's first novel, while taking pot-shots at the superficially similar *Two-Minute Warning* (1976). At first, I confused *Black Sunday* with Mario Bava's *La Maschera del Demonio* (1960), released in the U.S. as *Black Sunday*. I eventually sorted out the two *Black Sundays*, some time before I saw either movie. For the record, the Bava film doesn't feature either Bruce Dern or the Goodyear Blimp. Years later, I watched *Manhunter* (1986) on video. A box-office flop in the U.S., the film received a belated release in the U.K., drawing positive reviews but few filmgoers. While I liked *Manhunter*, I didn't realize it was based on Harris's *Red Dragon* (1981), the literary debut

1

of Dr. Hannibal Lecter. As played by Brian Cox, Lecter — respelled "Lecktor" — struck me as a fascinating character: repellent, hypnotic, barbaric, cultured, murderous, urbane, sneering, affable and utterly bad to the bone. It wasn't until *The Silence of the Lambs* (1991) hit cinemas that Thomas Harris finally impinged on my consciousness. The publication of *Hannibal* (1999), the long-awaited third installment of the Lecter saga, received saturation coverage in the media.

In *The Hannibal Files*, I described Harris as the Stanley Kubrick of popular crime fiction. Like the late director, Harris is a cultivated recluse, rarely granting interviews. Intentionally or not, he has created a mystique around his image. Curiously, given his commitment to privacy, Harris is unconcerned about being identified. There are no J.D. Salinger–style shots of Harris retreating in horror from a camera. Many editions of his books feature a photograph of him on the cover. The bespectacled Harris seems an affable figure, with a broad face, receding gray hair and a white beard. That said, biographical information on Harris is minimal. Born in 1940, or possibly 1941, Harris hails from Jackson, Tennessee. He grew up in his father's hometown of Rich, Mississippi, where Mr Harris Sr. returned to work as a farmer. Harris attended Clarksdale High School, where his mother taught biology. He spent much of his spare time reading and writing. His favorite authors included Ernest Hemingway, doyen of spare prose and unbridled machismo.

After college, Harris studied for a BA in English at Baylor University, Texas, and graduated in 1964. While still at Baylor, he wrote for a local newspaper, the *Herald-Tribune*, working on the night-shift. Employed as a police reporter, Harris found the job unexciting. He also met and married a fellow student named Harriet. They had one daughter, Anne, before divorcing later in the decade. After a sojourn in Europe, Harris became a full-time reporter, covering crime stories in the U.S. and Mexico. Between 1968 and 1974, he worked for the New York City branch of the Associated Press as a general-assignment reporter and editor. Harris continued to focus on crime stories, including several murders. Drawn to fiction, he started writing grisly short stories, selling them to magazines such as *True* and *Argosy*. Apparently, Harris was already noted for his attention to detail, one of his strengths as a writer.

Harris' output is minimal, to say the least. In 31 years, he has published just five books. Even Kubrick managed thirteen films during his career. The success of *Black Sunday* (1975) launched Harris on the literary scene. He devised the idea with fellow Associated Press employees Sam Maull and Dick Riley, and the book was planned as a three-way collaboration, but Harris soon took over the project. The story has Middle Eastern terrorists planning an attack on U.S. civilians, a plot sadly still relevant today. Harris used the real-life Palestinian group Black September, presumably unconcerned about repercussions. Despite mixed reviews, *Black Sunday* proved a bestseller. After the film rights were sold to Paramount, Harris became a full-time novelist. While the movie was a commercial disappointment, he never looked back. After *Red Dragon* introduced Hannibal Lecter to the world, Harris began his journey from successful thriller writer to literary phenomenon. After seven years, Lecter returned in *The Silence of the Lambs* (1988). Harris described his creation as "The adversary for anything like kindness and hope ... he's the dark side of the world." Readers couldn't get enough of the diabolical doctor, and Lecter assumed cult status. The much-delayed *Hannibal* (1999) was received as a major cultural event, resuming Lecter's story after eleven long years. Elevating his character to anti-hero status, Harris created an epic baroque narrative that transcended conventional genres. He conducted in-depth research in Italy, even attending the 1994 trial of serial killer Pietro Pacciardi, known as "Il Mostro di Firenze," The Monster of Florence. While the film version of *Hannibal* received a mixed reception, the Lecter bandwagon rolled ever onward. As readers waited for news of another Harris novel, Hollywood bridged the gap with *Red Dragon* (2002), an efficient yet redundant retread of *Manhunter*. Seven years after *Hannibal*, the fans' patience was rewarded with *Hannibal Rising* (2006), which expands *Hannibal*'s flashback to Lecter's formative years. For the first time, Harris was also to script the film adaptation. A multi-millionaire, Harris divides his time between homes in Rich, Mississippi; Miami, Florida; and Sag Harbor, Long Island, New York. Apparently, the garden of his Sag Harbor house contains a sculpture of a mutilated, limbless woman. Make of that what you will.

The Hannibal Lecter films have been extensively discussed, with numerous websites and multiple DVD special editions. There are endless debates among the fans: is *Manhunter* superior to *The Silence of the Lambs*?; is Brian Cox a better Hannibal Lecter — or Lecktor — than Anthony Hopkins?; does Julianne Moore's Clarice Starling compare with Jodie Foster's definitive portrayal? The original novels have received rather less attention, certainly in terms of serious critical study. This book offers a series of essays on Harris's work, examining his influences, themes, style and achievements. Inevitably, much of the focus must be on Lecter, despite his relatively small role in *Red Dragon*. How did a fictional cannibalistic serial killer become a popular icon? Why does this character resonate with readers worldwide? Is Lecter the most charismatic anti-hero of the modern age? A skilled storyteller, Harris plays with the thriller and horror genres, blending detailed police procedural with unflinching portrayals of psychosis. He excels at sympathetic, if flawed lead characters, whose encounters with Lecter can provoke both trauma and catharsis. If *Red Dragon*'s Will Graham is destroyed by Lecter's world, Clarice Starling ends up embracing it in *Hannibal*. Inspired by William Blake and The biblical Book of Revelation, *Red Dragon* is the narrative of cursed hero Graham, whose empathy with the psychopathic mind leads to his downfall. Wretched villain Francis Dolarhyde also earns our sympathy, despite his terrible actions. Born with a hare lip and cleft palate, Dolarhyde is a classic case of a victim — of child abuse — turned monstrous perpetrator. The small boy nicknamed "Cunt Face" is now the lethal "Tooth Fairy." He even tortures himself, threatening castration with false teeth as punishment for normal sexual desire. Despite obvious nods to *Psycho*'s Norman Bates, Dolarhyde is the one of the best-realized psychopaths in modern literature. Hannibal Lecter is a creature apart, scorning the standard serial killer profile. Lecter is a small man, with distinctive white teeth and maroon eyes. Having gutted Will Graham with a linoleum knife, he takes an almost paternal interest in the latter's health, personal life and return to active service. Lecter proves a father figure in the Cronos mould, devouring his own children figuratively, if not quite literally.

The Silence of the Lambs develops and refines many of the ideas in *Red Dragon*. Opening with quotes from Corinthians and John Donne's *Devotions*, Harris conjures a classic fairy tale of escape and rescue. The focal character is Clarice Starling, a trainee FBI agent. Like Will Graham, Starling has demons of her own, not to mention a daily struggle with institutional male chauvinism. Haunted by the memory of her murdered father, Starling's crusade to save victims stems from both moral conviction and personal need. Her quarry is Jame Gumb, the worst kind of mother's boy, seemingly born with a twisted soul. Butchering women to assume their shape — both mentally and physically — Gumb merits no pity and little understanding. The Death's Head Moth symbolism says it all. Lecter becomes Starling's mentor and confessor, pushing her to confront the past, herself and the clues that lead to Gumb. While Hannibal's grisly jail break underlines his true nature, he offers Starling more than any other man in her life. With Lecter's bizarre guidance, Starling breaks the case, proves her FBI worth and overcomes her inner torment. Unlike Harris's other books, *The Silence of the Lambs* gives its heroine the hope of a normal life. As the next book makes clear, this hope is soon taken away.

Hannibal saw Lecter complete his journey from show-stealing supporting player to co-star to full-fledged leading man. This time out, Starling needs to be rescued, as her fragile world is infected with disillusion and corruption. Conventional morality becomes almost meaningless. The U.S. law enforcement system is a bear pit of naked ambition, power-plays, jealousy, resentment and vindictiveness. This skewed vision is epitomized by child molester Mason Verger, a victim of Lecter infinitely more vile than Lecter himself. Imprisoned in his ruined body, Verger drinks the stolen tears of a young victim with a martini cocktail. The theme of child abuse touches on Lecter's own past, as his younger sister was murdered and devoured by German deserters during World War II. Forsaken by God, young Hannibal realized that the cruelties of mankind were nothing compared to the Supreme Being's whimsical malice. *Hannibal* is best read as Gothic romance or *Grand Guignol*, rather than a plausible psychological thriller. The Lecter-Starling "love story" gives the book a powerful, if melodramatic center, transcending the Florence travelogue, prolonged political intrigue, occasional purple prose and some questionable sexual stereotypes. Lecter and Starling are both orphans, two lost souls in need of healing. With Lecter's help, Starling completes her journey along the path to self-awareness.

In Hannibal Lecter, Thomas Harris created an archetypal nightmare figure, on a par with Count Dracula, Frankenstein's creature and Edward Hyde. Arguably, Lecter is Jekyll and Hyde simultaneously, his dark appetites acknowledged, embraced and indulged with relish. Harris's novels are the modern equivalent of The Brothers Grimm's fairy tales, reflecting universal fears of the dark in a fantastical, palatable form. With or without a big Amarone — or a nice Chianti.

Daniel O'Brien
Southampton, England
Fall 2007

Preface

Critical studies of Thomas Harris's works are sorely lacking, despite some successful attempts to juxtapose the texts with their cinematic adaptations. This book takes the next step in producing essays with larger themes and topics, targeting the academic community, and showcasing the unquestionable literary depth and value of the American author. I was very decisive in my choice of subject matter and worked closely with my essayists to ensure that each essay was both refreshingly new and produced a contemporary outlook on areas of Harris's writings which had received little study or acknowledgment in past literary excursions.

Thomas Harris is one of those authors in the field whom everybody — from reviewers to authors — has showered with constructive and unconstructive criticism, but has rarely received the professional criticism he deserves. Often, while reading his fiction, I found it jarring that there were never any essays or articles that sought to study his novels. Even as I am being entertained, I can not but help read with a critical eye and felt the need to correct this flaw. I am an analytically-minded person, especially in regard to literature, and of the mindset that once an author has become established as a professional and his or her works have undergone countless reprints, there is no time like the present to initiate critical studies.

This work is a collection of interpretive essays that explore Harris from a variety of positions, each essayist adopting a train of thought that is supported by empirical evidence. I have purposely avoided themes and topics which have been exhausted before, within the realm of magazines or journals, in order to ensure that the following essayists have delivered exempt of tireless examinations to determine the influence of one author upon another author or other such readings which are acceptable for readers already familiar with the writings of Harris, but not necessarily for the reader yet to enjoy his novels. This book is directed toward the learned reader who has either read Harris and wishes to see what bridges may be established from his writings to the field of academia, or to the established academic who has heard of Harris and is interested to know the merit his work possesses from a critical point of view, and thus wants to explore a study of his work in which his writings are center stage.

The essays in this collection have been formatted in accordance with the style conventions of the Modern Language Association. Essayists have chosen to directly cite from the most commonly available texts of Harris's writings, as the readers are unlikely to have access to original issues and first editions.

It is my hope that Thomas Harris will, sooner rather than later, be studied in the academic community and will remain an author worthy of study, within a university environment. In reading the essays written specifically for this book, as a reader, you will witness the genius of Thomas Harris as not only an author, but as a human being, showcasing the many layers of psychological, philosophical, literary, historical, theological and autobiographical elements that gave birth to the imagination behind his greatest works of fiction and undoubtedly contribute to the Western canon. *Dissecting Hannibal Lecter: Essays on the Novels of Thomas Harris* will hopefully open such a door and through its thought-provoking essays, initiate a long awaited critical acceptance.

— B.J.J.S.

Introduction

There are few authors as successful or as important as Thomas Harris, an author of only five novels since 1975. A statement as bold as this can be easily proven. As a publishing phenomena, he has sold millions upon millions of books and has been translated into over a dozen languages. His books are almost immediately adapted for cinematic release moments after they hit *any* bestseller's list. As a literary phenomenon, he created a subgenre of "psychological horror," bringing a refreshing originality to what at the time had become a worn-out field of literature, resulting in numerous clones and homages in an array of mediums, from comic books and novels, to television and movies. As a cultural phenomenon, it was Sir Anthony Hopkins's Oscar-winning performance in the cinematic adaptation of *The Silence of the Lambs* that concreted Harris's Hannibal Lecter as a villain future generations would both fear and be intrigued by. In fact, Lester is often voted as one of the best fictional villains of all time. That's some achievement.

Born in Jackson, Tennessee, in 1940, Thomas Harris is somewhat of a recluse. Harris decided early in his career — wisely, many feel — to avoid interviews, public forums, book tours and personal accounts of both his life and his literary works. What little that has been written about him is a combination of speculation, hearsay and what little is revealed by his publishers.

But it seems that this is how Harris wants it. Hannibal Lecter has, in many ways, shadowed his author — a reality which Harris undoubtedly appreciates. Lecter was surrounded by mystique, even in his creation. As Harris writes in the foreword to *The Hannibal Lecter Omnibus* (2001),

9

"Will Graham and I, approaching Dr. Lecter's cell. Graham was tense and I could smell fear on him. I thought Dr. Lecter was asleep and I jumped when he recognized Will Graham by scent without opening his eyes" (ix). Lecter was always there, in Harris's mind, waiting to be interviewed — waiting to be found, waiting to be released. All he needed was the inquisitive nature of a couple of Federal Bureau of Investigation agents.

Thomas Harris is an undisputed literary craftsman, for the four Hannibal Lecter novels — *Red Dragon*, *The Silence of the Lambs*, *Hannibal* and *Hannibal Rising* — realistically depict the evil that a human mind is capable of, while drawing inspiration from real cases of serial murders, forensic psychology, history, as well as the gothic genre. He founded an entire subgenre in crime thrillers and contributed a character to the realm of modern literature so horrifyingly real, with such psychological and philosophical depth, that Harris can rightly be said to have perfected the psychological suspense thriller.

Today, the criticism of Thomas Harris and his fiction are primarily fixed on the cinematic adaptations of his texts, rather then the texts themselves, a bittersweet curse shared by William Peter Blatty and Robert Bloch. While this work is interesting and insightful, the time has come to produce literary criticism on Harris's written work that is, longer than mere "notes" and focuses primarily on the written word.

Dissecting Hannibal Lecter: Essays on the Novels of Thomas Harris is, then, a thorough study of the many rich themes, topics and issues that exist within the diverse writings of the highly respected author, by leading Harris scholars and newcomers alike. While some may be familiar, each is as interesting and important as the other and all are fundamental to further studies.

Peter Messent's "American Gothic: Liminality and the Gothic in Thomas Harris's Hannibal Lecter Novels" opens the volume, discussing Harris's use of the Gothic genre and seeing the genre itself as a type of liminal space where both foreclosed cultural norms and (at a psychological level) repressed desires can be explored and interrogated to powerful effect.

John Goodrich continues with "Hannibal at the Lectern: A Textual Analysis of Dr. Hannibal Lecter's Character and Motivations in Thomas Harris's *Red Dragon* and *The Silence of the Lambs*," exploring Harris's much misunderstood character and seeking to explain his modus operandi.

In "Gothic Romance and Killer Couples in *Black Sunday* and *Hannibal*," Philip L. Simpson sees that Harris, beginning in 1975 with *Black*

Sunday and continuing through the *Hannibal* novels, has made a career of collapsing the boundary between binaries, including the opposition between "respectable" members of society and its outlaws, therefore, the bonding between Starling and Lecter into one murdering couple is quite predictable and fits well within the Gothic tradition.

Robert H. Waugh's engaging "The Butterfly and the Beast: The Imprisoned Soul in Thomas Harris's Lecter Trilogy," discusses motifs of butterflies, hounds, and labyrinths and such figures as the collector, the captive, and the transformed self, as seen in literary classics like Doyle's *The Hound of the Baskervilles*, Poe's "The Gold Bug," Fowles's *The Collector* and even Nabokov's *Lolita*. Also common to all these works are the implicit allusions to the Grecian myth of Theseus, and Waugh provides a very strong case for their association and what Harris achieved by both adopting and revising these antiquated themes and subject matter.

In "This Is the Blind Leading the Blind: Noir, Horror and Reality in Thomas Harris's *Red Dragon*," Davide Mana states that by adopting the newly coded and taxonomically defined "serial killer" as the mover of a fictional investigation, *Red Dragon* recalls, re-uses and updates the classical themes of noir, heralding the birth of neo-noir.

"From *Red Dragon* to *Manhunter*" by Tony Williams explores the archetypal pattern found within *Red Dragon*, commenting upon the character and motivations of Will Graham and the relationships he shares with the cast of characters. Williams also breaches the cinematic adaptation and discusses how the text changes and produces a new interpretation of the character.

S.T. Joshi, in "Suspense vs. Horror: The Case of Thomas Harris," considers Harris's precise place as a genre writer, beginning with the earliest works of fiction found between the mystery and the horror story, slowly working toward a discussion of Harris's four novels and asking the critical question of whether any of them contain sufficient elements of psychological terror to classify them within the realm of the weird tale.

In "Transmogrified Gothic: The Novels of Thomas Harris," Tony Magistrale follows the lead of Twitchell's *Dreadful Pleasures: An Anatomy of Modern Horror* (1987) by using Harris's first three novels to highlight the many characters — hero and villian — that undergo identity transitions and transmogrifications.

In his essay "*Hannibal Rising*: Look Back in Anger," Ali S. Karim explores the evolution of Hannibal Lecter in *Hannibal Rising*, weighing the positive and negative aspects of the novel and explaining what Harris was trying to achieve in a novel that surveys the formative years of the doctor.

"Before Her Lambs Were Silent: Reading Gender and the Feminine in *Red Dragon*" is Phillip A. Ellis's study of the often neglected main female characters of *Red Dragon,* who are often overlooked because of Clarice Starling's fame. Ellis defines the range of feminine responses in the novel, comparing and contrasting these with their corresponding masculine representations in *Red Dragon.*

Scott D. Briggs's "*Black Sunday,* Black September: Thomas Harris's Thriller, from Novel to Film, and the Terror of Reality" is a thorough study of Harris's pre–Hannibal Lecter novel *Black Sunday,* an understudied work that deserves recognition in light of the world's current political climate. Briggs explores the exhaustively research behind the novel and assesses its cinematic adaptation, which has become a cult classic.

Finally, in "Morbidity of the Soul: An Appreciation of *Hannibal,*" I describe my belief that regardless of the mainstream consensus that *Hannibal* did not live up to expectations, the novel warrants reconsideration. The study is a deconstruction of the many strengths *Hannibal* possesses and highlights the well researched train of thought Harris layered throughout every chapter of his underappreciated classic.

Dissecting Hannibal Lecter: Essays on the Novels of Thomas Harris is a study of author Thomas Harris's internationally known anti-hero Dr. Hannibal "the Cannibal" Lecter in *Red Dragon, The Silence of the Lambs, Hannibal* and *Hannibal Rising.* Where previous volumes studying Harris's writings have predominantly focused on the cinematic adaptations of his creations — by directors Michael Mann, Jonathan Demme, Ridley Scott, Brett Ratner and Peter Webber — my chief purpose has been to collect several scholarly essays focusing primarily on the texts themselves, to both spotlight and unearth the many rich themes, topics and issues that have haunted and intrigued readers for over a quarter of a century. Taken as a whole, the volume represents a pioneering attempt by many of the community's leading scholars to chart the development of Dr. Lecter's ascension from imprisoned monster to emancipated beast and his ever-lasting effect on the lives of Will Graham, Clarice Starling and many unsuspecting souls.

Benjamin Szumskyj
Melville, Western Australia
Fall 2007

1

American Gothic

Liminality and the Gothic in Thomas Harris's Hannibal Lecter Novels

PETER MESSENT

I. Liminality and Gothic Forms

Liminality refers primarily to the concept of the threshold, the area between two spaces. And that threshold is predominantly associated with provisionality, instability, intermediate forms; it is what lies between the known and unknown or "other." Noël Carroll writes (by way of Mary Douglas) that "things that are interstitial, that cross the boundaries of the deep categories of a culture's conceptual scheme, are impure ... cognitively threatening" (Tharp 111).[1] And the argument that danger lies in such a liminal area, where the distinctions by which we organize our lives and cultural systems are bought into question, is unsurprising.

However, we should remember that, in the words of Michael Taussig, "a threshold ... allows for illumination as well as extinction" (Veeder 33). Promise then, as well as threat, lies in the notion of the border area, and the possibility of crossover and transgression associated with it. Thus Bill Brown refers to "the mesmerizing power of genuine liminality, where the structures of normalcy and everyday security break down" (123).

In this essay I refer to the four novels by Thomas Harris that feature

This essay originally appeared in the Journal of American Culture *v. 25 i. 1 (23–35).*

Hannibal Lecter, *Red Dragon* (1981), *The Silence of the Lambs* (1988), *Hannibal* (1999) and *Hannibal Rising* (2006). For reasons of space, and because they represent the protagonist at the fullest stage of his development, I mainly focus on the 1988 and 1999 texts. Harris's novels engage with all kinds of threshold areas, thus providing a particularly useful site for an exploration of liminality. Here I briefly describe a number of such engagements — though the spatial limits of this essay require that other areas necessarily go untreated (e.g., gender difference). I focus my argument, however, around Harris's use of the Gothic genre, and follow William Veeder in seeing the genre itself as a type of liminal space where both foreclosed cultural norms and (at a psychological level) repressed desires can be explored and interrogated to powerful effect (23).[2] The boundary crossings that Harris represents in his texts, then, are tied in symbiotic connection to the Gothic forms he uses.

II. The Gothic as Boundary Breaker

Harris, though, also engages the thresholds between genres in his texts, and it is at that point that I commence. Harris's novels would normally be categorized as crime fiction. Thus, for instance, *The Silence of the Lambs* comes to be structured round Clarice Starlings successful quest to discover the identity and whereabouts of serial killer Jame Gumb ("Buffalo Bill") before he murders Catherine Baker Martin, the woman he has abducted. But Harris's is a peculiar type of crime fiction: a type of "antimystery" where, particularly in *Red Dragon* and *The Silence of the Lambs*, the detective "still seeks to unmask a murderer, [but where] the killer is known far in advance by the reader" (Simpson 7). Though the main crimes are successfully solved in these texts, the "sense of linearity," individualized character and epistemological authority normally associated with the genre are all placed under considerable strain (Richter 108). Serial murder (Harris's theme) evacuates much of that affect — that intensity of feeling, emotion and desire, the "charged density of motivation" in the close relationship between victim and criminal — of more traditional forms of detective narrative. In consequence, as Barry Taylor describes:

> The absence of any discernible motivated link between killer and victim ... leads to the criminological classification of serial murder as "motiveless," and so to the shattering of the links which forge the causal and narrative coherence of the "classic" murder. The serial murder is a crime about which no recognizable story can be told (and which therefore generates an apparently uncontainable desire for narration).... [Serial murder stands as] the sign

of a threatening randomness, of a disappearance of meaningful inter-subjective structures, of demotivated action, of the collapse of authoritative models of explanation and interpretation ... and of the disappearance of the subject [215, 216–17].

In Harris, the type of causal and narrative links that Taylor discusses are still recuperable in the cases of Francis Dolarhyde (in *Red Dragon*) and Jame Gumb, though not always by conventional means. The same — in terms of "recognizable story" — is not, though, true of Hannibal Lecter, at least until the final novel in the series.[3] For if detective fiction is about uncovering dark secrets and restoring a disrupted social normality, that is not quite what happens in either *The Silence of the Lambs* or *Hannibal.* The former novel, for instance, ends up with Lecter on the loose, the source of his monstrosity unknowable, his powerful aura overshadowing the social containment of Jame Gumb that provides (part of) the story's end. (That aura extends beyond the borders of the novel — and its film version — into another liminal space that opens up. Harris's texts bear a particularly unstable relationship to the contemporary world to which a book and screen protagonist can take on a cultural life that extends beyond the original representational limits of his performance; where "Hannibal the Cannibal ... has become a celebrity in his own right," Grixti 92.)[4]

It is this monstrousness that suggests that Harris's texts move beyond the borders of the detective genre into territories of the Gothic and Horror. Thus Taylor suggests that:

> Lecter ... is not a reviewed, placed and known subject, but a (fatal) object, some thing that happens (keeps happening) in an unrecuperable serial pre-sentness. Generically, the relationship of the Lecter narrative to the "classical" rationalist form of the detective story involves a shift toward the codes of Gothic and Horror [220].

This shift is given spatial form with — for example — Clarice's descent into the dungeon or labyrinth ("black warren" [345]) which is Gumb's base-ment (and toward the "oubliette" at its center, [329]) in the climactic scene of *The Silence of the Lambs.*[5]

Harris's Horror and Gothic antecedents are clear in the self-conscious inter-textuality that pervades his novels. The *National Tattler* features Clarice in their "Bride of Dracula" series (*The Silence of the Lambs* 346), thus unwittingly twinning her with the other victims into whom Lecter sinks his (in this particular case, metaphorical) teeth. Gumb is linked to Frankenstein in the patchwork monster, his new womanly self, he would make from the body parts (specifically the skin) of others (Young 30 n.17).

Both these references are part of Harris's general "cannibalisation" of the nineteenth century Gothic (Halberstam 51). Other allusions to Jekyll and Hyde, and, in *Hannibal*, to monstrous facial disfigurement (Mason), mock crucifixion scenes, and general visceral excess (disemboweling, man-eating pigs), fills out the Gothic and Horror landscape to which I refer here (I treat these as twinned genres, though it is Horror that is associated strongly with visceral excess).

The potential of the Gothic genre to move between, and to rupture, conventional generic and conceptual boundaries, is suggested by Maggie Kilgour (in her essay "Dr. Frankenstein Meets Dr. Freud") when she writes that the genre is "always a boundary breaker which erodes any neat distinctions between formats and modes, combining sentimentality and the grotesque, romance and terror ... philosophy and nonsense. This promiscuous generic cross-breeding is part of the Gothic's "subverting of stable norms" (40). One question we might ask here, triggered by Kilgour's view of this boundary-breaking capacity, is about the conclusions we might draw from the way Harris combines what we might call low and high culture within the liminal space of his Gothic texts. Jonathan Romney's review of the film version of *Hannibal* points directly to the disconcerting nature of this activity, commenting that:

> By counter pointing such horrors as man-eating boars against classical mnemonic systems, Harris served a finely balanced mixture of the sickening and the *soigné*, much as the cannibal gourmet Lecter himself lingered over the shallots and caper berries in his own ghoulish cuisine. [Lecter] is now in business in Florence as a Renaissance scholar ... darkly dispensing quotations from Dante's *La Vita Nuova*—a nightmare mix of Ted Bundy and George Steiner [3].

The "unstable affinity" between the aesthetic categories of "low" and "high" is now generally recognized. "'Art,'" in Elizabeth Young's words, "is only ever a relative term, subject to constant canonical erosion" (6). Stallybrass and White reinforce the point,[6] saying that the "bourgeois subject" has always:

> marked out ... [the] low ... as dirty, repulsive, noisy, contaminating. Yet that very act of exclusion was constitutive of its identity. The low was internalised under the sign of negation and disgust. But disgust always bears the imprint of desire [191].

In the Gothic space of Harris's text, high and low are juxtaposed, indeed clash violently. To focus just on *Hannibal*, we have on the one hand those wild boar making "a bloody dish" (423) of the face on which they feed;

descriptions of an exotic eel with "razor sharp teeth," "stuffed" (430) into a human mouth and seizing the tongue within to inevitable deadly effect. And, of course, we have Hannibal's cannibalism. On the other, we have the quoting of Dante's first sonnet in both Italian and English (122), an exposition of Dante's *Inferno* (195–97), references to Stephen Hawking's work on time and entropy (362–63) and to Frances A. Yates's *The Art of Memory* (see, for instance, 251–54). It is accordingly tempting to read the book as a type of hybrid monster, a "nightmare mix" (to recall Romney) of high and low (a phrase itself which takes us back to the Gothic and the notion of what we normally repress). But it must be recognized that the references to Hawking, Yates, and others are not just decorative flash and filigree. Rather they become an essential component of a text which builds toward Lecter's apparent success (with Clarice's help) in moving away from what Abraham and Torok call incorporation ("a trauma whose ... devastating emotional consequences are entombed" [99]).[7] For it seems that Lecter leaves the traumatic loss of his sister — and the cannibalism that comes to be associated with it[8] — finally behind him (though the heterosexual relationship with Clarice which replaces it seems very nearly as unhealthy: see my later discussion).

Harris's use of the Gothic allows him to bring together such materials and to challenge his audience's preconceptions concerning what is aesthetically appropriate in any given textual space. The success of such tactics remains problematic. The logic of the connections made may indeed be convincing, but the disparity of the types of discourse introduced, and the extreme nature of the gap between visceral and conceptual materials, may well prove too great for the majority of readers to bridge satisfactorily. It may, in turn, then be revealing that the film version of *Hannibal* omits the majority of references to the material culled from Hawkings and Yates, as well as any reference to the dead sister. On the other hand, this may only be a sign of Hollywood's flattening-out effect on an unusual and troubling text. The film's alteration of the book's ending can be read similarly.

III. Cannibalism in Harris's Texts

I return now, though, to Stallybrass and White and their reading of the "low" as "internalized under the sign of negation and disgust," a disgust that "always bears the imprint of desire." For this quote take us, not unexpectedly, to the subject of cannibalism and its function in Harris's texts. In *From Communion to Cannibalism: An Anatomy of Metaphors of*

Incorporation, Maggie Kilgour charts the type of binaries we use to produce meaning, that form the basis of the symbolic systems that structure our lives: cooked and raw, center and periphery, high and low, familiar and foreign, host and guest, and so on (3).[9] She discusses the positioning of these pairs in "a divided, hierarchically ordered, and yet apparently coherent system, in which order is guaranteed by the authoritative and superior term's control of the inferior" (3).[10] In Harris's Gothic novels, such binary relations break down in a textual space where both terms in such pairings are given equal authority. For as Barry Taylor writes:

> The novels [*Red Dragon* and *The Silence of the Lambs*] define Lecter through an oxymoronic implosion of definitions: brilliant scientist and bestial madman, a psychiatric case-study whom, as a psychiatrist himself, ridicules the models which his captors apply to him, the serial-killer who is consultant to the police. More fundamentally, Lecter confounds the monstrous and the civilised, the violence of nature and the refinements of culture, the raw and the cooked: he is a cannibal who we first see, in *Red Dragon*, reading Alexandre Dumas's *Grande Dictionnaire de Cuisine*.... [H]e is an ethical abomination with whom one is manoeuvered into identification [219–220].

I focus on the three binaries Taylor identifies — monstrous and civilized, nature and culture, the raw and the cooked — and what is implied by Lecter's cannibal status.[11]

The subject of cannibalism has moved right to the foreground of contemporary anthropological debate. Rather than attempting to follow the full paths of such debate, I highlight a number of key issues as I make my connections to Harris's novels. One recent anthropological controversy about cannibalism (anthropophagy) centers round the work of William Arens. In *The Man-Eating Myth* (1979), he claims that cannibalism (in Kilgour's words) "may never have existed as a ritualized practice, but is rather a myth used by races to assert their superiority over others." Anthropology itself, in its use of cannibalism, is then "a prime example of ... 'colonial discourse': the strategies through which imperialism justifies its own desire to absorb others by projecting that desire onto a demonized 'other'" ("The Function of Cannibalism at the Present Time," 239–240). Such a reading acts to disconcert our conventional dichotomy of civilized (culture) versus savage (nature).

If Arens's thesis is now seen as extreme, the analogy between related forms of desire is illuminating. It connects in turn with current debates based on the findings of archaeology: that cannibalism did exist and the imputation that it was widespread. For if *all* our ancestors were cannibalistic, then divisions between "us" and "them" (barbarous peoples) again start to collapse.

These debates can be linked in turn to a number of related but different readings of cannibalism. One of these is that associated with Montaigne, and his verdict (atypical in his time) that "I thinke there is more barbarisme in eating men alive, than to feed upon them being dead" (Bartolovich 213). Here, cannibalism is not in question, but the so-called savage act is now constructed as preferable to the "civilized" order that would replace it. Such an interpretation comes from a variety of sources. Cannibal societies can be seen as egalitarian communities, whereas in Europe (the source of Montaigne's comparisons) there existed "flagrant disparities within a civilised community based on unequal wealth and arbitrary laws" (Lestringant 2).[12] Cannibals, too — and rather differently — can be seen in their home (South American) context as part of the honorable forms of warfare. There, according to Lestringant, cannibalism functioned as a "symbolic system," an "honour-based warrior custom," (98) and contrasted with the brutal and acquisitive activities of the conquistadors, who left an empire in ruins, a people enslaved and millions dead, merely for "traffic in Pearls and Pepper" (105).[13] Cannibalism has been redefined and re-conceptualized in a more recent period but again in analogous terms. In the writing of Karl Marx, capitalism is metaphorically allied to cannibalism, feeding off the living bodies and blood of the workers. Analogies to vampirism and werewolves ("the werewolf like hunger for surplus labor") suggest the true nature of "capitalist appetite": that "the capitalist is a cannibal-manqué" (Bartolovich 212–13). Bartolovich here makes reference to vampirism, the werewolf, the parasite, and the cannibal as being part of the same continuum.

To sum up, in all these readings, cannibals, to use Bartolovich's words, "are sited by Western subjects *among themselves* rather than in a distant 'other' world" (234). Cannibalism, in other words, comes to lie at the center of civilization, not at its fringes. (Kilgour focuses on the construction of the modern subject as "'a cannibal ego' more insidious than any hottentot," 247).[14] And we should recall at this point Freudian theory, despite its very different base in the child-parent dynamic, with its belief, too, in "cannibalism [as] the basis of civilization." ("In the grim myth of *Totem and Taboo* [civilization] originates in the murder and eating of the father by his sons," 244). Cannibalism then becomes a *metaphor* (and the gap between the literal and the metaphorical is one to which I will return) for the worst aspects of western culture: the diverse forms of imperialism — or excessive appetites — through which we justify our "desire to absorb others" (240).

Such forms of imperialism, though, operate on an individual as well as group level, and it is here that the significance of Hannibal Lecter becomes most apparent. For Lecter, and I follow Kilgour's argument closely here, becomes:

> a literally cannibal ego ... the most exaggerated version of the modern Hobbesian individual, governed only by will and appetite, detached from the world and other humans, whom he sees only as objects for his own consumption [248].

Lecter's desire then cannot be contained within "proper" limits, violently incorporates the other, extends his own bodily territories in the pursuit of his own private needs. We might recall *Red Dragon* at this point and Tony Magistrale's analysis of the Blakean motifs in the text. The individualistic romantic urge to pursue "the lineaments of Gratified Desire" has now become perversely associated not with genuine artistic and imaginative fulfillment ("the creative will to assert and transform") but with "mere acts of degraded butchery" (30).

There is another side to this too, though, for cannibalism has both perpetrator and victim. And to identify with the latter is necessarily to fear the invasive appetite of the other, to be aware of the fragility and vulnerability of one's own bodily (and psychic) self. If on the one hand we have the image of the hungry and autonomous subject feeding off the world at his disposal, on the other, and equally, we have the fear of the loss of individual authority and control, of an "increasing sense of individual helplessness." Bodily mutilation, in such a reading, becomes a reminder of "the fragile nature of all limits and boundaries," of all that fearfully "shakes our sense of bourgeois identity." "Images of the bleeding body," Barbara Creed indicates, "point symbolically to the fragile nature of the self, its lack of secure boundaries, the ease with which it might lose definition, fall apart, or bleed into nothingness" (129, 157, 154, 144). Fears about extreme individualism and about "the fragmentation of the subject" (Jameson's phrase — [79–80] takes on added meaning here) both then feed into the texts that Harris writes. It is the Gothic use he makes of monstrousness, the variety of fears it arouses, and its relationship to the apparently normative that become my focus as my argument now develops.

IV. Harris and Monstrousness

The cannibalism motif develops in a number of ways in Harris's novels. First, I consider the pun about Hannibal Lecter's good taste that runs through the series. Staeger describes the pun as "a lawful disruption of traditional meanings." Her suggestion that wordplay of this type can "open up fissures in social categorising" (146) is apposite in terms of Harris's representation of Lecter as one who evades conventional interpretative judgments. Lecter is a man who appreciates the finer things in life. His taste is finely developed, both in the material and cultural senses — and has been greatly influenced (as illustrated in *Hannibal Rising*) by his relationship with Lady Murasaki, the Japanese wife of the uncle who takes Hannibal into his care, at his French chateau, after the boy has been orphaned in Lithuania during the latter stages of the second World War. Hannibal's fine taste as an adult is evidenced in his purchase of Chateau Petrus Bordeaux at $36,000 a case; in the way he checks the Scarlatti played by the Florence Chamber Orchestra against a 1688 version of the score on hand-copied parchment (*Hannibal* 262, 179). Two forms of his taste, one admirable (cultured) and the other (for human flesh) abominable, meet when the "infuriatingly inept" viola player in the Florence Orchestra goes "oddly missing," to be savored, we can assume, at least in part, by Lecter in the form of edible delicacy.

In the fissures in categorization that open up here, Harris would appear to indicate that cannibalism is our civilization's "dark secret": that "the pretence of refinement masks a secret and increased appetite for flesh." Real and metaphorical cannibalism intertwine in the suggestion that our original appetites, "our ferocious buried hungers," still drive us, and that the process of sublimation (the replacement of lower by higher forms of behavior) is a fraud: "Man-eating is a reality — it is civilisation that is the myth" (Kilgore, "The Function of Cannibalism at the Present Time" 249, 259). Harris's Gothic forms allow us to recognize hungers, desires, and raw appetites that are usually denied or repressed.

A second way in which the cannibalism motif plays throughout these texts is in the doubling that occurs with more legitimate forms of activity. If cannibalism enacts the ingestion of one body by another, a transgression of boundaries, and the destruction of identity, then the workings of what we suppose to be "civilization" offer an analogy for such processes. Lecter is a psychiatrist by profession, a career path metaphorically twinned with his cannibalistic activities. So, in Elizabeth Young's words, "the characterisation of the Freudian Dr. Lecter as serial killer offers a purposeful unmasking of the authority of the Freudian master" (24). Lecter penetrates the minds as well as the bodies of others (see for instance his effect on Miggs in *The Silence of the Lambs*): "he specializes in getting ... into one's thoughts [as well as "under one's skin"] and he makes little of the classic body / mind split as he eats bodies and sucks minds dry" (Halberstam 39). Young notes that in *Silence of the Lambs*, Hannibal the "male invader ... acts as an invasive reader of Clarice Starling" (28 n.6).[15] Again, here, what we take for refinement (the analyst as benevolent imperialist; a doctor who colonizes the mind rather than the body) is revealed as something rather different, as "the psychological imperialist turns out to be a real cannibal.... Analysis and cannibalism thus form a continuum.... [T]o see into the minds of others is an act of aggression, a psychic imperialist invasion, which leads to a physical consumption" ("The Function of Cannibalism at the Present Time" 249–250).

The motifs of invasive surveillance associated here with psychoanalysis elide with the act of physical consumption (though this time in animal, not human, form) in *Hannibal*, where Mason's deformities are the result of Lecter's peculiar brand of "therapy." For Lecter suggests (this time, using powerful drugs to achieve his effect) that Mason peel off his own face with a shard of glass from the mirror before which he narcissistically performs. Mason then feeds his face to the dogs (loosed by Lecter) that he keeps for his own sadistic investigative ends (60–62).

There is one further point that should be made here, and that involves the continuum implicit in Harris (and particularly in *Hannibal*) not just between mind and body, but also between the psychological and the social. If Freud imagined himself as a detective ("The Function of Cannibalism at the Present Time" 250), then Clarice is one.[16] She is not however a Private Eye but a public one. Young notes that in *The Silence of the Lambs*, Clarice's "feminist tal[e] of triumphant individualism" is in part undermined by the fact that the final status she gains as (FBI) "agent" is in "the most reactionary of political settings." She continues:

> The success of her coming-of-age as an FBI agent means that she is now fully trained to enforce the power of the state through modes of invasion, surveillance, entrapment, discipline and punishment that not only parallel but literalise, as Foucault's work helps to remind us, the operative modes of psychoanalysis itself [25].

In *Hannibal*, however, it is Clarice's own life that is subject to the ruthless monitorings of the Bureau. Krendler subjects Staling to close surveillance, boxes her into a "little low-ceiling life" (454), metaphorically gets right under her skin. The invasive scopic authority of both psychoanalysis and FBI are part of a piece, an extension, so Harris would metaphorically suggest of other, more physical, forms of cannibalistic feedings. Clarice's final evasion of "authority and taboo" (454), when she literally ingests (part of) Krendler's body and rids his influence from her life, provides an appropriate conclusion to the chains of connection thus developed. A taboo form of invasive activity cancels out that which is official and licit as the two meet together in ironic juxtaposition.

The type of doubling that occurs in the novel (here, cannibalism and psychoanalysis, psychoanalysis and investigative state agency) is typical of the Gothic form. Indeed, doubling appears throughout Harris's texts in his representations of the monstrous-civilized relation. I focus very briefly here on the figure of Mason Verger in *Hannibal* as exemplar. Mason Verger is monstrous in appearance. With a single, lidless eyeball, "noseless and lipless, with no soft tissue on his face ... all teeth, like a creature of the deep, deep ocean" (57), his features are a measure of his primal viciousness. Verger, like Hannibal, is in the meat business, as to an extent is Clarice, who "from early life ... had known much more than she wished to know about meat processing" (*The Silence of the Lambs* 26). Present head of a meat-packing dynasty, the Verger family fortune is based in part on a mixture of business malpractice and political corruption. Capitalist corporate America functions, so Harris implies, through cannibalistic practices, here literalized (though displaced onto, or into, the bodies of the consumer) when we are told:

> The "embalmed beef" scandal in the Spanish-American War hardly touched the Vergers. When Upton Sinclair and the muckrakers investigated dangerous packing-plant conditions in Chicago, they found that several Verger employees had been rendered into lard inadvertently, canned and sold as Durham's Pure Leaf Lard, a favorite of bakers. The blame did not stick to the Vergers. The matter cost them not a single government contract [52].

A sadist and in the past a pedophile too (or so it is strongly suggested), and also the incestuous abuser of his sister, Mason's social respectability, power and ability to manipulate both other individuals and the law for entirely selfish and evil ends leaves the supposed space between monstrous and civilized in absolute question. The contrast between Mason's abuse of his sister and Lecter's trauma that results from the loss of Mischa (and from his *unwitting* "abuse" of her) is also pertinent.

In *Red Dragon*, FBI man Will Graham's ability to solve violent crime is based not on logic but on instinct, the uncomfortable affinity between his imagination and that of his quarry. Serial murderer and law-enforcer are (almost) twinned in symbiotic connection:

> Graham understood murder uncomfortably well....
>   He wondered if, in the great body of humankind, in the minds of men set on civilization, the vicious urges we control in ourselves and the dark instinctive knowledge of those urges function like the crippled virus the body arms against.
>   He wondered if the old, awful urges are the virus that makes vaccine [354].

The relation between virus and vaccine progressively slips as Harris's series continues. In *The Silence of the Lambs*, Lecter literally wears a (very mangled) policemen's face (232), torn from his victim as disguise, when he escapes from Memphis. In *Hannibal*, it is he who first punishes Mason for his "crimes." Harris destabilizes the relationship between hunter and hunted, criminality and law, throughout his texts.

V. Another View of Hannibal

At this point of my argument, I return to *Hannibal* (but by way of *Hannibal Rising*) to examine the series of linked textual moves that come to complicate his earlier representations of cannibalism and the monstrous. Hannibal, in the first three books in the series, is described as "the monster," an unknowable and red-eyed (*Silence* 15) satanic figure with an aura of pure malevolence around him ("Can you stand to say I'm evil ... Officer Starling?" 20). In *Hannibal*, unexpectedly, we are given an explanation for the type of person he is.[17] His own cannibalism (it is implied — though the details given are of such brevity that any interpretative move can only be tentative here) may be a type of repetition compulsion, stemming from events that occurred in Lithuania in 1944 when he was six years old, and starving army deserters took his sister Mischa for food following the collapse of the (German's) Eastern Front (see 255–56).

This explanatory framework is considerably expanded in *Hannibal Rising*, the retrospective story of Hannibal's childhood and young adulthood, from eight to (some) eighteen years old. We are now given a much fuller description of Mischa's death, which now occurs just slightly later in Hannibal's life. Indeed, part of the text's narrative movement lies in the account of Hannibal's difficult recovery of this repressed traumatic memory, and his failure fully to recover from the effects of what for him stands as an affective primal scene. The army deserters are given more fully-rounded form here as 'Hiwis' (Lithuanians who worked for the Nazis and who then, as the Russian Army advanced and beat the Germans back, killed and looted for their own private and predatory ends). Their killing (and eating) of Mischa, and Hannibal's own return to his childhood home and rediscovery of his sister's remains — the image of her baby teeth seen in the "reeking stool pit" carried over from *Hannibal* (255) turns out to be a false memory — form the prelude to what is essentially a revenge narrative: one which concludes with Hannibal slashing and screaming as he carves the initials of his dead sister's name on the dying body of her murderer.[18]

Harris threads his way carefully here between criminal act and the representation of excess (Hannibal's murderous acts of revenge) as they begin in psychologically explicable terms, and end in pure evil, sheer monstrousness. But it is important to recognize that this psychological groundwork *is* now laid, creating readerly empathy for Hannibal, and retrospectively creating connections between him and the Clarice of *The Silence of the Lambs*: both orphans, neither able to do anything to help the innocent lambs whose deaths have so affected them (Mischa now takes on this symbolic role). But Hannibal's acts of revenge are shown as strongly motivated and a product of his distressed emotional and mental state. His cannibalistic acts may consequently be read as a compulsive replaying of the savagery that others have loosed on his family, and part of the necessary payback he intends. Thus when the chef at his uncle's chateau tells Hannibal that "the best morsels of the fish are the cheeks. This is true of many creatures" (107), the reader is more than ready (given her or his knowledge of the prior Hannibal Lecter novels) for what inevitably follows. Hannibal, now thirteen, kills the local butcher, Paul, for his gratuitous sexual insults directed at Lady Murasaki. A type of doubling occurs here as Hannibal has, at this moment, a flash-back of Grutas (the leader of the deserters) just before Mischa's death (93), and as he plays out — this time more successfully — the role of protector of delicate womanhood that (in his sister's case) had been impossible. Murasaki then discovers Paul's decapitated head, but with the cheeks missing (110).[19] Later, when Hannibal kills Dortlich (the first of his sister's killers to be hunted down), he completes the act by cooking, and — we assume — eating, "a brochette, cheeks and morels" (228), the former ingredient taken from his victim.

But if Harris "explains" Lecter's murderous and cannibalistic actions in this way, he also makes it clear that this history, and Hannibal's feelings and consequent actions, have made him — at this point — finally and fatally monstrous. We see him, for most of *Hannibal Rising*, in what (again) we might call a liminal position. A functioning member of the surrounding social world, and apparently building a relationship with his (now-widowed) aunt-by-marriage (Murasaki) that seems to promise sexual and emotional fulfillment, he is at the same time driven in an (opposite) murderous and savage direction by the traumatic childhood event, and his need to avenge it. And if Inspector Popil recognizes something "Other" (122) in Hannibal almost as soon as he meets him, by the end of the narrative Hannibal is fully positioned outside the community, with — as Murasaki recognizes — nothing now left in him to love (303), seemingly frozen inside forever (308), "entered [upon] his heart's long winter ... not visited in dreams as humans are" (310). The couplet from *Faust* introducing the final section of the book ("I'd yield me to the Devil instantly, / Did it not happen that myself am he!" 311) indicates that the initial psychological cause has resulted (despite Murasaki's seeming promise of redemption) in a final monstrous otherness. And this is reinforced as Hannibal, now started on his American career as an intern at Johns Hopkins, ends the book with the final revenge killing for his sister while he is on vacation in Quebec: "He was not torn at all by anger anymore, or tortured by dream. This was a holiday, and killing Grenz was preferable to skiing" (322).

The knowledge we have of Lecter's past, given in extreme brevity in *Hannibal* and in more detail (and given in slightly different form) in *Hannibal Rising*, is essential background for an understanding of Lecter's connection with Clarice as it is represented much later in his life, in *Hannibal*. Cannibalism plays its part in their developing relationship, too, but here (and this is what I have been moving toward) it is represented in rather a different light. For one of the most genuinely shocking scenes in *Hannibal* is when Clarice feeds — together with Lecter — on Krendler's brain. Krendler typifies aggressive male sexuality and its relationship to institutional power, as Chilton did to lesser extent in *The Silence of the Lambs*. He is primarily responsible for the reducing of Clarice's agency (as FBI employee, though the term signifies it is done more widely) to a shadow. The scene, in chapter 100 of the novel, provides a reminder that cannibalism, or at least the act of ingestion and incorporation of which cannibalism consists, can have other implications than those I have described previously. For it is now represented as echoes of a communion service, with Clarice and Hannibal as joint communicants.

The Catholic communion service is a sacramental rite where the bread and wine consumed are the body and blood of Christ "transubstantiated," offered to mankind for its redemption. The words used by the priest, echoing Christ's own, are "This Is My Body. This Is My Blood." In "The Function of Cannibalism at the Present Time," Kilgour describes the communion service as "a banquet at which host and guest can come together without one subsuming the other, as both eat and are eaten."[20] For, as the body of Christ is consumed by the individual, so he or she becomes part of Christ, and of the body of the Church which the latter represents:

> The individual bodies of the members of the community are identified with the corporate body of the Church, which in turn is identified with the individual body of the sacrificed Christ. The two essential characteristics of the early rite are that it is a sacrifice and a corporate act [Kilgour 79–80].

The eating of Krendler's body — with "the flames of candles," "creamy napery" and "a screen of flowers" (468) providing appropriate appurtenances to the ceremony — is both a type of ritual sacrifice (though not one to which the victim agrees) and communal act. What we have here is an odd parody of the communion service, and one that, at first glance, does not easily fit the depictions of cannibalism in the earlier novels about the "adult" Hannibal (where it is the very sign of Lecter's rapacious male ego, his monstrous appetite for others). For here, the taboo Clarice breaks, as she sups with Lecter, appears symbolically to release her from repressive and corrupt "authority." From this point she enters into a community of two — marked by her heterosexual relationship with Lecter — at one remove from the lack of opportunities, injustices and misogynies of life in the normative American social and professional world.[21]

Another strange episode (chapter 101) then immediately follows. Here Clarice re-directs Lecter's desire to "make a place for [his dead sister] Mischa in the world ... the place now occupied by Clarice Starling" (436) by suggesting that such room be found within his mind, rather than in outside reality, in her own substitute form (476). Her suggestion that Hannibal might have been required to give up feeding at his mother's breast too soon (relinquished to Mischa) is then followed by her freeing her own breast and Lecter bending "his dark sleek head ... to her coral and cream in the firelight" (477).

Well, just what are we supposed to make of this? It seems that Harris here plays deliberately on Freud. (The text, then, is apparently contradictory in that the attack on psychoanalysis and the Freudian master gives way to a reliance on those same Freudian models. And an apparent cure also replaces invasion in Lecter's act of literally digging up Clarice's father's body in order for her to come to terms with his dead presence; to move beyond her Electra complex. A more convincing reading of this, of course, is to see Lecter helping Clarice to replace one authority figure with another — that of Lecter himself). Freud characterizes the "oral phase of sexual development" as "cannibalistic existence." The infant, in this phase:

> has no sense of its own separation from the world: it is aware only of the mother's breast, which it does not see as a separate object but, as it can be taken inside itself, as part of itself. The individual's original existence ... is thus described as a cannibalistic experience of fluid boundaries between self and world, who are joined in a symbiotic oneness ["The Function of Cannibalism at the Present Time," 244].[22]

What Clarice does in the scene described is, apparently, to re-create for Lecter that original form of (cannibal) satisfaction. Such oral cannibalism functions as "ritual of re-union," repairing the gap between self and other, self and world ("The Function of Cannibalism at the Present Time," 247). The implication here is that Lecter's relationship with his mother was been broken off too quickly in infancy. What Clarice then does here is to translate Freudian theory to literal practice. Taking the place of the too-soon-departed mother she allows Lecter to re-create a childhood primal scene (which has occurred before, and which now replaces the alternative primal scene of Mischa's murder).

The interpretation of both these episodes must be provisional and indeterminate. We can read them, though, to suggest that Lecter can, through Clarice's actions (this time successfully) separate from the mother, and can now — to push this reading to its limits — re-take a place in a (relatively) normal sexual and social world, leaving both forms of cannibalism behind him. To see it thus is to see Clarice allowing Lecter to remember his dismembered self, curing him by making him whole.[23] However, it is equally, and perhaps more, likely that this description of the act of breast-feeding might be seen to symbolize some kind of retreat on Lecter's part into the realm of fantasy or madness.

To put this last suggestion another way, the actions and relationships in the two related scenes I have just described are not interpretatively transparent. In particular, the matter of Clarice's agency is indeterminate and unclear. On the one hand, Clarice does appear — as in the breast-feeding scene — to exercise some authority and responsibility for what occurs. And for other hints of her autonomy in these chapters, one might point to Lecter's wondering whether she has chosen (my word) to carry her gun (466) and to her ability to redirect Lecter's way of thinking with what appears to be an authoritative intervention (476). But on the other, and this I would suggest is the predominant emphasis, Clarice seems to have been fashioned (by Lecter) for the part she now plays. There are a number of references made to the drugs he gives her (see 439, 450, 484) and, at a slightly earlier point, to the fact that she is "both herself and not herself" (441). In other words, Lecter's rapacious appetites may now have simply changed direction, to focus carnally (rather than carnivorously) on Clarice; and he (in an odd and highly indeterminate sense) may have programmed her to enable his own transformation from one cannibal identity to a similar, but metaphorical, other one: as voracious sexual partner. Harris's disturbing description that Lecter and Clarice's "relationship has a great deal to do with the penetration of Clarice Starling, which she avidly welcomes and encourages" (483), with its connotations of invasive violence, then makes more sense. So, too, do the words that follow the example of her "resource" in suggesting the different form that Mischa's "place in the world" might take, in the immediate check given to any assumption of self-determination. For here a Frankensteinian echo enters into the text with the words, "perhaps [Lecter] felt a vague concern that he had built [Clarice] better then he knew" (476–77). We are left between a number of possibilities here, some of which are troubling. But to see these scenes as a logical conclusion to Lecter's designs on both Clarice's mind and her body certainly does not seem inappropriate.[24]

VI. Cannibalism and Monstrosity as Metaphorically Suggestive

Of course it would be easy to accuse me, or Harris, or both of us, of writing twaddle here. And it might be pointed out that the pair of scenes I describe also feature Krendler, still conscious, the top of his skull surgically removed, exclaiming "Smells great!" as his brains are literally fried (473)! Freudian theory is used above, it might be argued, to make an entirely implausible case about the relationship between two forms of cannibalism (metaphoric and literal). Moreover I (and perhaps Harris) give two distinct accounts for the sources of Lecter's aberrant behavior, via the sister's death and the mother's breast, thus leaving us with a conflicted "explanation." This, though, takes us back to my start in the notion of the Gothic as "boundary breaker ... combining ... philosophy [or in this case psychology] and nonsense."

And at one level I would not argue against the accusation of "nonsense." Neither, though, would I dismiss the serious and thoughtful nature of the ideas contained within the text. In the final part of my argument I finally return to the notion of the liminal — though my entire essay has implicitly addressed this subject with its focus on transgression, instability, and the crossing of limits. But it is the liminality of the Gothic mode that is particularly important here, and its consequent ability to contain just the type of provocative, even illuminating, contradictions and correspondences I have described to this point.

As my argument has proceeded I have found myself moving repeatedly from the literal to the metaphoric and back again, and it is that move that provides the springboard for this final section. Harris's texts, and the Gothic generally, use a strategy of "transformation of [the] figurative to [the] literal." Thus Miggs's act, for instance, of throwing his semen in Clarice's face in *The Silence of the Lambs* is a literalization of Chilton's "more socially acceptable" "come-on" to her. Jame Gumb's house, with labyrinthine cellar and pit, is a "literal prison-house of gender" (Young 10). Dolarhyde in *Red Dragon* eats the William Blake painting, "The Great Red Dragon," that has inspired him (298), literally — as he assumes — to ingest the physical and sexual power it represents. Pazzi in *Hannibal* pays for his avarice as his "greedy guts" are sent spilling from his body (203, 210). Lecter takes the metaphor "good enough to eat" absolutely at face value.

Throughout this essay, when I have been discussing cannibalism, I have read Lecter's literal tearings of the flesh in metaphorical terms (as a figure for capitalism, psychoanalysis, child-mother relationships, etc.). Maggie Kilgour gives a brilliant reading of the metaphors (including that of cannibalism) that cluster round the activity of eating and incorporation in the introduction of her *From Communion to Cannibalism*. The extensive range of such metaphorical activity becomes clear as she does so. And it would be easy to extend the range of cannibal metaphors one can apply as we discuss Harris's novels. The hint in Lecter's name, the many references to the excesses of tabloid journalism and its obsessive interest in serial killers, and, in *Hannibal*, to the "collectors of hideous arcana" who buy the bootlegged police photos of Lecter's "outrages" (47), indicate that Harris is warning his readers of their own cannibalistic tendencies, asking in what ways they are gratified as they feed voraciously off stories of monstrous and violently perverse acts, and what this says about their own good taste. Reviewing the film version of *Hannibal* in the London *Evening Standard* (15 February 2001) Alexander Walker says that "It's ... pretty repugnant to think that a movie costing millions of dollars is being hyped by millions more, all to sell voyeuristic cruelty as entertainment to a world already spilling over with insensate real-life crimes" (29). It is tempting too, as Kilgour does in "The Function of Cannibalism at the Present Time," to apply the cannibalistic metaphor to the literary (and film) critic too: "eager to sink his teeth into fresh kill" (242).[25]

But this is where I return to liminality. I have shown the way in which Harris's Gothic texts use literal acts of cannibalism and monstrosity as metaphorically suggestive. Those metaphors are then used to undermine a series of boundaries and differences that we would normally take for granted. Thus the line is blurred between the taboo act of cannibalism and the deepest instinctual needs that drive human beings as a species (the murderous desires at the heart of all "civilized" beings). The boundaries between this latter psychological realm and the social are also crossed and blurred, for monstrous individuality is linked to a social order that uses its powers to feed (as well as to challenge) such individual needs, and whose larger corporate appetites threaten to chew up, and then to spit out as pulp, the majority of its subjects. Psychoanalysis stands here as one point of interchange between these two worlds, controlling the excesses of private desire but to the benefit either of the therapist himself or of the invasive and reductive public order which he ultimately may be seen to represent.

But this is exactly the point at which we need to step back, to remind ourselves that metaphor is "a suspiciously dualistic trope that yet collapses opposition," and that it is built on the principle of *difference* as well as similarity (*From Communion to Cannibalism* 16). There is in fact a difference between the deepest of instinctual desires (if we accept such a version of the psyche) and practiced forms of behavior. Cannibalism is the abnormal exception to the world's rule. There is a difference too between all metaphoric representations of excess and the base from which they depart. Psychiatry, the state, the political and business community, cannot *only* be associated with self-serving and immoral action and with a scopic invasiveness that bolsters those in authority at the expense of the figurative life-blood of others. For the social order (at least as it operates in western democracies) must also be credited with the desire for, and attempt at, communion: to realize communal best interest in an imperfect world in the best possible way. What the Gothic does, in its use of the literalization of metaphor and of doubling (where monstrousness interpenetrates all the way from the deepest self to the outer social order), is to set up a liminal fictional space where each side of this equation — inner and outer, subject and society — can be brought together in a type of "third space" — and there explored at one and the same time. In this liminal space, the Gothic can do what it does best, challenge our fixed preconceptions, make us aware of possibilities and configurations we would otherwise deny. As Veeder puts it:

> What makes the Gothic a potential [or "third"] space [a transitional, intermediate, liminal generic area] is its commitment to the simultaneous exploration of inner and outer, the psychological and the social.... [G]othic is, of all fiction's genres, the one most intensely concerned with simultaneously liberating repressed emotions and exploring foreclosed social issues, since gothic presents most aggressively the range of outré emotions conventionally considered beyond the pale — incest, patricide, familial dysfunction, archaic rage, homoerotic desire [22–23].

In Harris's case we can add fratricide, pedophilia, mutilation, murder, cannibalism, and the animal consumption of human flesh to this list. But Veeder's words stand as an almost exact description of what he succeeds in doing in his highly successful Gothic novels.

VII. Coda

I end, however, with a very brief coda. For in the work I do here as a critic, I echo the processes traditionally associated with the Gothic novel itself. I open up Harris's ideas only to offer the comfort of a rational way out; separate out the ends of the metaphors he uses to re-establish a version of a safely normative social "reality." In the odd moves of the ending of *Hannibal*, however, this is exactly what Harris himself refuses his reader, leaving her or him in a fictional world where social and moral disruption still remains, where we are not allowed a comforting ending that lays anxiety to rest. For the retreat into the fantasy cum madness (if this is what it is) of the "communion" scene is not where the novel ends. Rather, the novel is closed off by the scene in which we are once more given Clarice and Lecter in the larger world of social "reality," living in Buenos Aires: the embodiment of evil still on the loose, now with "bride" in tow. The ambiguity and interpretive indeterminacy of the previous scenes have given way here to a final sense of threat and nightmare. Most especially, the notion that we get, through Will Graham in *Red Dragon*, that the savage and the civilized are not the same whatever the metaphors used — that knowing we can be / were "cannibalistic" is what gives us the chance not to be again — is now completely hidden from view. We are left instead with a moment of genuine liminal frisson.[26] My critical assertions of metaphoric difference remain then in final tension with the darker note of transgressive excess with which Harris ends his text. Infection here appears triumphant, any glimpse of vaccine removed. We are left with unspeakable Gothic energies still inhabiting this fictional world, still threatening our everyday conceptions of normality to powerful effect:

> We'll withdraw now, while [Lecter and Clarice] are dancing on the terrace.... For *either* of them [my emphasis] to discover us would be fatal.
> We can only learn so much and live" [484].

Notes

1. The slippage here between the term "interstitial" and the idea of boundary crossing may be inherent in the notion of the liminal itself, and the undecidable nature of its spatial status.

2. Veeder uses such terms in "The Nurture of the Gothic" (23). Also, see the full quotation that appears near the end of this essay. He does not use the word liminality but his concept (via D.W. Winnicott's *Playing and Reality*) of a "third" or "potential" space is remarkably similar.

3. Where the eighteen-year-old Hannibal carries out his acts of revenge on those who killed his younger sister a decade previously. It is here, too, that (despite the figure of Inspector Popil) Harris moves furthest away from the detective fiction form.

4. Such instability between text and surrounding world is worryingly extended in the space where fictions about serial killers meet their real-life counterparts. See especially Nicola Nixon (217–36).

5. Where appropriate, page references from Harris's novels follow quotations henceforth. The term "oubliette" signifies powerfully here, for the relationships between what is remembered and what is forgotten play a crucial part in Harris's texts. See, for instance, the Prologue to *Hannibal Rising*.

6. Though they are not discussing the realm of aesthetics here, the argument is transferable.

7. Peter Nicholls applies this term (and its therapeutic opposite, introjection) in "The Belated Postmodern: History, Phantoms, and Toni Morrison." The use of the word "incorporation" here has specific and different connotations than at other points in my argument.

8. If we see Krendler's death as a possible end to such activity.

9. The effect of poststructuralism, as she fully recognizes, has been to show "that any meaning constructed by differences defined as absolute antitheses needs constant questioning" (3).

10. See too Janet Staeger's comment that "hierarchies reproduce themselves across various symbolic systems such as psychic forms, the human body, geographical spaces, and social orders" (145).

11. The raw-cooked opposition is a touch misleading as the food Lecter ingests is, when he has time and opportunity, carefully prepared: he sautées slices of Krendler's brain, dredged in fresh brioche crumbs, till "just brown on each side" (*Hannibal* 473).

12. Lestringant bases this comment on Montaigne's account of the actual presence of Brazilian cannibals in Rouen in 1562, as juxtaposed with the king's recapture of the city from the Protestants, and the harshness of the accompanying punishments, just previously. Montaigne's words would seem first and foremost to have referred to western practices of usury, thus allowing a connection with Marx (see later).

13. Cannibalism (and warfare) here have nothing here to do with the acquisition of food or territories but with self-giving, a display of "the stoical 'generosity' of the warrior prisoners." Cannibalism then becomes "a sign that the vanquishers absorb into themselves ... an acknowledgement and confession that [the warrior prisoners] are vanquished" (Lestringant 101–02). I just describe two of a large number of (often contradictory) readings of cannibalism here. See too, for instance, endocannibalism (the cannibalism of relatives): "human flesh [as] a physical channel for communicating social value and procreative fertility from one generation to the next" (Peggy Reeves Sanday 7).

14. This and the quotes immediately following are from "The Function of Cannibalism at the Present Time."

15. See Young, too, on "the misogynistic potential of psychoanalysis" (9). Kilgour reminds us that Freud's childhood hero was Hannibal, in "The Function of Cannibalism at the Present Time" (249).

16. See Kilgour, too, on the relation between detective and (literary) critic in "Dr. Frankenstein Meets Dr. Freud" (50–51).

17. See Joseph Grixti, for instance, on Harris's (early) "compartmentalising [of serial killers] into two distinct types. The first is the psychopathic loner, who turns into a vicious beast, largely as a consequence of serious gender identity problems [i.e., who is psychologically explainable]. The second is the serial killer as enigmatic devil and modern embodiment of evil [i.e., whose motives and actions are inexplicable]" ("Consuming Cannibals" 91).

18. Hannibal's normal calm and self-controlled manner has been shattered here by Grutas's revelation that he himself had committed a cannibalistic act, had been fed the broth made from his sister's body; "'You are her, half-conscious your lips were greedy around the spoon.' Hannibal screamed at the ceiling, 'NOOOOO!' and ran to Grutas ... and slashed" (302).

19. Again, Murasaki's Japanese influence on Hannibal plays a major part in the text as, in the manner of the Japanese warrior tradition (see 80), he kills Paul with the samurai sword of Murasaki's ancestor (103–4, 110).

20. See this same essay (79–85) for a brief explanation of the complicated history concerning the representative nature of the bread and wine, and its importance in terms of Catholic-Protestant religious difference.

21. The positive (and communal) note one might read here is, as I go on to describe, in good part, undermined by this "remove," and by the thoroughly ambiguous nature of the scene. However, this might also be constructed as a step toward "reconnection" for Hannibal, the unfreezing of the heart in a relationship reminiscent of that with Lady Murasaki so much earlier (in chronological though not textual time). In both cases, however, such interconnection exists outside the margins of conventional morality and the law (for there is at least a suggestion, at that earlier time, that Murasaki's aesthetic taste can partially accommodate the ritualized killing associated with Hannibal's revenge). As I go on to suggest, there is a complex linked relationship here between Mischa, Murasaki and Clarice.

22. Veeder's description of the Gothic, via Winnicot, in terms of that "third space" that lies between the psyche and the social, between the maternal introject and the mother, between dream and reality, provides a fascinating point of connection here between theme and form. See "The Nurture of the Gothic" (21–22).

23. This is close to a direct quote from Maggie Kilgour on the role of the Freudian analyst in "Dr. Frankenstein Meets Dr. Freud" (41). We are left here with incestuous implications (Clarice as mother/ sister?/lover). We are also left with the paradoxical link of cannibalism to cure.

24. Hannibal and Hannibal Rising both connect and differ here. If we can tentatively see a connection between Clarice and Murasaki, this is cemented both by Hannibal and Clarice's act of shared cannibalism and by the implied sense of manipulation on Lecter's part. The direct link back to Lecter's mother made in Hannibal is underemphasized in Hannibal Rising (though see 7). Murasaki's role as a substitute mother-projected lover does, however, fit the Freudian paradigm I use to interpret Clarice's role in the earlier novel.

25. See too Kilgour's other comments on the critic as gothic detective and mad scientist, "Dr. Frankenstein Meets Dr. Freud" (50–51). She also presents a quite different reading, of "The Critic as Host" (via J. Hillis Miller, from whom the latter quote is taken): the avoidance of critical cannibalism by communion, a group of readers sharing a mutually enjoyable "verbal feast"—"Reading becomes a new form of communion, involving a triple reciprocity, for not only do the readers share the text among them, but, as it informs them individually and unites them as a group, so each transforms it" (From Communion to Cannibalism 16).

26. And one that the step back to Hannibal's childhood in the most recent novel does nothing to dissipate.

Works Consulted

Abraham, Nicholas, and Torok, Maria. *The Shell and the Kernel*, vol. 1, ed. and trans. Nicholas T. Rand. Chicago: University of Chicago Press, 1994. [Editor's note.]

Aguirre, Manuel, Quance, Roberta, and Sutton, Philip. *Margins and Thresholds: An Enquiry into the Concept of Liminality in Text Studies.* Madrid: Gateway Press, 2000.

Bartolovich, Crystal. "The Cultural Logic of Late Cannibalism," in Francis Barker, Peter Hulme, and Margaret Iversen (eds.), *Cannibalism and the Colonial World.* Cambridge: Cambridge University Press, 1998.

Brown, Bill. *The Material Unconscious: American Amusement, Stephen Crane, and the Economies of Play.* Cambridge, Mass.: Harvard University Press, 1996.

Creed, Barbara. "Horror and the Carnivalesque: The Body-monstrous," in Leslie Devereux, and Roger Hillman (eds.), *Fields of Vision: Essays in Film Studies, Visual Anthropology, and Photography*. Berkeley: University of California Press 1995.

Grixti, Joseph. "Consuming Cannibals: Psychopathic Killers as Archetypes and Cultural Icons." *Journal of American Culture*, vol. 18, no. 1 (1995).

Halberstam, Judith. "Skinflick: Posthuman Gender in Jonathan Demme's *The Silence of the Lambs*." *Camera Obscura: A Journal of Feminism and Film Theory*, Fall 1991.

Harris, Thomas. *Hannibal*. London: William Heinemann, 1999.

_____. *Hannibal Rising*. London: William Heinemann, 2006.

_____. *Red Dragon*. London: Corgi, 1983 [1981].

_____. *The Silence of the Lambs*. London: Mandarin, 1991 [1988].

Jameson, Fredric. "Postmodernism, or the Cultural Logic of Late Capitalism." *New Left Review*, 146 (July–August 1984).

Kilgour, Maggie. "Dr. Frankenstein Meets Dr. Freud," in Robert K. Martin and Eric Savoy (eds.), *American Gothic: New Interventions in a National Narrative*. Iowa City: University of Iowa Press, 1998.

_____. *From Communion to Cannibalism: An Anatomy of Metaphors of Incorporation*. Princeton, N.J.: Princeton University Press, 1990.

_____. "The Function of Cannibalism at the Present Time," in Francis Barker, Peter Francis Hulme, and Margaret Iversen (eds.), *Cannibalism and the Colonial World*. Cambridge: Cambridge University Press, 1998.

Lestringant, Frank. *Cannibals: The Discovery and Representation of the Cannibal from Columbus to Jules Verne*. Oxford: Polity Press, 1997.

Magistrale, Tony. "Transmogrified Gothic: The Novels of Thomas Harris," in Tony Magistrale and Michael A. Morrison (eds.), *A Dark Night's Dreaming: Contemporary American Horror Fiction*. Columbia: University of South Carolina Press, 1996.

Nicholls, Peter. "The Belated Postmodern: History, Phantoms, and Toni Morrison." *Borderlines: Studies in American Culture*, vol. 1, no. 3 (March 1994).

Nixon, Nicola. "Making Monsters, or Serializing Killers," in Robert K. Martin and Eric Savoy (eds.), *American Gothic: New Interventions in a National Narrative*. Iowa City: University of Iowa Press, 1998.

Reeves Sanday, Peggy. *Divine Hunger: Cannibalism as a Cultural System*. Cambridge: Cambridge University Press, 1996.

Richter, David. "Murder in Jest: Serial Killing in the Post-Modern Detective Story." *Journal of Narrative Technique*, vol. 19, no. 1 (1989).

Romney, Jonathan. "Ridley Bites Off More Than He Can Chew...." London *Independent on Sunday* (Culture Section), 18 Feb. 2001.

Simpson, Philip. "The Contagion of Murder: Thomas Harris' *Red Dragon*." *Notes on Contemporary Literature*, vol. 25, no. 1 (January 1995).

Staeger, Janet. "Taboos and Totems: Cultural Meanings of *The Silence of the Lambs*," in Jim Collins, Hilary Radner, and Ava Preacher Collins (eds.), *Film Theory Goes to the Movies*. New York: Routledge, 1993.

Stallybrass, Peter, and White, Allon. *The Politics and Poetics of Transgression*. London: Methuen, 1986.

Taylor, Barry. "The Violence of the Event: Hannibal Lecter in the Lyotardian Sublime," in Earnshaw Steven (ed.), *Postmodern Surroundings*. Amsterdam and Atlanta, Ga.: Rodopi, 1994.

Tharp, Julie "The Transvestite as Monster: Gender Horror in *The Silence of the Lambs* and *Psycho*." *Journal of Popular Film and Television*, vol. 19, no. 3 (Fall 1991).

Veeder, William. "The Nurture of the Gothic, or How Can a Text Be Both Popular and Subversive?" in Robert K. Martin and Eric Savoy (eds.), *American Gothic: New Interventions in a National Narrative.* Iowa City: University of Iowa Press, 1998. [Quoting Michael Taussig, *Shamanism, Colonialism, and the Wild Man,* 1987.]

Walker, Alexander. "Hannibal." *Evening Standard.* 15 Feb. 2001.

Young, Elizabeth. "*The Silence of the Lambs* and the Flaying of Feminist Theory." *Camera Obscura: A Journal of Feminism and Film Theory,* Fall 1991.

2

Hannibal at the Lectern

A Textual Analysis of Dr. Hannibal Lecter's Character and Motivations in Thomas Harris's Red Dragon *and* The Silence of the Lambs

JOHN GOODRICH

Thomas Harris's most famous creation, the character of man-eating psychiatrist Hannibal "the Cannibal" Lecter, fires the imagination as few characters in contemporary literature have. The inherent contradiction of a highly intelligent, highly accomplished, and polite character performing such uncivilized acts as murdering and eating people has had a profound effect on the American popular thrillers. In Lecter, the stock trope serial killer has moved from an unreasoning psychotic into a more nuanced, more human character. Intelligent, even demonic, genius serial killers, such as John Doe from *Seven*, or Pat Bateman from Bret Ellis's *American Psycho,* stand in marked contrast to such socially maladjusted, downtrodden nonentities as Norman Bates from Robert Bloch's *Psycho* or Hans Beckert from Fritz Lang's *M*. And yet, for all his influence, Dr. Hannibal Lecter seems to be very consistently misunderstood.

For a character so feared and imitated, however, Doctor Lecter's true character remains very opaque. What sort of character did Thomas Harris create, and how can we then account for his astonishing popularity?

To start off with, the character's very name gives us some clue as to his function in the novels. His first name, Hannibal, allows Harris to give the character the delicious, almost pulp fiction–like, rhyming moniker, "Hannibal the Cannibal." With such care given to the first name, can this famous character's last name be trivial, or random? "Lecter" suggests the roots of "lecture" and "lectern," from L. *lectus*, pluperfect of *legere,* "to read." Given that Dr. Lecter's previous profession was that of a psychiatrist, the reader may infer that he is a reader of men, something borne out by his interactions with both Will Graham and Clarice Starling.

Despite his most obvious and terrifying features, Dr. Lecter's character is profoundly mysterious. Although his disturbing personality traits — he is a killer and a cannibal — stand out, they are not the heart of the character. Consider this exchange between Lecter and Clarice Starling from *The Silence of the Lambs*:

> "What does he do, this man you want?"
> "He kills —"
> "Ah —" [Dr. Lecter] said sharply, averting his face for a moment from her wrongheadedness. "That's incidental. What is the first and principal thing he does, what need does he serve by killing?" [227].

If we are to understand who the character is, we need to understand what needs he serves in his actions. In the first two novels, Dr. Lecter is at an interesting point. Although he is repeatedly referred to as impenetrable and impossible to evaluate, his actions are severely limited because he is in prison. Like an organism in a lab setting, Dr. Lecter has very few options open to him, while he is incarcerated, and thus we may compare like actions to like, especially with the format in which Dr. Lecter is approached being so similar in *Red Dragon* and *The Silence of the Lambs*.

The character of Hannibal Lecter is first introduced in *Red Dragon*, in which he is visited by FBI consultant Will Graham. Graham only spends a single chapter speaking with Dr. Lecter, although he is often the topic of conversation. These two characters have a history together; Graham exposed Dr. Lecter as a murderer. When Graham comes to see him in his cell, Dr. Lecter speaks with Graham if he were not precisely an equal, but at least as someone interesting to have a conversation with. Dr. Chilton, on the other hand, merits no such courtesy. This is an interesting contradiction — Dr. Lecter seems to hold no obvious grudge against Will Graham. There must be something about Graham which for Dr. Lecter overcomes the humiliation of speaking with the man who is responsible for Dr. Lecter's incarceration. Something that Graham has that Dr. Chilton does not. Consider Dr, Lecter's questions about him to Will Graham from *Red Dragon*:

"Chilton. You must have seen him when you came in. Gruesome, isn't it? Tell me the truth, he fumbles at your head like a freshman pulling at a panty girdle, doesn't he? Watched you out of the corner of his eye. Picked *that* up, didn't you?"

From this, it is clear that one of the things Dr. Lecter values is the ability to "read" and quickly understand people, something Graham has demonstrated, and shows all through the book. Yet, at the same time, Dr. Lecter is pressing Graham to answer a question.

> "A layman ... layman — layman. Interesting term." Lecter said. "So many learned fellows going about. So many *experts* on government grants. And you say you're a layman. But it was you who caught me, wasn't it, Will? Do you know how you did it?"
> "I'm sure you've read the transcript. It's all in there."
> "No it's not. Do you know how you did it, Will?"
> "It's in the transcript. What does it matter now?"
> "It doesn't matter to *me*, Will" [63–64].

Graham will not engage Dr. Lecter with this question, however. But at the end of the meeting, Lecter answers the question himself: "The reason you caught me is that we're *just alike*" was the last thing Graham heard as the steel door closed behind him" (67).

Exactly what Lecter is trying to accomplish with this piece of information is obscure, until we compare it to his actions in *The Silence of the Lambs*. Why is Lecter asking Graham a question if he already knows the answer? If Lecter himself does not hope to gain information from asking the question, then he must want Graham to work the answer out for himself. This is a technique used by mentors and teachers around the world; if the student makes the connection in their own mind, they are much more likely to remember the solution. This combines tellingly with an interesting paragraph that comes just a few pages before their conversation: "Graham was a natural procrastinator, and he knew it. Long ago in school he had made up for it with speed. He was not in school now" (*Red Dragon* 57). Why would an author as notoriously meticulous about his manuscripts invoke school just before this encounter? Perhaps to have the echoes of the school image in the reader's mind as Graham goes to speak with Lecter.

In *The Silence of the Lambs*, Dr. Lecter's role is much larger. He and Clarice Starling have five separate conversations, and more importantly, Starling and Dr. Lecter have no initial relationship, allowing the reader to observe their interactions from the very beginning. This initial building of the relationship is very informative for the characters of Clarice Starling, and more importantly to this essay, Dr. Hannibal Lecter.

Clarice Starling is a very different character from Will Graham. She is untried, where Graham is well-known to the characters he interacts with. She is also young, as opposed to the older, more experienced Will Graham. However, we know that she is someone who reads people, although she is not yet proficient at it. Before she meets Dr. Lecter, she speaks with his keeper, Dr. Chilton. After giving him a brusque brush-off, she reprimands herself: "*Dammit, she should have read him better, quicker. He might not be a total jerk. He might know something useful. It wouldn't have hurt her to simper once, even if she wasn't good at it*" (9). Harris has let us know here that Starling at least expects herself to be able to understand a person fairly quickly, although she considers that she has failed in this particular attempt. This is a skill that will prove very useful to her as an FBI agent, and it is what someone who wants to be a profiler needs to have — the ability to quickly understand another person's point of view. Starling has a formal background in counseling, similar to Lecter's background as a psychiatrist, something Will Graham, does not share. Graham may not understand how he caught Dr. Lecter, but with Clarice, Hannibal shares the language of human psychology.

Starling and Lecter's first encounter, the third chapter of *The Silence of the Lambs*, is something like a seminar. The two of them assess each other, getting to know the other person in the way that two fencers approach each other cautiously, making feints, trying to get a feel for the other's reactions before moving in to make any serious attacks. The initial feel of the conversation is steady, measured and polite until Starling makes a clumsy transition concerning the reason she has been sent. It is at this point that Dr. Lecter's gift for human understanding comes on display:

> No. No, that's stupid and wrong. Never use wit in a segue. Listen, understanding a witticism and replying to it makes your subject perform a fast, detached scan that is inimical to mood. It is on the plank of mood that we proceed. You were doing fine, you'd been courteous and receptive to courtesy, you'd established trust buy telling an embarrassing truth about Miggs, and then you come in with this ham-handed segue into your questionnaire. It won't do" [19].

This is a beautiful piece of writing, one of Harris's most striking. Aside from showcasing Dr. Lecter's grasp of conversational dynamics, it demonstrates that he cannot resist chiding wrong-headedness, and will attempt to correct it. This is his first attempt to "push her buttons," to prod her and discover what sort of person exists underneath the calm exterior of Clarice Starling. What he finds is strength. She replies to him directly, rather than getting angry or attacking him in retaliation

Dr. Lecter, you're an experienced clinical psychiatrist. Do you think I'm dumb enough to try to run some kind of mood scam on you? Give me some credit. I'm asking you to respond to the questionnaire and you will or you won't. Would it hurt you to look at the thing?" [19].

Here we have the first two cuts of the bout. Hannibal has attacked her directly, chastising her, although this is not the full-on assault he later subjects her to, and she has smartly replied. The tenor of the conversation changes — Lecter is now willing to discuss the FBI, and tests her knowledge of serial killer psychology. She has passed his first test.

It is later, after some guarded conversation about the serial killer dubbed "Buffalo Bill," that Lecter performs a full-on emotional assault on Clarice. He subjects her to the full brunt of his appraisal, and tells her in unkind but definite terms what he sees in her. The effect of this must be devastating, as he divines Starling's past, digs out the reason for her ambition, and brings her insecurities to light, sprinkling the truth of his observations with condescension. Such a blistering assault would reduce some to tears, but Starling is not to be beaten, and she again replies to him. Her counterattack is fairly strong, considering the circumstances, but she doesn't become angry, remaining professional and continues to try to get him an answer a questionnaire she has been assigned to give him. This done, there is again an alteration in Dr. Lecter's manner and conversation as displayed in a scene from *The Silence of the Lambs*:

"You're tough, aren't you, Officer Starling?"
"Reasonably so, yes."
"And you'd hate to think that you were common, wouldn't that sting? My! Well you're far from common, Officer Starling. All you have is fear of it" [23].

Clearly, the verbal abuse was another test, and again Starling has passed. While we are not told if Dr. Lecter is pleased, he does begin to reward Clarice for her patience. He makes a suggestion for what she can do with the tacky jewelry he so recently scoffed at, and says that he will consider giving her something she can use. Lecter's neat package of acute condescension and absolute control over the situation is disrupted when Miggs throws semen on Clarice as she is leaving. Lecter apparently feels responsible for dragging Starling down there, and wishes to offer her something as an apology. Not having much else to offer, and only a little time, he gives her what he had only considered giving her previously. This is an interesting quirk of Lecter's, that rudeness is so anathema to him that he will forego his 'fun' of stringing her along in order to make up for it.

Clarice's return to Dr. Lecter's cell in chapter nine is probably the most significant act in the book. She has already demonstrated that she is smarter and more resilient than Dr. Lecter's average visitor. "'Would you like a chair?' Barney asked her. 'We could have had one, but he never — well, usually nobody needs to stay that long'" (17). It seems that few people would return to see Dr. Lecter. Those he wishes to converse with could be subjected to the same scorn that he heaped so accurately on Clarice Starling in chapter three. And that is if he is interested in them. Dr. Lecter demonstrates that he is perfectly able of completely ignoring anyone with whom he does not want to speak.

But Starling is not welcomed on her return. Despite Dr. Lecter's decided lack of conversational opportunities, he does not jump at the chance to speak with her again. Instead, he again tests her, this time to see if she can wait. She is cold and wet, she has no chair, and Dr. Lecter is unseen in his darkened cell. In this dungeon-like setting, time must crawl, especially since she is wet and miserable. But he does eventually reward her patience and determination; he sends out a towel for her to dry off with, and a second conversation begins.

This conversation is completely different from the previous one. Most of it is straight business, Hannibal filling Starling in on what she has found. It begins with an exchange that establishes the way each should address the other; she calls him Dr. Lecter, and he refers to her as Clarice. This protocol is dictated by Dr. Lecter, and once it has been established, the characters do not deviate from it.

Still, this conversation is also the beginning of Hannibal's mentoring of Clarice. One of the first things he does is to correct an imprecise statement on her part:

"Dr. Lecter, you started this. Now please tell me about the person in the Packard."

"You found an entire person? Odd. I only saw a head. Where do you suppose the rest came from?"

"All right. Whose *head* was it?" [58].

Here, Lecter uses his considerable powers of sarcasm and personal abuse to correct Starling. However, once she acknowledges his correctness, he is full of information. Having tested Starling's grit and worthiness in the previous encounter, he proceeds to demonstrate his own worthiness for continued contact. Lecter has a lot of information about the head Starling found, and shares most of it fairly easily.

Once his use as a source of good information has been established, Lecter moves onto a new topic, asks Starling if she thinks Crawford desires her sexually, and follows up by asking if she thinks Lecter himself is interested in eating her. These are very unusual questions, but taken together, the two negatives state that the men in question are not interested in her for her body. A logical conclusion follows that they are pay attention to her because of her mind, although neither of them states this outright. What he has done is to, again, pay Starling an interesting compliment, somewhat like the previously quoted statement from page twenty-three that she is not common.

It becomes fairly clear with the second conversation that Dr. Lecter intends to become something of a personal mentor to Clarice Starling. His intention is to teach her becomes clear at this point. He corrects her once for speaking imprecisely, and brings a speech trait that makes her sound overly studied to her attention: "Your interrogative case often has that proper subjunctive in it. With your accent, it stinks of the lamp" (61). This is possibly a statement that Starling should tailor her speech to her audience in order to give a proper impression. If this is the statement he is making, it works; on page eighty-two, Starling uses her background as part of the Appalachian working-class in the funeral home in West Virginia to her advantage.

Further evidence that Starling is growing under Dr. Lecter's tutelage comes just before she returns for a third conversation with Dr. Lecter, in chapter twenty-two. Lecter's keeper, Dr. Chilton, attempts to block Starling's access:

> "I'm not a turnkey here, Miss Starling. I don't come running down here at night just to let people in and out. I had a ticket to *Holiday on Ice*."
>
> He realized he'd said *a* ticket. In that instant, Starling saw his life, and he knew it.
>
> She saw his bleak refrigerator, the crumbs on the TV tray where he ate alone, and still piles his things stayed in for months until he moved them — she felt the ache of his yellow-smiling Sen-Sen lonesome life — and switchblade quick she knew not to spare him, not to talk on or look away. She stared into his face, and with the smallest tilt of her head, she gave him her good looks and bored hew knowledge in, speared him with it, knowing he couldn't stand for the conversation to go on [141].

Clearly, Clarice is learning from Dr. Lecter. The head-tilt is reminiscent of a similar movement Dr. Lecter makes in *Red Dragon*, during his discussion with Will Graham. "Dr. Lecter seldom holds his head upright. He tilts it as he asks a question, as though he were screwing an auger of curiosity into your face" (65). In this, Clarice's first conscious imitation of Doctor Lecter, we have the very first inklings of her eventual fate in *Hannibal*. Lecter has taken an interest in her, has begin to mold her. Will Graham was too canny to allow this sort of personal invasion, but Clarice, although intelligent, strong, and very good at reading people, is simply not prepared for the precise insight and personal manipulation of Dr. Hannibal Lecter.

As she enters the hallway which leads to Dr. Lecter's cell, Clarice inadvertently misquotes T.S. Elliot's "Ash Wednesday" poem aloud. "Teach us to care and not to care, teach us to be still" (*The Silence of the Lambs*, 142). On her last visit, Dr. Lecter taught her how to be still, or at least tester her ability to remain still and patient. Even if she is not consciously aware of it, Starling definitely knows that she is being guided by the madman she cannot seem to stay away from.

After acknowledging her presence, Doctor Lecter's first comment is "You're up late for a school night" (144). Although Harris does not shower us with school metaphors, they do appear with fair regularity when Clarice and Dr. Lecter speak. It is especially apt in this encounter, since it is here that Dr. Lecter really begins to teach Clarice.

After the initial discussion of the specific case of Buffalo Bill, Lecter returns to his hobby of finding out about Clarice; how she handled being confronted with a dead body, and if she was getting anywhere in her own analysis of the serial killer's behavior. Since she has not, he starts on a very long and roundabout lesson concerning a new patient, Sammie. In a single lecture, Dr. Lecter ridicules Dr. Chilton's diagnosis, and at the same time, provides Starling with a memorable lesson in the analysis of mental illness. After provoking Sammie into giving Starling a show, Lecter asks for a diagnosis of his condition, which she provides to his satisfaction. Again, she has passed a test — now Dr. Lecter is sure that he can provide her with psychological insights that will not be wasted on an imperceptive mind.

This is also the first visit in which the quid pro quo exchanged is used, Dr. Lecter trading bits of information in return for personal experiences from Clarice Starling. This is an interesting moment, and one that can be read several ways. Harris states specifically, when Dr. Lecter meets Senator Martin, that Dr. Lecter enjoys watching other peoples' anguish. "When her pupils darkened, Dr. Lecter took a single sip of her pain and found it exquisite. That was enough for today" (201). However, this is not narratively revealed when Dr. Lecter is speaking with Clarice. All of those scenes are written from Starling's perspective, rather than Dr. Lecter's.

It is possible that Doctor Lecter is intruding on Clarice Starling's inner turmoil for his own amusement, like the moth that lives only on tears.

This is Jack Crawford's assessment. "Second, we remember that Lecter looks only for the fun. Never forget the fun" (130). And again, on the same page, Jack Crawford still talking:

> He'd have the most fun by waiting and acting like he's trying to remember week after week, getting Senator Martin's hopes up and letting Catherine die, and then tormenting the next mother, and the next getting their hopes up always just about to remember — that would be better than having a view. It's the kind of thing he lives on. It's his nourishment [130].

However, we must also remember that Dr. Lecter is also a trained psychiatrist. One of the tenets of psychiatry is that if we speak about the things that are painful, and by dealing with them, keep them from becoming major problems, or at least easing the ill effect painful memories have on a patient's current self. Since Dr. Lecter does seem to gain nourishment, or at least pleasure from seeing other people suffer, then psychiatry was the perfect career choice for him. And yet his practice was said to be very successful, so Dr. Lecter must have been able to help at least some people. Certainly with the acuity he displays in the novels, Dr. Lecter would have been an excellent psychiatrist. In fact, the two would not be exclusive at all, with Dr. Lecter divining and bringing to the surface the patient's most painful memories, taking pleasure in their pain, while they worked through that pain.

So it is possible that even as Dr. Lecter enjoys Starling's pain, he devises the quid pro quo format partially in order to assist Starling. He has found her to be canny, perceptive, and intelligent, but perhaps in his judgment, she may benefit from a little encouragement and mental housecleaning, made stronger by confronting her demons. Or perhaps the analysis he gives and the compliments he gives here are merely honeyed bait for the trap he places in her mind, to be taken advantage of years later, during *Hannibal*.

Regardless of his motivations, Dr. Lecter gives Clarice better value for her memories than she will immediately give him credit for. Dr. Lecter's desire seems to be to give her information in order that she can understand serial killers generally, where she is interested mainly in the one in front of her. This disconnect reinforces the teacher-student motif that comes along with the school imagery. Lecter, as the teacher, is far more experienced, and is trying to instill in Clarice a set of skills. Starling just wants the answers to next week's test.

Starling and Lecter's fourth encounter, may be the most significant in their relationship, because it is the point in which Clarice demonstrates exactly how much she has learned from Dr. Lecter. The chapter in *The*

Silence of the Lambs begins with uncommonly plain instance of school imagery:

> "Excuse me," Barney said. "If you've got a lot of papers to wrestle, there's a one-armed desk, a school desk, in the closet here that the shrinks use. Want it?" [161].

She does accept the desk. Starling has come to Dr. Lecter with an offer from Senator Martin, which she knows is fictitious. Starling is perfectly aware that Senator Martin has not made this offer, and so her account of it is entirely as lie to Lecter. Clarice has learned, and quickly, how to judge people, and how to use her knowledge of them to deceive. It is certainly to be expected that she first use her wiles to deceive her teacher, but it is quite apparent that he is not expecting her to have done so. He says, as they discuss the painful subject of Clarice's father: "I'll know if you lie" (165). He has caught her in lies and evasions before this, he does not catch her in this one. He gives good, well thought-out information about how to catch Jame Gumb without giving the entire game away.

The fifth encounter has a different tenor from the previous two. Dr. Lecter and Clarice see each other much more as equals as before. In fact, he could be described as somewhat wary, perhaps even guarded. "I'll have to be careful doing business with you" (227), Dr. Lecter says, confronting her with the fact that she has lied to him. She, in turn, desperately seeking any scrap of information she can pry out of him to save Catherine Martin, shows him how well she knows him:

> But today you happened to remember just one detail. He'd had elephant ivory anthrax. You should have seen them jump when Atlanta said it's a disease of knifemakers. They ate it up, just like you knew they would.... I think maybe you didn't meet him and Raspail told you about him. Second hand stuff wouldn't sell as well to Senator Martin, would it?" [226].

Where this relationship began with Lecter being the "sage on the stage," laying down the rules of the relationship, Clarice has passed all of his tests, has come to know him well enough to know what he likes, even know him enough to deceive him, and possibly even sparked his respect in doing so. She has proven herself to be a student worthy of his time, possibly even learning faster than he anticipated. Despite this, Dr. Lecter still presents himself as the teacher, and is still condescending to Clarice when he says: "When you show the odd flash of contextual intelligence, I forget that your generation can't read" (226–227). As with the previous lesson with Sammie in their third encounter, Dr. Lecter walks his pupil through a lesson on Marcus Aurelius and the importance of first principles.

It is indeed this final lesson which, combined with the note he leaves in the case file, allows Starling to locate Jame Gumb. With her rescue of Catherine Martin, Hannibal's lesson is more or less complete — Starling has passed her self-imposed exam by rescuing Catherine Martin.

Hannibal's nature is that of an intelligent, perceptive aesthete with a drive to murder and devour. This combination of traits also drives him to teach; Lecter likes the finer things in life, and knows the disappointment of having those finer things ruined by the thoughtless, the dull, and the ignorant. "Being smart ruins a lot of things, doesn't it? And taste isn't kind" (23). Lecter is forced to teach because his only opportunity to speak with someone with common experience is to create it. Dr. Lecter is so incredibly far off the normal human spectrum as to be unique in a world of billions. This is the motivating factor for him to push the unwanted knowledge onto Graham. It is for this reason that he forms a relationship with Clarice Starling, teaches her to be a reader of individuals, and eventually devours her: in order to stave off his own loneliness. This is the basic, fundamental need for companionship. Lecter knows he is unlikely to meet anyone like himself, and so he must make someone.

And yet, there is still one more question regarding Dr. Lecter's motivations, which cannot be divined from Harris's text. Has Dr. Hannibal Lecter found some sort of liberating self-actualization? Is he pulling his companion upward and out of a Platonic cave, introducing the two of them to a brilliant light of his new morality, unshackling them from the dull fears of the unenlightened society? Or is Lecter like Milton's damned Satan, seeking companions in his suffering, so that it might seem the less? Within the three currently released books (as of this writing, the fourth has been announced, but is not yet available), it is difficult to say. Dr. Lecter spends time unhappily in prison, but he escapes. He finds his companion, but she does not join her of her own free will. On this, Harris's text is silent. Where the other characters in the novels play fairly close to morality-tale lines; the serial killers are themselves killed, the FBI investigators live, and Dr. Lecter, murderer of eight, escapes at the end of *The Silence of the Lambs*, and remains free at the end of *Hannibal*. Like Shiloh at the end of *Red Dragon*, Harris refuses to judge the actions of Dr. Hannibal Lecter.

Works Consulted

Bloch, Robert. *Psycho*. New York: Tom Doherty Associates, 1991.
Ellis, Bret Easton. *American Psycho*. New York: Vintage Contemporaries, 1991.
Harris, Thomas. *Red Dragon*. New York: Dell, 1981.
_____. *The Silence of the Lambs*. New York: St. Martin's Press, 1988.

_____. *Hannibal.* New York: Delacorte, 1999. *M*, dir Fritz Lang. Criterion, 2004. DVD.

Milton, John. *Paradise Lost, Paradise Regained*, ed. Christopher Ricks. New York: Signet Classic, 2001.

Plato. *The Republic*, trans. Allan Bloom. New York: Basic Books, 1991. *Ravenous*, dir. Antonia Bird. 20th Century–Fox, 1999. DVD. *Seven*, dir. David Fincher. New Line Cinema, 1995. DVD.

3

Gothic Romance and Killer Couples in *Black Sunday* and *Hannibal*

PHILIP L. SIMPSON

After the best-selling success of Thomas Harris's 1988 novel *The Silence of the Lambs* and its Oscar-winning film adaptation in 1991, fans of the paternalistic, semi-romantic relationship between fictional FBI trainee Clarice Starling and cannibalistic serial killer Hannibal Lecter had to wait another eleven years for Harris's rumored sequel. Though no hints were forthcoming from the reclusive Harris, the rumors suggested, at least according to Robert Winder, that the new story would pit Starling and the FBI against the at-large Lecter, who has begun a new "career" by killing serial killers in an ingenious ploy to simultaneously help Starling and mock her (44). When Thomas Harris began showing up in Florence, Italy, for the trial of a suspected serial killer, the rumors regarding Lecter and other serial killers intensified. Another early rumor had it that the new story would feature Starling rescuing Lecter from a serial killer who targets other serial killers as victims. Rumor and speculation drove anticipation to ever higher levels. However, when the novel was finally published in June of 1999 and the actual storyline known, fan and critical reaction was decidedly mixed.

Hannibal centers on the efforts of a former Lecter victim, the paralyzed and faceless multi-millionaire meat-packing magnate Mason Verger, to enlist the aid of corrupt Italian cops, snuff-film makers, pig trainers, and sleazy Justice Department official Paul Krendler in capturing Lecter and then feeding him alive to a herd of swine. Even that story arc, as unlikely as it sounded in synopsis, did not put off those who were familiar with Harris's previous melodramas. What did draw criticism was Harris's continued pathologizing of homosexuality in his latest novel.[1]

Other readers were disturbed that the evil Dr. Lecter had now been given a facile childhood trauma — witnessing his beloved sister Mischa being eaten by starving German soldiers in 1944 war-torn Lithuania — to explain his cannibalism.[2] However, what led to the most negative reactions was the novel's climax, which places Starling and Lecter in a mutually cannibalistic and romantic union.[3] Many readers from the general public, some of whose reactions are sampled in an essay by Stephen Fuller (819, 832), expressed almost apoplectic levels of outrage.[4]

Undoubtedly, then, Harris succeeded in shocking many of his readers, who were otherwise quite accustomed to the grisly and macabre from his earlier works. For the dedicated and compassionate Clarice Starling, who so agonized over rescuing Catherine Martin from serial killer Buffalo Bill in the previous story, to become the cannibalistic consort of another serial killer does, at first blush, seem like quite a stretch. But is the ending of *Hannibal*, with its symbolic if not literal marriage between Lecter and Starling, really so unexpected? Does the ending truly constitute a betrayal of the characters, as those angry readers indignantly protest? In actuality, as Stephen Fuller argues, the seemingly bizarre romantic ending completes and fulfills the converging character dynamic established between fellow outsiders and social exiles Starling and Lecter in *The Silence of the Lambs* and anticipated before that by the dissolution of the boundaries between law-enforcement hero and serial-killing antihero in *Red Dragon* (829). In fact, Harris's first published novel, *Black Sunday*, dramatizes another lethal romantic pairing, this one also between a mass murderer acolyte and a sexually liberating tutor. The relationship between ex-military pilot Michael Lander and Arab terrorist Dahlia Iyad parallels the Starling-Lecter alliance but precedes it by decades. Harris, beginning in 1975 with *Black Sunday* and continuing through the *Hannibal* novels, has made a career of collapsing the boundary between binaries, including the opposition between "respectable" members of society and its outlaws. From this longitudinal overview of Harris's work, the bonding between Starling and Lecter into one murdering couple is quite predictable and fits well within the Gothic tradition.[5]

Readers familiar with the conventions of Gothic or neo–Gothic fiction should not be surprised at all to find Starling taking her alliance with

Lecter to such an extreme, or that in *Black Sunday* a disgraced combat veteran would team up with a Black September terrorist to attempt to detonate an aerial bomb over the Super Bowl. The Gothic, after all, is the true genre residence of Harris's fiction, as Tony Magistrale points out (27–28), and not the "political thriller" or "crime novel." Peter Messent concurs that Harris "engages the thresholds between genres in his texts" (23) and "moves beyond the borders of the detective genre into territories of the Gothic/Horror" (24). The textual movement into the Gothic allows Harris to reject linear Classical neatness and order in favor of the disordered, the exaggerated, the transformative, the chaotic, the endlessly doubling, and the primitive. Therefore, Harris plots feature decidedly outlandish characters and events involved in most extreme acts of violence: a blimp piloted by an insane Vietnam veteran and a ruthless Arab terrorist crashing into Tulane Stadium in New Orleans, a weightlifting madman with a cleft palate who murders entire families, a failed transsexual who murders women in order to wear their skins, and a cannibalistic psychiatrist who has a pattern of feeding enemies' internal organs to people at swank dinner parties.

Further, the narrative space so created is a liminal one, according to Messent, in which binary categories such as high culture and low culture are "juxtaposed, indeed they clash violently" (24). This collision of binaries is a prominent feature of *Black Sunday*, primarily in the union-of-convenience of Michael Lander, an ex-military man with no interest in politics but a fierce desire to murder thousands of Americans in the ultimate act of contempt and spite for a nation that rejected him, and Dahlia Iyad, a political ideologue who has a fierce desire to murder thousands of Americans in the ultimate act of hatred for a nation that has helped victimize her people. The apotheosis of this trend in Harris's fiction is, of course, Hannibal Lecter. His intellectual and cultural sophistication starkly contrasts with his consumption of human organs and even his choice of mate, the "white trash" Starling from West Virginia.

Altered states of reality are a consistent feature of the Gothic, and also abound in Harris's fiction. Much of Harris's novels is told from the point of view of the killers, with their fantastical perspectives. These killers are visionaries seeking mystic transport away from society and earth itself, and Harris's technique takes us into those mental landscapes as complicit partners. Lander, for one, has yearned since the age of eight and his first sight of a dirigible to fly above the earth in the magical lighter-than-air blimp. He learns to fly a Piper Cub so that he can be one with the gravity-defying machine and lose his sense of injured self: "At the controls he saw nothing of Lander, but he saw the little plane banking, stalling, diving, and its shape was his and its grace and strength was his and he could feel the wind on it and he was free" (64). Similarly, Lecter can free himself of reality by retreating into what Harris calls his memory palace. A typical such moment in *Hannibal* occurs when Lecter transcends the discomfort of a trans-Atlantic flight: "Dr. Lecter could overcome his surroundings. He could make it all go away.... As he had done in his cell so many times, Dr. Lecter put his head back, closed his eyes and retired for relief into the quiet of his memory palace, a place that is quite beautiful for the most part ... so we will go with him now into the palace of his mind" (251). Just as "we" the readers are complicit in the fantasies, we then become partners in the acts of murder these visionaries commit. They contemplate and use murder, with its Cain-like associations of social exile, as the mechanism for achieving that godlike transcendence. Sex and the absorption into other will also serve as a means to that end, but within the minds of Harris's murderous mystics, sex and death have become inextricably intertwined. Lander's vision of sex with the deadly Dahlia as erasure of the self is typical: "Lander felt that he was falling into those bottomless eyes. He remembered as a child lying in the grass on clear summer nights, looking into heavens suddenly dimensional and deep. Looking up until there was no up and he was falling out into the stars" (26). Linda Mizejewski observes that the infamous conclusion of *Hannibal* is similarly vertiginous: "When the pursuit and rescue plotlines have ended, *Hannibal* takes a turn toward the poetic and surreal. Lecter begins studying astrophysics in order to reverse time and make broken teacups fly together again. And the novel's gruesome revenge scene is a bizarre Mad Hatter's gourmet dinner/tea party ... [the novel] ends in a far more dreamy style and mise-en-scene. Its conclusion in Buenos Aires resembles South American magical realism" (189). From these examples, one can observe that the Gothic narrative space in Harris's work is very often dream-like and hallucinatory.

Doubling also occurs throughout Harris's fiction, in which killers not only reflect but display key behavioral traits of cultural enforcement agents and vice versa. This fusion or blurring of character boundary is given even more dramatic weight by perversely sexual unions between killer couples from opposite ends of the social spectrum, brought together by a shared interest in murder. Lander is from the relatively privileged American middle class. Dahlia is from an impoverished refugee family in a third-world region. They unite to take revenge on the same culture, albeit for dramatically different reasons, but both based on an outraged sense of social justice. Lecter originates within the aristocratic European class, Starling from the American "third world" of West Virginia. Lecter's sense of social justice compels him to eat the rude and inflict Dante-esque poetic justice upon the clods of the world, while Starling must endure institutional sexual harassment and professional isolation from the "old boy's network" types like Paul Krendler and as such, is ripe for Lecter's brand of therapy. So, while many readers were clearly outraged by the sexual relationship between Hannibal Lecter and Clarice Starling, in context of Harris's work and the larger neo-Gothic tradition, the development is not only logical but inevitable. One need only look to Harris's first killer couple, Michael Lander and Dahlia Iyad.

Dahlia is a woman defined by dangerous sexuality, a signature Harris leitmotif. A female terrorist in a traditionally patriarchal Arab culture, she is introduced in the opening scenes of *Black Sunday* as a smartly dressed, assertive woman who uses her sexuality as a useful tool to manipulate the men around her in service of her political agenda. Her Westernized appearance disconcerts her three terrorist colleagues in Beirut even as they skeptically press her with questions about the suitability of ex prisoner-of-war Michael Lander as key instrument of the attack they are plotting against the United States. She states matter-of-factly to one of the tribunal that she has cured Lander's impotence: "It is not a matter of credit, Comrade. It is a matter of control. My body is useful in maintaining that control. If a gun worked better, I would use a gun" (3). Her lethality, utter commitment to ideology, and high rank in the terrorist organization are established through the memory of one of the men questioning her: "Dahlia had helped train the three Japanese terrorists who struck at Lod airport in Tel Aviv, slaying at random. Originally there had been four Japanese terrorists. One had lost his nerve in training, and, with the other three watching, Dahlia blew his head off with a Schmeisser machine pistol" (3). Clearly, on the evidence of these scenes that juxtapose sexual desirability with ruthlessness, Dahlia is the narrative's femme fatale.

The scene where the terrorist tribunal questions Dahlia about her specific sexual experiences with Lander, ostensibly part of the tribunal's overall agenda to confirm Lander's malleability, introduces another primary Gothic theme — the power of the past to haunt the present. Dahlia's graphic descriptions excite the three men, and from her perspective, "it seemed to Dahlia that there was a smell in the room. Real or imagined, it took her back to the Palestinian refugee camp at Tyre when she was eight years old, folding the wet bedroll where her mother and the man who brought food groaned together in the dark" (5). Significantly, Dahlia's unpleasant childhood memory of the smell of sex is inextricably intertwined with her visceral experience of social injustice and now influences her adult interactions with men who she believes can help her even the scales of justice. Much later in the book, just prior to her suicide mission with Lander, she weeps for herself and steels herself for death and slaughter with memories of her mother's pain in the refugee camp: "She went through her mother's final agonies, the thin woman, old at 35, writhing in the ragged tent. Dahlia was ten, and she could do nothing but keep the flies off her mother's face" (291–92). These details from Dahlia's past establish the importance of early trauma as a determining factor in the development of murderous adult characters in Harris's work.[6]

Dahlia's fusion of sexuality with the politics of terrorism is further cemented in the scene after the tribunal dismisses. Invited back to the apartment of Hafez Najeer, the head of Al-Fatah's intelligence unit, Dahlia records a tape to be used by Black September after the attack to claim responsibility, but beyond its practical application the tape serves as a key device in death-fetishized foreplay. As she records the tape and speaks of the death of thousands, she is naked and becomes visibly sexually aroused, then makes love to Najeer. Only minutes later, as she showers, her lover is killed by Israeli commandos led by Major David Kabakov. She survives only because Kabakov, not realizing her status as member of Black September, allows her to escape. Much of the rest of the novel's plot centers on Dahlia's urge to take revenge not only on the United States and Israel as enemy nations, but this particular Israeli as agent of the latest trauma in her life.[7] Because she can only take her revenge by allying herself with deadly men, she manipulates those such as Lander through sex, one of the many tools in her lethal arsenal.

Yet as deadly as Dahlia is, she is not without her nurturing side. This paradox in her character is encapsulated in Harris's description of her as she tends Lander during a bout with pneumonia late in the narrative: "No man ever had a kinder, deadlier nurse than Dahlia Iyad" (263). Her sexual relationship with Lander is, in its own perverse and manipulative way, therapeutic.[8] It begins with their first meeting in a public pool, where she has been sent by Black September to interview the American who has been trying to contact the organization. Lander's admission to her — that he is looking for 1200 pounds of plastic explosive to detonate in the Super Bowl — is difficult to say, "as hard as opening up to a shrink." Dahlia's acceptance of his admission makes him feel safe at last in his release of socially unacceptable and repressed feelings: "She looked at him as though he had painfully admitted a sexual aberration that she particularly enjoyed. Calm and kindly compassion, suppressed excitement. Welcome home"

(55). As their sexual relationship commences, Dahlia often uses powerful drugs to render him nearly insensible and more susceptible to influence — a "first draft" of Lecter's sexual and pharmaceutical treatment of Starling's neuroses in *Hannibal*: "[Dahlia] believed in the genuine understanding and affection she shared with Lander, and she believed in the 50 milligrams of chlorpromazine she had dissolved in his coffee" (116). Whenever Lander feels that he can no longer control his murderous rage, Dahlia cleverly finds ways, verbal or sexual or chemical, to defuse him.

She does so not only out of compassion for his pain, but also so he can keep himself together long enough to carry out his suicide mission. For example, when Lander has to go to the Veteran's Administration hospital for a routine check-in to maintain his pilot's license, Dahlia ensures he won't fail the check-in by reminding him brutally of what's at stake: "All right, are you crazy today? Are you going to spoil it? Are you going to grab a VA clerk and kill him and let the others hold you down...? You don't have to get them one at a time, Michael" (18, 19). Upon his return from the VA check-in, Dahlia ensures he will remain calm by giving him water laced with an opium paregoric and then making love to him on the same bed where Lander once witnessed his wife's infidelity. As part of foreplay, she passes him a hash pipe, so their subsequent lovemaking takes on an almost dreamlike quality in which Dahlia's eyes transport Lander to celestial heights. The scene makes clear not only the depth of Dahlia's control of Lander but the methodology by which she dulls his enraged memories of past abuses. Just as she is embittered by her past, so is he, and thus do the Palestinian terrorist and the American ex-serviceman find a common murderous identity. She sees him as a "splendid machine with a homicidal child at the controls" (57), but ironically, so is she.

For his part, Lander is a man easily manipulated by women. He is by far the weaker character in the dynamic established between him and Dahlia. Like Dahlia, he has suffered wrongs and injustice, beginning with a childhood of repression in a strict, religious Southern home. His father is a minister tolerated by the rough-and-tumble male parishioners but never respected — perceived as soft, useless, and effeminate. Lander's mother, by contrast, is an overbearing and overweight woman who publicly humiliates the boy on more than one occasion, most notably when she angrily drags him away from the football field where he has tried to dispel his scholarly reputation by trying out for the team.[9] By the age of fifteen, Lander hates his family, the church, and everyone around him, but has learned the art of masking his inner rage and inadequacy beneath a compliant and soft-spoken demeanor — the perfect camouflage for the future killer: "He cannot bear personal competition. He has never experienced the gradients of controlled aggression that allow most of us to survive.... Lander understands limited aggression objectively, but he cannot take part in it. Emotionally, for him there is no middle ground between a pleasant, uncompetitive atmosphere and total war to the death with the corpse defiled and burned. So he has no outlet. And he has swallowed his poison longer than most could have done" (63). He maintains the mask of normalcy long enough to marry, though the future "bliss" of this relationship is foreshadowed by their marriage in a chapel at Lakehurst, site of the Hindenburg disaster. Lander quickly alienates his wife, Margaret, with his extremes of mood and shows "flashes of cruelty that terrified her" (67). Even as he withdraws emotionally and physically from her, he becomes jealous and paranoid of her, then overcompensates by showering her with gifts. Thus, long before his bitter combat experience in the Vietnam War, Lander is choked with unseen but building rage that he cannot safely vent. When his anger and coldness manifests itself nevertheless, he tries desperately to conceal his inner self with external acts of solicitousness. In many ways, Lander is a template for the damaged serial killers that will become Harris's later claim to literary fame.

Once Lander goes off to war, his journey toward homicidal madness accelerates. Based on his early aptitude for machinery and flying, Lander becomes a navy pilot but is unfortunately shot down on a rescue mission in Vietnam. His hand injured in the crash, he is taken captive by the Vietnamese and then offered treatment for his hand if he agrees to denounce the United States of America in a written confession read before a group of his fellow prisoners. The scene where he reads the confession before his countrymen and a movie camera is a poignant counterpoint to an earlier scene where Lander as a boy was forced to read his prize essay to a decidedly unappreciative audience of his resentful classmates. Thus, a thematic bridge is established between the youthful ostracism of Lander and his adult ostracism in the dehumanizing environment of a POW camp: "His disgrace before the other prisoners, the isolation that came later, were all the old, bad times come again" (72). His one friend, Jergens, is removed from his company, completing Lander's social exile. Significantly, toward the novel's end, it is news of Jurgen's suicide, conveyed to Lander by his ex-wife, that drives Lander into a self-destructive drinking binge that results in his contracting pneumonia, and thus panicking terrorist mastermind Muhammad Fasil into precipitous action to replace Lander. Fasil's clumsy attempt draws Kabakov's focus upon the true nature and target of the plot and ultimately undoes it when Lander recovers enough to fly the blimp. Lander's grandly designed murder-suicide falls far short of what he intended because of his own failings aggravated years before by intense psychological abuse in the Vietnamese POW camp.

Lander is a man who can find no escape from an escalating cycle of abuse in whatever setting he finds himself. His return to the United States from Vietnam does not bring him any relief. He is brought up on charges of collaboration with the enemy, a legal continuation of his humiliation which only his resignation from the military ceases. He finds no refuge at home, where his marriage suffers because of his physical impotence and his increasing jealousy of his wife. His marriage ends when, in a fit of jealous rage, he kills his wife's kitten by shoving it into a running garbage disposal. Immediately remorseful, he tries to make amends with Margaret and returns to the house with a new kitten, but discovers Margaret having sex with a man in their bedroom. At that moment, Lander feels his last shred of sanity die and devotes himself to only one cause: killing as many as he can in his own act of suicide. Harris's description of the "reborn" Lander could apply just as well to Dolarhyde, the child-man of *Red Dragon*: "The man functioned perfectly because the child needed him, needed his quick brain and clever fingers. To find its own relief. By killing and killing and killing and killing. And dying" (82). Lander's descent into homicidal insanity is now complete; he awaits only his partner to fulfill Harris's formula for Gothic romance and to bring the murder plot to its climax. The means for Lander's mass murder-suicide is an aerial assault using the blimp he flies for the fictional Aldrich company, but he lacks the explosive to make the attack truly devastating. He cannot succeed without Dahlia "completing" him by bringing the plastic explosive to America, so their alliance in mass murder becomes a metaphor for their mutually reinforcing brands of madness.

Twenty-four years later, Harris's fascination with romantic dalliances between killers continues in *Hannibal*, where the stalwart law-enforcement heroine Clarice Starling, beloved by millions after her portrayal by Jodie Foster in the film version of *The Silence of the Lambs*, reveals her dogged pursuit of justice to be little more than a raging Electra complex that lends itself easily to Lecter's unique style of therapy. To be fair to Harris, this dynamic was clearly established in *The Silence of the Lambs* and its pathology implied even then. In the follow-up novel, Lecter engages in a protracted stalking, followed by successful seduction, of Clarice Starling. His method is to exacerbate her pre-existing isolation and, eventually, to turn her into a cannibal herself. She is predisposed to accept his seduction because she is working in an alienating patriarchal setting (the

FBI) where her initiative is frowned upon and she has been targeted for professional ruin by her nemesis Paul Krendler. Krendler hates Starling for two primary reasons: first, he "had never forgiven her for finding the serial killer Jame Gumb ahead of him" (94), and second, he is sexually attracted to her but resents Starling for rebuffing a clumsy, drunken pass he once made at her. (As the novel progresses, Krendler's frustrated sexual hostility toward Starling finds expression in his ugly reference to her as "cornpone country pussy" [265]). Over the years, Starling gradually realizes that "her early triumph in catching the serial murderer Jame Gumb was part of her undoing in the Bureau. She was a rising star that stuck on the way up. In the process of catching Gumb, she had made at least one powerful enemy [Krendler] and excited the jealousy of a number of her male contemporaries.... Finally, deemed too irascible to work with groups, she was a tech agent" (50). Ultimately, she leaves behind not only the FBI, but also society itself, as a result of her symbiotic relationship with Lecter. By finally succumbing to Lecter's seduction under the influence of hypnotic drugs, she has removed herself from her own oppressive culture forever and joined him in his culture as a new matriarchal bogeywoman. She is the Final Girl that Carol Clover writes of, whose murderous potential and affinity with the Gothic predator has always been implicit, turned full-fledged monster, or at least willing consort of a monster. She transforms from passive victim to active aggressor and becomes what the fictional tabloid *National Tattler* in *The Silence of the Lambs* prophetically called "The Bride of Frankenstein." But in so doing, she redeems Lecter, the final beneficiary of her moral martyrdom, by literally offering up her breast to his hungry (but in this case not cannibalistic) mouth.

Starling ends up as Lecter's "bosom" companion because the novel's opening shootout begins the process of isolating Starling from her two male mentors in the FBI. (Former Senator Martin, Starling's only powerful female ally, is no longer in office and is thus unable to protect her either.) Jack Crawford, of course, is one of those mentors. BATF Special Agent John Brigham — Starling's firearms coach, close friend, and could-have-been lover — is the other. However, Crawford has been ineffectual in getting Starling assigned to Behavioral Science and, with retirement looming, is no longer a power to be reckoned with in the FBI hierarchy. Brigham, who is younger but equally unable to do much for Starling's moribund career, is removed from Starling's life in a much more dramatic and final way. In the opening scene, Brigham is fatally gunned down by drug-dealer Evelda Drumgo in a raid gone disastrously wrong. In the resulting melee, broadcast from an orbiting news helicopter and photographed by nearby reporters, Starling kills five people, including Drumgo, who happens to be carrying her infant with her when Starling kills her. The infant is covered with his mother's blood but is otherwise unharmed; however, the media reaction is to publish photographs of Starling washing the blood off the infant and to declare her a "Death Angel" and a "Killing Machine" who may face departmental and civil liability in the death of the mother. The Guinness Book of World Records even takes notice, sending her a questionnaire in order "to list her as having killed more criminals than any other female law enforcement officer in United States history" (95).

As the unfavorable publicity mounts, FBI Director Tunberry informs Starling's sole remaining protector, Jack Crawford, that Starling must be sacrificed to Judiciary Oversight to save the FBI from further repercussions. Justice Department official Paul Krendler, Starling's chief antagonist, has convinced Tunberry that Starling's ruin is necessary. Tunberry, in turn, orders Crawford to not interfere. Starling is then completely alone and vulnerable before the wrath of public opinion and the professional animosity represented primarily by Paul Krendler — a development that compels the smitten Lecter, at the risk of his own life and freedom, to reach back into Starling's life via letter all the way from his exile in Florence, Italy. So, just as Starling loses her patriarchal protectors within the FBI, serial killer Lecter ironically establishes himself as Starling's new guiding mentor through the suddenly treacherous landscape of the FBI. In turn, Starling herself has now taken on the aura of a killer, albeit an officially (though briefly) sanctioned one. The two are moving closer together.

Of course, the prime mover in this relationship is Lecter, befitting his status as the older and more experienced killer. His courtship from afar continues the psychological manipulation begun in Dr. Chilton's asylum. Lecter's first communication to Starling in seven years begins by invoking the memory of Starling's dead father: "In our discussions down in the dungeon, it was apparent to me that your father ... figures large in your value system. I think your success in putting an end to Jame Gumb's career ... pleased you most because you could imagine your father doing it.... Have you always imagined your father ahead of you there [at the FBI].... And now do you see him shamed and crushed by your disgrace?" (30) Lecter, having reminded Starling of her most basic motivations, then tries to reassure her that the loss of a career in the FBI is not as devastating a loss as she feels it to be: "Have your superiors demonstrated any values, Clarice? How about your parents, did they demonstrate any? If so, are those values the same...? Have you failed your dead family? Would they want you to suck up?" Lecter concludes his pep talk to his future lover by reminding her that the shootout with Drumgo ended well, no matter what her critics say: "You are a warrior, Clarice. The enemy is dead, the baby safe. You are a warrior" (32).

Lecter's encouragement betrays the depth of his emotional commitment to Starling, and his earnest desire to help her in ways that Brigham and Crawford, from their respectable niches within society, could never do. His rhetorical emphasis upon the image of Starling's father also indicates his awareness of the primary reason that Starling remains isolated and sexless — she is in thrall to the memory of a dead father, just as Lecter is psychologically imprisoned by his memories of his dead sister Mischa, who was cannibalized by starving soldiers during World War II. Both are traumatized by the brutal deaths of loved ones early in life, and both see in each other the earthly continuation of the essence of the dead loved one. Later in the novel, a psychologist named Dr. Doemling, who has been enlisted by Verger to explain why Starling and Lecter are attracted to each other, elaborates: "I think the woman Starling may have a lasting attachment to her father, an *imago*, that prevents her from easily forming sexual relationships and may incline her to Dr. Lecter in some kind of transference, which in his perversity he would seize on at once" (271). Dr. Doemling's explanation, while simplistic and too dismissive of Lecter's emotional attachment to Starling, touches upon at least part of the truth regarding the complex relationship between the younger female FBI agent and the older male serial killer — supposedly one another's mortal enemies.

Lecter's fatherly words restore Starling's self-confidence for her confrontational meeting with Krendler and her hostile FBI supervisors. However, his message also exposes Lecter to the danger of capture from the various forces arrayed against him. Lecter is aware that the FBI and the employees of Mason Verger are scouring the world hunting for him, and he also knows that Starling, at this point, will still share his message with his pursuers and thus give the competing investigations renewed impetus to find him. However, Lecter is willing to take the chance because of his attraction to Starling, who represents the memory of his lost sister Mischa just as much as Lecter represents a dark father-figure to Starling. Indeed, the jeopardy that Lecter faces in the last third of the novel arises directly out of his initial contact with Starling, but in turn Lecter has given Starling a brief reprieve from professional death. The Lecter message gives mentor Crawford one last opportunity to intercede covertly on Starling's behalf. The meeting at which "Death Angel" Starling is to be sacrificed to male political cowardice ends abruptly, leaving Starling in limbo but, at least momentarily, with her shaky career still in place. Afterward, Crawford tells Starling privately, "They were going to throw you away, Starling, clean up with you like you were a rag. You would have been wasted just like John Brigham. Just to save some bureaucrats at BATF.... I had somebody drop a dime to [Mason Verger] and tell him how much it would hurt the hunt for Lecter if you got canned. Whatever else happened, who Mason might have called after that, I don't want to know" (49–50). Thus begins the novel's primary story arc — the attempt of the grotesquely injured Mason Verger to use Starling as bait to lure Lecter into the grisly if implausible fate (death by man-eating pig) Verger has planned for the man who made Verger feed his own face to a pack of dogs and then paralyzed him. Lecter escapes from Verger twice — the first time in Florence, effortlessly and unaided. But when Lecter allows his guard to slip as he comes to the United States to pursue Starling, Verger is able to capture Lecter and nearly carry out his plan to feed Lecter to the pigs. Starling, true to form as established in *The Silence of the Lambs*, descends into hell in order to rescue another helpless victim from a monstrous villain. Ironically, this time the victim is Dr. Lecter.

Part II of the novel, entitled "Florence," details Lecter's first escape from Verger's forces and demonstrates the extent of his crafty intelligence unleashed from the confines of a jail cell. A professionally disgraced Italian investigator named Rinaldo Pazzi has inadvertently identified Lecter behind his assumed identity as Dr. Fell, new curator of the Palazzo Capponi, and rather than formally arrest him, decides to turn Lecter over to Verger's representatives. As the noose draws tighter around Lecter, he unconcernedly spends his off-hours watching for news of Starling in the tabloids and on the FBI's home page, sketching her as a griffin and writing a note to her calling her "the honey in the lion," and shipping bath oils and lotions to Starling — all demonstrating the depth of his attraction to his dream-lover and surrogate sister, Starling. When Pazzi makes his move against Lecter, Lecter easily kills Pazzi, among others involved in the trap, and disappears again. The Florence interlude establishes that Lecter, undistracted by the intoxicating presence of Starling, is quite capable of bloodily defending his life and freedom and is still the quintessential super-demon of Harris's other two serial-killer novels. Only as Lecter moves closer to Starling does his physical jeopardy increase — establishing that the Gothic link between romance and danger cuts both ways, endangering not only the Maiden but the Shadow as well.

Following the murder of Pazzi, Lecter heads via jetliner to the New World with Starling's home address retrieved from his memory palace and nightmares of Mischa's death becoming more vivid as he nears Starling. Meanwhile, Starling, back at the FBI and with her career temporarily reprieved by the revival of the Lecter case, begins tracking Lecter. More isolated than ever in her institutional cubicle, she has an epiphany on the subject of "taste" that enables her to find the ghost trail of Lecter's movements. She has come to realize in her professional tribulations that she no longer has faith in institutional technique borne from rigorous training and education of the sort she devoted herself to in the FBI. Rather, she now turns to "her own visceral reactions to things, without quantifying them or restricting them to words.... Within the framework of her mind, ... she felt as though she were giving in to a delicious perversion ... the sea change inside her ... sped her toward the idea that Dr. Lecter's taste for rarified things, things in a small market, might be the monster's dorsal fin, cutting the surface and making him visible" (225–26). By rediscovering and trusting in her "gut" instincts, she has bridged the formerly vast conceptual abyss between her and the killer Lecter, in which instinctual savagery and educated intellect co-exist in equilibrium. She is one step closer to becoming Lecter's lover — even without the drugs and hypnosis he uses to make that final crossover complete.

The remainder of the novel traces the stages in Starling's final exile from society. Verger's second trap, the one that nearly succeeds, is sprung shortly after Starling begins to track Lecter through his exotic purchases. Dr. Doemling, Verger's hired psychological gun, advises Verger to place Starling in jeopardy again — to finish the professional ruination that was abruptly halted earlier in the novel — to bring Lecter out into the open. Verger orders Krendler to break Starling on a false charge: that she tried to warn Lecter of his danger in Florence through a classified ad in the Milan daily newspaper. (Verger himself placed the ad.) Unaware of Verger's latest move, Starling goes about her daily routine as Lecter surreptitiously spies on her (even breaking into her car to sniff her steering wheel) and then returns to his new home in Maryland to savor the images and smells of her as he plays his harpsichord. In the matrix of associations Lecter holds within his memory palace, Starling and Mischa conflate into an image of an arrow-wounded deer led to the slaughter by the same men who killed and ate Mischa — a traumatic association that compels Lecter to kill and dress a poacher and bowhunter he first encounters at a gun and knife show and then follows into the woods. When Starling is called to the northern Virginia morgue where the mutilated hunter's body has been taken, she links the latest murder with Lecter's sixth victim — also a bowhunter. Even before DNA testing on a hair sample from the arrow taken from the hunter's body confirms it, Starling knows now that Lecter has returned home.

Krendler and Verger, also learning of Lecter's confirmed return, make their final move against Starling by setting up a hearing where Assistant FBI Director Noonan and Krendler expel protector Crawford from her side, place her on administrative leave on the basis of Verger's planted ad, and take away her badge and weapon. Before she surrenders her weapon, Starling entertains a brief fantasy of killing all four of her professional tormentors — yet another indication of how much closer her isolation has moved her to Lecter. To further aggravate Starling's alienation, Crawford suffers a heart attack shortly after the hearing. Finally, the media, in full scandal mode as a result of the Clinton impeachment hearings and alerted by Krendler to further bloodsport, eagerly publicize Starling's latest professional disgrace. Lecter, seeing Starling's exile broadcast on television, realizes that the time is right for his seduction of Starling and so steals a number of sedatives, anesthetics, and powerful mind-altering drugs necessary for what he has planned for Starling and Krendler. However, his guard down because of his pursuit of Starling, Lecter is abducted by Verger's minions and taken to Verger's rural compound. Witnessing the kidnapping and knowing what Verger has in mind for Lecter, she realizes she cannot tolerate Lecter being tortured to death: "she shied from it as she had from the slaughter of the lambs and the horses so long ago.... Almost as ugly as the act itself was the fact that Mason would do this with the tacit agreement of men sworn to uphold the law" (397). So she decides to go against her the dishonorable men of her profession and finds liberation in her rebellion — she realizes that "she was not quite herself, and she was glad" (398). Verger's trap for Lecter, in a strange way, is about to free Starling from the tyranny of the past.

The stage is therefore set for Shadow and Maiden to work together — for Starling to rescue Lecter from his enemy, Verger, and for Lecter to rescue Starling from her enemy, Krendler. Using a gun secretly vouchsafed to her by dead father-surrogate Brigham, Starling does indeed save the helplessly bound Lecter from Verger's men while Verger himself is gruesomely killed by his own sister. In the melee, however, Starling is shot with a tranquilizer dart and Lecter, in turn, carries the unconscious Starling safely away from Verger's farm and takes her to his home on the Chesapeake. The final section of the novel — the part which outrages the largest number of readers — describes Lecter's "therapeutic" treatment of Starling, through hypnosis and powerful drugs, for her father fixation and Starling's equally therapeutic treatment of Lecter for his sister fixation. Lecter's therapy includes forcing Starling to confront, quite literally, the skeletonized remains of Starling's father, which Lecter has earlier exhumed and brought to his home. Through this confrontation, Starling finally acknowledges her unspoken anger at her father's ignorance, low ambitions, and abandonment of his family. But in the macabre course of treatment prescribed by Dr. Lecter, one last hurdle remains before she can fully integrate the savage and civilized halves of her psyche. She must partake in the murder of Krendler, who as an older male out to sexually harass and ruin her symbolizes all of her darkest feelings about her dead father.

Lecter prepares her for the shared act of murder by lecturing to her about his theory of the balance between savagery and civilization: "Clarice, dinner appeals to taste and smell, the oldest senses and the closest to the center of the mind. Taste and smell are housed in parts of the mind that precede pity, and pity has no place at my table.... This evening you will see yourself from a distance for a while. You will see what is just, you will say what is true. You've never lacked the courage to say what you think, but you've been hampered by constraints. I will tell you again, pity has no place at this table" (466). When Lecter brings out the bound and lobotomized Krendler for the main course, Starling has "progressed" far enough in her therapy to confront her nemesis, who represents the unspoken envies and forbidden sexual desires underlying her simultaneous attraction and repulsion to paternalism: "You know, Mr. Krendler, every time you leered at me, I had the nagging feeling I had done something to deserve it.... I *didn't* deserve it. Every time you wrote something negative in my personnel folder, I resented it, but still I searched myself. I doubted myself for a moment, and tried to scratch this tiny itch that said Daddy knows best.... You *don't* know best, Mr. Krendler. In fact, you don't know anything.... You are forever an ... an *oaf,* and beneath notice" (471). For the rest of dinner, as Starling and Lecter dine on brains dished from the still-living Krendler's cranium, Krendler indeed is mostly beneath notice, singing scraps of childhood rhyme hidden behind a funerary flower arrangement until Lecter forever silences him with a crossbow bolt. Lecter also verbally imprints the susceptible Starling with an association between the sound of the crossbow string and her complete liberation from thralldom to Lecter — suggesting that the Shadow is learning to respect his lover's autonomy even as he manipulates her.

The dinner scene then concludes with Starling's reciprocal therapy for her Shadow lover Lecter's obsessive desire to reverse time and bring his cannibalized sister Mischa back into the world. Starling says: "If a prime place in the world is required for Mischa, ... what's the matter with your place? It's well occupied and I know you would never deny her. She and I could be like sisters. And if, as you say, there's room in my for my father, why is there not room in you for Mischa...? Hannibal Lecter, did your mother feed you at her breast...? Did you ever feel you had to relinquish the breast to Mischa...? You don't have to give up this one" (476–77). With that, Starling bares her breast to Lecter and allows him to nurse, thus simultaneously freeing herself and Lecter from their mutually shared sexual frigidity while confronting the incest taboos that have paralyzed both from a young age. In the years that follow, Starling and Lecter live the cultured life in Buenos Aires, freed of the demons of their pasts and choosing to remember only that which is good for both. Lecter symbolically has his sister back and Starling has managed to cultivate a satisfying personal relationship with a father figure. Both need each other, and yet both are fiercely independent at the same time, as Harris concludes: "Clarice Starling's memory palace is building as well. It shares some rooms with Dr. Lecter's own memory palace — he has discovered her in there several times — but her own palace grows on its own. It is full of new things. She can visit her father there.... Jack Crawford is there, when she chooses to see him bent over at his desk" (483). The two have healed through a shared monstrosity.

In conclusion, those readers and critics who were horrified that Starling turned into a cannibal, however drugged and hypnotized and coerced, are overlooking one of Harris's most obvious literary conceits — the intermingling of culture and primitivism central to the Gothic tradition. The novels in Harris's canon are constructed on such binaries. His mass-murdering and serial-killing protagonists display superior degrees of intelligence and professional, public service twisted into private missions driven by fantasies of slaughter and memories of past injury. Michael Lander, once such a promising student and superb pilot, is driven by family dysfunction and social humiliation to use his gifts to strike back against the middle-class America that he both feels superior to and shunned by. Dahlia Iyad feeds her ideological commitment to the Palestinian cause with bloodlust fueled by childhood memories of her family's destruction in the refugee camps. Together, Lander and Dahlia unite in rage to harm a country that they hate for differing but complementary reasons. Hannibal Lecter, born with an almost supernatural intelligence and outward physical markers of his exceptionality (the extra sixth finger on one hand, the maroon-tinted eyes), is motivated at least in part by being orphaned in World War II and then seeing his sister taken away from him and eaten by starving soldiers. Clarice Starling, also an orphan, becomes an FBI agent to redeem her father's meaningless death but learns she must look within her self and away from the kind of institutional authority that so betrays her. What she finds within herself is a child's anger, hatred, and brutality — qualities that her final tutor, Lecter, no stranger to obsessive reliving of childhood trauma, eagerly helps to liberate. Lecter's privileged insights into life show Starling the way toward her personal freedom in this fallen world of savagery. Thus, through the union of hurt souls, Harris shows us all that the monsters are not so different from us as we may wish.

Notes

1. Robert Plunket exclaims in *The Advocate*: "In fact, never has a mainstream thriller been quite so fraught with stereotypically homosexual themes and motifs. Among the more prominent: opera, bodybuilding, pornography, fussy entertaining, drugs, cosmetic surgery, the daddy obsession, and — I swear to God — a lesbian couple contemplating artificial insemination" (74).

2. Paul Gray writes, "Having created a character of unadulterated evil, Harris has now proceeded to adulterate him, giving Lecter a traumatic childhood experience to explain the wicked path he later trod" (72). Similarly, Terry Teachout laments, "What possessed Harris to tell us such a thing? With this wholly unexpected revelation, the dignified demon ... shrivels before our eyes into yet another sympathy-seeking victim, the sort of fellow whose pain Bill Clinton would hasten to feel" (53).

3. A typical scathing review comes from Annabelle Villanueva: "Ever since I finished reading *Hannibal* two days ago, I've tried to quiet my anger long enough to write a level-headed, fair review. Unfortunately, that's been really hard, because this sequel ... may be the most loathsome book I've ever encountered, with surely one of the most obscene endings ever written.... I've never seen a writer so thoroughly betray his characters. It's amazingly ridiculous — Clarice Starling, as Harris created her, would never become the person she becomes in the novel's final pages" (par. 1, 5).

4. Apparently, Jodie Foster, who played Starling in the 1991 film, agreed. She publicly refused to have anything to do with the film adaptation of *Hannibal*, which led to a frantic series of script rewrites that eliminated Starling's drug-induced cannibalism and thralldom to Lecter but failed to lure Foster away from her commitment to another film. *Hannibal* as a film directed by Ridley Scott stars Julianne Moore as Starling and returns Anthony Hopkins to the Lecter role that he made so famous. The film does place Starling in the morally ambiguous position of allowing Lecter to escape police custody at the film's conclusion but absolves her of cannibalistic complicity in the grotesque death of Paul Krendler. This plot revision is probably responsible for the financial success and more favorable public and critical reaction of the film as opposed to the source novel. For an examination of *Hannibal*'s status as Hollywood blockbuster, see my own essay, "The Horror 'Event' Movie: *The Mummy, Hannibal,* and *Signs.*"

5. For an overview of how the Gothic tradition informs and structures conventions within the fiction of serial murder, see my own *Psycho Paths*, pages 27–35.

6. Tony Magistrale elaborates on the role of victimization in *Black Sunday*: "Lander and the members of the radical terrorist group ... are the cyclical products of historical violence and political betrayals" (33).

7. To this end, she risks the entire Super Bowl mission by attempting to kill Kabakov in a U.S. hospital where he is recuperating from injuries sustained in a bomb blast.

8. With the advantage of hindsight, one is tempted to see here, in embryonic form, the same type of metaphoric therapist-client relationship as that between Lecter and Starling in *The Silence of the Lambs* and *Hannibal*.

9. The reversed gender stereotypes — a "womanly" father and a masculine mother — are another persistent theme in Harris's fiction of identity transmutation.

Works Consulted

Fuller, Stephen M. "Deposing an American Cultural Totem: Clarice Starling and Postmodern Heroism in Thomas Harris's *Red Dragon, The Silence of the Lambs,* and *Hannibal." The Journal of Popular Culture,* vol. 38, no. 5 (August 2005).

Gray, Paul. "Desert, Anyone?" *Time,* 21 June, 1999.

Harris, Thomas. *Black Sunday.* 1975. Reprint. New York: Bantam, 1977.

_____. *Hannibal.* New York: Delacorte Press, 1999.

Hutchings, Peter. "Tearing Your Soul Apart: Horror's New Monsters," in Victor Sage and Allan Lloyd Smith (eds.), *Modern Gothic: A Reader.* Manchester: Manchester University Press, 1996.

Magistrale, Tony. "Transmogrified Gothic: The Novels of Thomas Harris," in Tony Magistrale and Michael A. Morrison (eds.), *A Dark Night's Dreaming: Contemporary American Horror Fiction.* Columbia, S.C.: University of South Carolina Press, 1996.

Messent, Peter. "American Gothic: Liminality in Thomas Harris's Hannibal Lecter Novels." *Journal of American and Comparative Cultures,* vol. 23, no. 4 (Winter 2000).

Mizejewski, Linda. *Hardboiled and High Heeled: The Woman Detective in Popular Culture.* New York: Routledge, 2004.

Plunket, Robert. "Eating Our Own." *Advocate,* 31 Aug. 1999.

Simpson, Philip L. "The Horror 'Event' Movie: *The Mummy, Hannibal,* and *Signs,*" in Steffen Hantke (ed.), *Horror Film: Creating and Marketing Fear.* Jackson, Miss.: University Press of Mississippi, 2004.

_____. *Psycho Paths: Tracking the Serial Killer through Contemporary American Film and Fiction.* Carbondale: Southern Illinois University Press, 2000.

Teachout, Terry. "Feel His Pain." *National Review,* vol. 51, no. 3 (1999).

Villanueva, Annabelle. "*Hannibal* (rev.)." *Cinescape Online,* June 1999. .

Winder, Robert. "A Contemporary Dracula." *New Statesman,* vol. 128 (1999).

4

The Butterfly and the Beast

The Imprisoned Soul in
Thomas Harris's Lecter Trilogy

ROBERT H. WAUGH

The maniac of *The Silence of the Lambs* puts a death's-head moth in the mouths of his victims, a bizarre action that Stapleton, the criminal butterfly-collector who stands behind the beast in *The Hound of the Baskervilles,* would understand. Between these two thrillers several works play with motifs of butterflies, hounds, and labyrinths and with such figures as the collector, the captive, and the transformed self. The prototype of these figures is Stapleton in Arthur Conan Doyle's novel; related to him is the eccentric Legrand of Edgar Allan Poe's "The Gold Bug," in which the theme of the sacred nature of the scarab becomes apparent. The class implications of these motifs are developed in John Fowles's novel *The Collector,* and significant elements also appear in *Lolita,* written by a well-known butterfly-collector. With these works in mind we can see Thomas Harris's Hannibal Lecter tetralogy in a new light as he plays with these tropes. Common to all these works are their implicit allusions to the myth of Theseus, who threads his way through the labyrinth on the island of Crete by means of a clue to defeat the Minotaur, winning and deserting Ariadne, who in some versions of the myth is then won by Dionysus, who translates her crown into the heavens (Graves 1.339–40). In a duplication of the story, Theseus descends into the underworld, braving the beast Cerberus in an attempt to win Persephone. Lurid and magical, these works demonstrate that beauty, murder, filth and transformation are "Blown past the marsh where the butterflies play" (Lindsay 180).

I. Imagery in the Tetralogy

More than fifty years after Doyle's story of the butterfly-collector and the hound, Thomas Harris returned the material to its unsavory place in the bog of the popular thriller. His tetralogy is loosely connected by the figure of Hannibal Lecter, a secondary character in the first novel *Red Dragon* and a central character in the second, third, and fourth novels; but although he was originally a secondary character, a number of details already made him compelling. One of the most striking is that in a novel narrated through the traditional past tense he is presented in the present tense. He "has" maroon eyes, he "is" lithe, and his teeth "are" small (69–70). Though he acts in the past tense, he exists in a mythic present that Harris employs throughout the four books; he uses the present tense for his antagonists also, but only in terms of their loose monologues — their lives are never mythic. How can they be, since they are almost speechless? They very much resemble Frederick Clegg in *The Collector*, who denies his name in favor of Ferdinand; but vis-à-vis his captive, Miranda, he is Caliban. "Thou earth, thou! Speak," Prospero commands Caliban (The Tempest, 1.2.314), and Clegg does (cleog means "clay" according to the *Oxford English Dictionary*), usurping the role of Prospero: he teaches Miranda a lesson, and at the end of the novel plans to teach his new butterfly how to pose for pornographic photographs (304–05). The new world of the middle class cages or destroys all beauty before which it stands impotent — impotent, that is, as long as beauty is alive, errant, unclassifiable; for Clegg believes in his potency with the photographs that don't "talk back" (109).

Like Clegg, Dolarhyde in *Red Dragon* and Gumb in *The Silence of the Lambs* are explicable, but Lecter is inexplicable within the terms of any psychiatric framework; he is a sociopath "because they don't know what else to call him" (*Red Dragon* 62). Both as myth and as sociopath he is private. Like Sherlock Holmes with his powerful sense of smell, Lecter behaves as though he were a sleuth, a hound that smells out his prey. In *The Hound of the Baskervilles* the first trace of Stapleton occurs when Holmes smells the perfume of Mrs. Stapleton on her anonymous letter (15; 897). Holmes has a fine sense of smell; and like the hell-hound he breathes smoke — through his pipe. In the second novel Lecter's sense of scent becomes a means of seduction, in the third a means of romanticizing the world, and in the fourth of discovering it. But although Lecter is a hound and a detective, he definitely lacks one quality that Graham and Starling, the protagonists of the novels, possess fully, the curse of being able to empathize with victims and madmen. Empathy, his great lack, becomes one of the themes of the tetralogy.

Dr. Lecter is also, in a democratic age, an elitist. Is it a surprise that in *Hannibal Rising* we learn he is the son of a count, though we would rather that he be in this as in so much else *sui generis.* His tastes, even when he feeds upon his victims, are refined. Confined to an ascetic cell that his guards watch with extreme care, he guards it himself with a fastidious awareness. Like Holmes and Stapleton he is careful about his appearance. Furthermore, he is a doctor of psychoanalysis, the man in charge of the new confessional, in which he learns secrets by which to destroy his patients. More importantly he is an aesthete who heroically despises the world as given (Fowler 3).

Imprisoned as he is, Lecter must send forth emissaries. He sends Dolarhyde, his pilgrim, to kill Graham, Molly, and her son. "Kill them all" (*Red Dragon* 130), he writes, with a swift, gratuitous viciousness that Graham, Starling, and a reader should never overlook. Stapleton is also recognizable through his emissaries: the typist Laura Lyons, betrayed by her husband and father; and Stapleton's sister, in fact his wife, both of them women he pimps for his own loveless purposes. But Holmes doubles also, for he sends forth Watson, whose function is emphasized through his narrative, his letters, and his diary. His being sent forth by Holmes approximates his figure to that of Mrs. Stapleton and Mrs. Lyons. Like them he is duped, so much that he says to Holmes, "You use me, and yet do not trust me...! I think that I have deserved better at your hands" (12; 868–69). He is Holmes's butterfly anima and plays Ariadne to Holmes's Theseus; for despite Holmes's deprecation, Watson is important to the solution of the case.

Graham is an emissary of Crawford, who sends out Starling as his emissary in the next two novels. Cursed by his empathy, Graham is leery of picking up his work again; it is only his awareness that more people shall die if he holds back from involving himself in the murderous complex of the killer that compels him to take action. But this work is an affront to his imagination; in an allusion to imagery that pervades the trilogy, "often his thoughts were not tasty" (26). His empathy becomes very strong when he senses that he and the murderer are "doing the same things," eating, showering, or sleeping at the same time (192–93).

In the matter of empathy we must discriminate between Graham's talent and Holmes's. Often Holmes insists upon the need to imagine what a criminal might have done, but his use of the word "imagine" makes clear that it is a voluntary, rational act of picturing the criminal; he is not like Legrand, who tentatively solves the puzzle of the skeletons that sprawled across the treasure through being as imaginatively capable of bludgeoning Jupiter and the doctor as Captain Kidd was capable of killing his two assistants (Hoffman 131–32). Insofar as Graham suffers his talent for empathy he is much closer to the roots of mayhem than Holmes. In *Hannibal*, on the other hand, Starling, who has a touch of empathy herself, believes that "it's hard and ugly to know somebody can understand you without even liking you" (48). The understanding Lecter shows when dealing with his patients does not prevent him from murdering them.

The tabloid photographer Lounds, who has a modicum of understanding, introduces a theme important to the three novels, the use of film and various optical apparatus to spy upon victims, because the antagonists of the novels need distance. This motif seems innocent in Doyle's and Poe's works, in which Watson and Legrand make use of telescopes, but it is considerably less innocent in Fowles' novel. Clegg and Harris's antagonists are voyeurs who believe they can master a situation through film; Dolarhyde like Clegg masturbates to the films he has taken of his murders. Lounds also represents another kind of character found throughout the trilogy, the vulgarian who does not believe in anything except his own career; he does not understand the idealistic insanity of Dolarhyde or Lecter or the idealistic sanity of Graham. Dr. Chilton is the main example of this kind of character in the second novel, and Krendler the main example in the third, both of whom lust after Starling without Lecter's odd intensity; their lust is quotidian, as are their lives. In their arrogance neither can believe in Lecter's unreadability. Because of his disbelief Dolarhyde captures Lounds and sets him aflame, rolling down the street like a fireball, its "flames blown back like wings" (177). He is turned into a demonic butterfly, the Red Dragon that Dolarhyde hopes to become.

The imagery of various insects is rich in the novel. When Graham and Willy feed the dogs, moths are batting at the screen (19). Reba has no fear of the bees attracted by the rotting apples around Dolarhyde's house (259). A caterpillar hangs near the tree behind the Jacobi house; and just before Graham finds the sign of the Red Dragon a beagle begins to bark and a cicada to buzz (92). As a child Dolarhyde keeps "a bright beetle in a pill bottle" (214), a phrase striking for its balance and pararhyme. When he chooses his victims the film seems to "jump against his palm like a cricket" (220). Gagged and tied in Dolarhyde's van Reba can hear the crickets (313). Graham thinks Mrs. Leeds drew her killer "as surely as a singing cricket attracts death from the red-eyed fly" (48), a more percipient image than he knows given Dolarhyde's red goggles (78). Graham feels that Lecter can see through his head, "his attention ... like a fly walking around in there" (70). All of the insects associated with transformation are imprisoned, those not are vicious.

This imagery is basic to our study. The butterfly is an ancient symbol of the psyche as it escapes the cocoon of the body; but it is not the only insect that symbolizes this moment, for cicadas and crickets also appear in crucial moments. Odysseus holds out to Cerberus a cicada, and cicadas and crickets are involved in the rebirth myths of Arion, Memnon, and Tithonus (Bachofen 368). The bee and the scarab offer the same hope. There is no butterfly in Poe's story; but there is a scarab and a labyrinth. The mystification of the bug (844) is of a piece with the hoaxes that riddle Poe's career. Yet how profoundly the scarab works when it exchanges places with the death's-head on the other side of the page that contains the cipher. Other references to insects belie the mystification. The cipher may be read, "Shoot from the left eye of the death's-head a bee line from the tree" (839), and when Legrand sees the death's head and his own drawing of the gold bug he experiences "a glow-worm–like conception" of the truth (829). Bee and glow-worm suggest intellectual enlightenment and renewal. The significance of the scarab in Egyptian religion is telling: "The god who begets himself is depicted ... as the scarab or dung beetle. Because he rolls a ball of dung before him, this beetle was venerated as the sun-moving principle.... He buries the sun-ball in a hole in the ground and dies, and in the following spring the new beetle creeps out of the ball as the new sun" (Neumann, *Origins* 236). Its self-originating nature makes the scarab emblematic of the heart animating the body. It represents that tension between value and valuelessness, which confronts any desire of renewal. In this story dung materializes as the filthy lucre into which Jupiter buries his arms "as if enjoying the luxury of a bath" (826) and which Legrand and the narrator so carefully collect.

Like the insects, the dog is scattered throughout *Red Dragon*. Obsessed with dogs, Graham can sense madness "like a bloodhound sniffs a shirt" (22). In a home movie the dog Scotty barks silently to announce Mrs. Leeds (50). Dogs are involved in Graham's Augustinian theft of a watermelon, when he was pursued by a swineherd and the dogs (53). Comic as these instances are, they point up the complex feelings Dolarhyde brings to his choice of victims. Given to hurting animals and pets as a young boy, he becomes excited when his film of the Shermans shows him their small dog. Standing in front of the labyrinth and the night-journey into the underworld, the hound is as central to the myth as the butterfly; and in *The Hound of the Baskervilles* the hound remains supernatural despite Holmes's scorn for the legend, for the hound and the moor become indistinguishable. Doyle used a bit of local folklore that implies the myth of Cerberus, Hades, and Persephone, conflated with the myth of Theseus and Ariadne who solve the labyrinth in order to slay the Minotaur. The divided nature of the Minotaur, human and bestial, the offspring of queen Pasiphae and the bull from the sea, reveals itself as the dichotomy between the butterfly and beast. Mythologically Holmes is unsuccessful; for though he hopes "to drag this great dog to the light of day" (12; 876) as Hercules did Cerberus, he merely kills it and demystifies its fire.

The great threat Dolarhyde presents, who aspires as much to become a hound as a dragon, is to his blind colleague Reba. Her blindness works in a number of ways. It becomes a motif in the next novel, in which Gumb pursues his prey and Starling in the darkness of his basement as he uses infrared glasses, his symbol of weakness and of power, as are the glasses of Dolarhyde. But Reba's blindness is also a grace; she is relieved from the control that comes from too great a reliance on the sense of sight, the preeminent sense of knowledge in the Western world. The four books conduct a dialectic between the sense of sight and the senses of taste, smell, touch, and hearing, which are so intimate in their effect but which we have denigrated as the senses of the beast — we have noted how important smell is to the hound. Deprived of a world that seems objectively given, Reba nevertheless moves with a confidence and courage that allow her to save herself.

II. Motifs of Regression

In the second novel Jame Gumb has for a short time worked for the Hide leather company. He has a poodle that serves as a blind for the actual hound of the novel, Dr. Lecter (*Red Dragon* 69; *The Silence of the Lambs* 131), who attacks like a dog killing a rat (*The Silence of the Lambs* 218). Much more than the compulsive Gumb, it is the beast Lecter who takes a good deal of pride in the events of the story and who sends Gumb forth and benefits from his actions. Gumb gums his victims to death, starving them in a pit; Lecter savors.

Gumb shares a number of qualities with Clegg, the drab life, the photography, the van, and the cellar "like the maze that thwarts us in

dreams" (186), where mannequins clothed in human skin stand "like broken classic statuary green beneath the sea" (187). His aggression, however,
differs: Gumb wishes to become his victims by wearing their skins; Clegg
despises the notion of mouthing his victim's ideas, although he envies her
class privilege and style. The death's-head of "The Gold Bug" becomes
the death's-head moth that Gumb places in the mouths of his victims. But
to identify the moth Starling must regress, consulting the scientists in the
natural history museum, as Legrand had to consult the linguistic history
of South Carolina and Holmes had to live among the prehistoric huts dot-
ting the moor.

Regression is a frequent motif of this myth. Perhaps Stapleton is most
clearly revealed when Holmes covers the portrait of Stapleton's ancestor
to show that the man is a throwback, primitive as the people who once
lived in the huts. The portrait of the Cavalier, with his "firm-set, thin-
lipped mouth, and a coldly intolerant eye," reveals that the ancestor, who
collects women, and his descendant, who collects butterflies, share the
same obsessive personality.

Lecter is a reader, possessed of information that taints his New-
Critical purity. In charge of the sacred texts of psychiatry, which he scorns,
with more insight into their meaning than the doctors attempting to read
him, he lectures Starling. And he is our surrogate, devouring the text with
full complicity. Holmes is very like him in this respect. The Baskerville
legend that Watson finds moving is to Holmes merely of interest "to a collector of fairy-tales" (2; 790). His "cold, incisive, ironical voice" dissolves
the horror (12; 867). He exhibits no interest in outré prose styles; in mock-
ing them he represents the voice of reason in a novel that strives towards
the sensationalism of the Gothic. Lecter also is a critic, critical of any pre-
tension Starling might betray (*The Silence of the Lambs* 20, 208), although
he grants her a modicum of taste. Much more than Gumb (97), Lecter
lives on tears (207), like a moth (96); he sips pain (184). Chilton also
drinks pain, but like "a thirsty chicken" (11). He does not have the style
of a moth. Lecter also represents an aggressive theology, boasting: "I collect church collapses, recreationally. Did you see the recent one in Sicily?
Marvelous! The facade fell on sixty-five grandmothers at a special Mass.
Was that evil? If so, who did it? If He's up there, He just loves it" (19).
Like Satan, Lecter enjoys "going to and fro in his suite and walking up
and down in it" (251; Job 1.7), an allusion that Harris repeats in the third
novel but with a different accent, for there Lecter becomes the accuser of
human insufficiency (*Hannibal* 99). His tilted head is a symbol of the critical stance that he never releases (*Red Dragon* 71).

These metaphysics resemble concepts developed in *The Collector*. The only God that Miranda confesses is cold: "perhaps God has created the world and the fundamental laws of matter and evolution. But he can't care about individuals" (239). God is in the image of Clegg, who is "an empty space designed as a human" (240). These speculations are not to be found in Doyle, Poe, or Nabokov. Theology is quite beside the point for Holmes. Poe is not unmetaphysical, but the mysteries of this world are sufficient for the display of human intellect. Nabokov finds God in bad taste. Only for such post-holocaust authors as Fowles and Harris does the language of evil make sense. The God of *The Collector* resembles the Quiet into which Browning's Caliban speculates Setebos may molt "As grubs grow butterflies: else, here we are, / And there is He, and nowhere help at all" (*The Tempest*, ll. 248–49; 394). God masturbates over the bodies of the dead beauty his maze imprisons, for the labyrinth implies the sexual failure of Minos. Clegg has no way out of himself; his euphemisms create a maze that confines him and his victim, so at the end of the novel he is hardly transformed into a new life. Instead he degenerates to a compulsive, featureless object, rather like Dolarhyde, Gumb, and Mason.

But Lecter is more than demonic personality and hound. He is a butterfly, for his extra finger and the two colors of his eyes indicate that he is a sport. His "mask and the black vest suspended by its nape from the coat tree" (*The Silence of the Lambs* 205–6) and his trick of wearing Pembry's face in the ambulance suggest that he is molting into a new form. This language is introduced early in the novel, for Crawford has changed his style: "neat but drab, as though he were molting" (2); but he is molting into death.

As a neophyte Starling does not know everything, although she knows a good deal. Like Miranda in *The Collector* she is pressing her maturity; not independence so much as a clear vision is at stake. She is doubly sent forth. Crawford sends her to Lecter, who sends her through a labyrinth to Gumb; but she has been sent already by her father, whose place both Crawford and Lecter assume (Magistrale 38). Keen as a beagle (3), she becomes the transformed protagonist of the novel; but until then she is not a star but a starling, one tough bird. The imagery of the star, however, sprinkled through this novel and *Red Dragon*—Reba has "a small star-shaped scar" on her nose (*Red Dragon* 225)— suggests that not only does Starling have promise, she has always been promised. It is also suggestive to note that the "startling live movements" (261) of Reba in bed, recalled later by Dolarhyde as "her startling and harmless mobility" (304), promise that which characterizes Starling to Lecter, her ability to surprise him. In the third novel, before he captures her, he nevertheless possesses a sensibility that is "startling and gratifying to the scent merchants" of Florence (*Hannibal* 187). Arriving at Crawford's office "after a fast walk" (*The Silence of the Lambs* 1), she is in motion from the moment Harris introduces her; in this novel and the next her typical tableau is running.

The implicit comparison between Starling and Reba needs to be made more explicit. Just as Reba is deprived of sight, Starling has been deprived of a broad cultural background. Just as Reba moves with confidence and courage, so does Starling; and just as Reba is tricked by Dolarhyde, we should consider the possibility that Starling is tricked by Lecter. She attempts to remind herself conscientiously what he is, but at the conclusion of the third novel he collects her. Meanwhile, although she does sleep in peace at the end of the novel, the hunt surrounds her. The divided viewpoint that Starling and Lecter share comes to a kind of reconciliation by which each of them enjoys a partial release. She can sleep for a time; he can walk at large. She regresses to the waters (324); he flies.

III. Dilemmas of the Third and Fourth Novels

There is a shift in tone between the first two and the second two novels, perhaps accented by the fact that in the second two we find no pitiable antagonist like Dolarhyde or Gumb. Mason is too rich and too powerful, and so are Grutas and Kolnas, so that none need fear the police; they are free. But even Mason, as we shall see, is driven by various compulsions; Grutas and Kolnas are driven by nothing but greed. And the great difference between the two pairs of novels is that in the second pair Lecter does not suffer incarceration; though he must still be wary of the police, he no longer finds himself cast back upon his inner resources.

Several problems make the third novel, *Hannibal*, unsatisfying, albeit illuminating. Chief among them is Harris's betrayal of Lecter's unreadability when he offers a cheap psychoanalytic account of Lecter's childhood at the expense of his mythic power. If we consider that story soberly, the tale of a Lithuanian child whose sister is eaten by soldiers, we realize that the Lecter of the first two novels would have considered it in the worst of taste, just as Holmes disapproved of the style of the Baskerville legend. As Pooh-Bah puts the matter, Harris deploys "corroborative detail, intended to give artistic verisimilitude to an otherwise bald and unconvincing narrative" (Gilbert 390); it is a sentimental tale that raises more questions than it answers. Rather than psychoanalyze him we must take him at his word: "Nothing happened to me.... *I* happened. You can't reduce me to a set of influences" (*The Silence of the Lambs* 19), defying anyone to pluck out the heart of his mystery (*Hamlet* 3.2.351–52); he insists that evil exists. At the conclusion of the novel he collects Starling, and she has little chance of escape; rather, she consents to her new life as an object of elegant beauty. She is no longer a warrior but a Miranda.

Lecter identifies Starling as a butterfly when he thinks that "he could feed the caterpillar, he could whisper through the chrysalis; what hatched out followed its own nature and was beyond him" (*Hannibal* 466). In his memory palace Lecter collects her materials beneath a painting of St. Francis "feeding a moth to a starling" (253). She is "a butterfly lit on an armored fist" (458). But the fist will not set her free, anxious as it is that she fly beyond it. Perhaps most significant is Lecter's observation of her running, the light "blurring her outline as though she had been dusted with pollen" (282), a sight that recalls his young sister, "white cabbage butterflies around her" (283). But whom has Lecter captured? His sister he still possesses within his memory palace, perhaps in a more intimate fashion than that of the soldiers who ate her, and Starling he possesses at the conclusion of the novel as his mistress. In *The Hound of the Baskervilles* Stapleton imprisons the woman that he pretends is his sister but that is actually his wife; her joy is immense when she sets Holmes on her husband's trail through the labyrinth of the Grimpen Mire.

This sensory complex of Starling and his sister is similar to Humbert Humbert's view of Lolita as she plays tennis; with some ambivalence both dense moments suggest a transcendence of time that acknowledges time's power. Nabokov himself is a text as well as an author, a myth of the modern author as self-bewildered labyrinth-maker; and as a collector of butterflies it is easy to displace him into his own fiction.

For Nabokov a butterfly's "mysteries of mimicry had a special attraction" (*Conclusive Evidence* 83), its "luxury far in excess of a predator's power of appreciation" (84) and thus a metaphor of his own luxuriant style. The image of the butterfly is implicit in his sensuous aesthetics. Humbert's first meeting with Lolita has "that flash, that shiver, that impact of passionate recognition" in which she eclipses her prototype (41). Her tennis game, which she plays only for the sake of keeping the ball in play, is the high point of "the art of make-believe" because "it was the very geometry of basic reality" (233). The passage seems to insist upon the freedom of the artistic act.

On the other hand, although Humbert despises a camp where "some gaudy moth or butterfly, still alive, [is] safely pinned to the wall" (112), he does hope "to fix once for all the perilous magic of nymphets" (136), the borderline where "the beastly and beautiful" merge (137). This ineffable borderline Lolita embodies, first as the butterfly that Nabokov captured near Dolores, Colorado (Butler 61–63, 70–72). Studies of Nabokov notoriously make too much of details, so only in this study do we feel a frisson at the sight of "an elf-like girl on an insect-like bicycle, and a dog, a bit too large proportionately" (214). With Quilty we jeer, "Maeterlinck-Schmetterling" (303). But none of the foolery denies the happy accident at the conclusion of Humbert's words on art when "an inquisitive butterfly passed, dipping, between us" (236). Humbert embodies the borderline also as he attempts to write his account. It is a difficult place to live: "I talk in a daze, I walk in a maze, / I cannot get out, said the starling" (257) — which returns us to the events of *Hannibal*.

Taking place on the shores of the Chesapeake, many of these events evoke the sea. Theseus had to cross the sea to find the labyrinth, and this landscape is central to the mythic worlds of Doyle, Poe, and Fowles. The moor in Doyle is characterized by its prehistoric huts and their long-dead dwellers, "forced to accept that which none other would occupy" (8; 834), and by oceanic imagery, "undulating downs, long green rollers, with crests of jagged granite foaming up into fantastic surges" (7; 827), where the distant howl of the hound is "like the low, constant murmur of the sea" (12; 871). In Poe the story takes place on an island off the Carolina coast, where Legrand lives defended from the mainland by "a wilderness of reeds and slime" (807), accompanied by a Newfoundland called Wolf and a former slave, Jupiter, hunting for "shells or entomological specimens — his collection of the latter might have been envied by a Swammerdamm" (807). In Fowles the marine landscape is provided by the several references to *The Tempest*. For Harris the great maze is Muskrat Farm (or marshrat as many of the locals might say). And the dog has been supplanted in its bog by sixteen hogs, specially bred to devour Lecter. It is well to remember that one of Theseus's feats is the slaying of the Crommyonian sow (Graves 1.330–31). The image of the hog has appeared earlier in the series. Dolarhyde confessed that he was "rooting piglike with his bottom turned carelessly to the camera" (*Red Dragon* 83). Attacking the gas attendant who stares up Reba's skirt he refers to the man's "pig eyes" (263). Several other characters act out the part of the dog, most significant among them Krendler who turns his head "to her on his long neck as though he were locating her by scent" (*Hannibal* 352).

Mason Verger is engaged in capturing his own butterfly, Lecter. Mason, however, for all his verbal violence and taste for a martini salted by the tears of children (66), is only partially visible. He is a vulgarian, as we know from the sadistic, guiltless religiosity he preaches. Faceless, because his psychoanalyst Dr. Lecter had persuaded him to feed his face to dogs, and living now in semi-darkness, he is Hades. Confined to his bed and relying upon video-hookups for a connection to the world, he sends forth his emissary Carlo, always recognizable from "the rank boar-sausage smell of his head" (376). If the hogs stand in the place of the dog in this novel, Carlo is the Cerberus they incarnate. The mastiff that imprisons a lady in Doyle's "The Adventure of the Copper Beeches" is named Carlo (373); and in "The Adventure of the Sussex Vampire" a spaniel is named Carlo also (1225). The hogs, however, will not attack Lecter, but worship him as though he were the true Hades of the novel (427).

Many characteristics are the same in Lecter, but one strongly emphasized now is his memory palace, which he learned at the knees of Simonides, Cicero, and Giordano Bruno (253), who erected his interior palace as a means of grasping the universe. Harris, however, extends this magical image to include the oubliettes that dramatize Lecter's inner terrors. Unless he exerts a severe control the stench of the oubliette, centering on the death of his sister, overcomes him. The basement underworld in which he had been confined still accompanies him; but he no longer requires it as urgently as he had when incarcerated.

A further nuance to this characterization is Lecter's pseudonym, Dr. Fell, an allusion to the famous epigram that begins, "I do not like thee, Dr. Fell." Much more swiftly than Pazzi the reader knows why one should not like the erudite Doctor. But the word *fell* bears other meanings. It may refer to a moor, or to a hide or pelt; it may imply violence. The word compresses the several themes we have been concerned with. According to Mason in a nice word-play, Lecter looks like James Mason (62), who played Humbert Humbert in Stanley Kubrick's *Lolita*; we need to put Anthony Hopkins out of mind.

Although another characteristic was surely implicit in the earlier Lecter, it is still surprising in this third novel that he "very much liked to shop" (288). He shops for a wide variety of elite items, the paths by which Starling shall find him because his taste leads to him. Money and class are as important to Lecter as they are to Dolarhyde, Gumb, Legrand, and Clegg. Stephen King strews his novels with the brand names of the middle class; but Thomas Harris, in a more expensive appeal to consumerism, strews this third novel with the brand names of the upper class and by doing so makes more pressing the dilemma we face in the novels: Which shall it be, the vulgarians represented by Lounds, Chilton, Krendler, and Mason, or the elite represented by Lecter and the transformed Starling?

This dilemma allows a reader little space. We cannot side with the vulgarians, whose delectable deaths we are allowed a taste of; but neither can we side with an elite whose various murders, heightened by a nice taste in grotesqueries, are simply a part of the side show of the contemporary thriller. The power of Harris's novels resides in part in this moral dilemma.

On the other hand, a part of that power may be diluted by the style, which often seems to assume Lecter's point of view: "You may labor under the misconception that all Protestants look alike. Not so. Just as one Caribbean person can often tell the specific island of another, Starling, raised by the Lutherans, looked at [Inelle] and said to herself, *Church of Christ, maybe a Nazarene at the outside*" (68). Or consider this passage: "Now that ceaseless exposure has calloused us to the lewd and the vulgar, it is instructive to see what still seems wicked to us. What still slaps the clammy flesh of our submissive consciousness hard enough to get our attention?" (127). This narrative voice could well be Lecter's introduction to the exhibit of Atrocious Torture Instruments, which he attends in order to watch the faces of the self-righteous vulgarians who attend it; but the voice also functions as an accusation of anyone reading the novel. No doubt the vulgarians, the "free-range rude" (87) as Lecter calls them, are culpable, and Lecter, the mass murderer, is morally superior to them; and no doubt that audience represents the avid readers of the trilogy. Although we may pretend to be the knowledgeable equals of Lecter, the stance of the book identifies us as vulgarians, indicted as members of a mediocre culture (Van 45).

Different as this last novel is from the first two, it does take up one theme central to all three, the argument with God. The opening of Job is repeated twice, and Blake, so important to the first novel because of his picture of the Red Dragon, is alluded to again in the third (56). Both Blake and the author of Job, which Blake illustrated, are central figures in the argument that the Western world wages with God. In the first novel Dolarhyde is impressed by a tiger's "terrible striped face" (246) and arranges for Reba to feel it anaesthetized; her hands on its chest, she can hear "the tiger heart's bright thunder" (253). This is Blake's tiger, which elicits the question, "Did he who made the lamb make thee?" Is the God of love also the God of destruction? The question is so pressing and so difficult that it occasioned the first heresy, Marcion's decision that the God of the Old Testament, the evil maker of an evil world, could not be the God to whom Jesus refers. Until Starling transforms him, Lecter believes only in the God of mayhem. Starling does possess such power, symbolized by the tiger's eyes that Lecter recommends to pick up the color of her eyes and the highlights in her hair (*The Silence of the Lambs* 21).

But can she transform him, if she herself is not transformed? She resembles Miranda in *The Collector,* who becomes an object and then dies. Although aware of the desperate battle in which life is pitted against Thanatos, she dies untransformed; no other life exists than this. It is a dead beauty that Clegg imprisons. Miranda cannot become more than a chrysalis, because he keeps death prisoner (93): each is a death, each a projection of the theological and social case. In "The Gold-Bug" the labyrinth reveals that this "moneygrubbing nation of merchant materialists" know nothing of real wealth and that "the most valuable coins comprise a mystery within the mystery, being so old and worn there isn't even a secret writing on their face for Legrand to translate" (Hoffman 129). This blank at the center assures the prehistory of code and treasure. The maze of the code is a surround; the maze of the universe is bounded and all there is. Minos made the labyrinth in order to conceal his shame and in order to kill anyone who entered it. Theseus and Ariadne escape, but we are becoming less and less convinced that anyone in the labyrinth of these works has that chance.

As for Starling, lovely as the décor is at the conclusion of *Hannibal,* she seems half-drugged. We do not trust the vague assurance of the narrator that "the drugs that held her in the first days have had no part in their lives for a long time" (484). Is it possible that Lecter behaves in this way because he fears that he may be a false dog, like Humbert. Lolita pets a spaniel and rises, "leaving the dog as she would leave me some day" (120). A dog appears as Humbert drives away from Lolita, loping beside the car, "but he was too heavy and old, and very soon gave up" (282). Humbert is a lapdog aspiring to become the redoubtable hound of the moors, and elegant as he is Lecter may fear his age also. He has lived through more than twenty years of the novels devoted to him.

IV. Hannibal's Early Years

Though the whiskers on Kolnas's face gleam "like hog bristles" (247), the hogs that worshipped Hannibal in the third novel are tamed in *Hannibal Rising* to become the heraldic sign of the Lecters, and the jewels of Hannibal's mother are hidden in a boar's head (219); the false dog thus continues his amiable existence early in the novel. Mastiff bitches do not become sinister despite the allusion to Coleridge's *Christabel* (71); the one that wags its tail on the estate of Hannibal's father, Count Lecter, does not protect the family from the attack of the six deserters, and the one that guards the estate of Hannibal's uncle wags its tail after it receives the new addition to the family. More important to the novel are the collection of dog tags Hannibal employs to track down his enemies. It takes some time, however, before that Hannibal is empowered to undertake his mission, for the Hannibal of this novel is not the Hannibal of the saga until its final pages, at which the motifs with which we are familiar suddenly appear, after being carefully placed earlier. After he kills Grutas a dog barks (303).

Grutas, the ultimate antagonist of the novel, lives most of the time on a boat that moves up and down the labyrinth of the Essonne. He is a Charon who prostitutes women and delivers them to the criminal underworld. Though his eyes are blue, his one pale blue eye that looks in on the children (37) is possibly reminiscent of the vulture eye, "a pale blue eye, with a film over it," that destroys the protagonist of Poe's "The Tell-Tale Heart" (792). Smeared with blood and feathers Grutas's eyes resemble the fiery wheels of Charon's eyes in Dante's infernal world (*Inferno* 3.99). This motif of blood and feathers, repeated several times in the novel, suggest that the image of the butterfly is generalized here to all birds: the black swans of the Lecter estate that a Panzer destroys (20); the goose Paul Momund draws and perhaps the chicken whose innards Hannibal smashes into his face (92–93); and the ortolans that Lecter frees, after their unmistakable chirps inform him where Grutas holds Lady Murasaki as a captive (286)— they are the one delicacy that Hannibal does not partake of, for he is not yet the Hannibal we know from the other books.

Another form of the butterfly are the many crickets that appear in the novel and become a major symbol. Chiyoh plays her lute "when the crickets faltered" (89), but she effectively leaves the novel to marry in Japan. In a scene introduced by a spider that captures a beetle (101), Hannibal frees Momund's crickets after he kills him (104), just as he shall free the ortolans. He finds a suzumushi cricket for Lady Murasaki (133–36). Inspector Popil tells Hannibal that in the French Resistance a cricket clicker, clicked twice, meant "I'm a friend, don't shoot" (282). Moths flutter about the *Christabel* as a sign of the deaths that Hannibal shall soon commit, but it is too early for the crickets to sing (297). Recalling for a moment the moths "like derelict snowflakes" (*Lolita* 294) that accompany Humbert Humbert to his confrontation with Quilty, we realize that moths are not butterflies; they do not signify rebirth but a ghostly death.

A more benign butterfly, though never identified as such, is Lady Murasaki, whether she dresses in a kimono or in the more sinister black leather as she takes to her motorcycle. In the black leather she functions as Hannibal's emissary, though he does not realize yet his need of someone to send forth. On the motorcycle she takes Mumond's head to place it with some humor in front of the barbershop. When, however, she follows the lead of Chiyoh and returns to Japan, realizing that she can do nothing for her Oedipal step-nephew, she does not escape into transformation because he cannot accept her invitation to step onto her bridge of dreams. He, however, throughout the novel "is growing and changing, or perhaps emerging as what he has ever been" and aligns himself with Dolarhyde and Gumb as a demonic butterfly, opposed to Grutas, "the beast that panted its hot breath on his and Mischa's skins" (159).

This beast reminds us that a very important motif throughout the series is the compulsion to devour other people, so it is proper that it alludes to Humperdinck and Wette's opera of *Hänsel und Gretel* when Grutas sings the first lines of the little man in his purple mantle (72). This innocent riddle in the opera becomes ominous in the novel where many people are wrapped in blood. But the opera is not innocent as far as hunger is concerned. It opens on the theme of the children's hunger: "Ei, wie beißt mich der Hunger!" [Oh, how hunger bites me] (1.1), Gretel sings, and her father affirms, "Hunger ist der beste Koch" (Hunger is the best cook) (1.3), adding more bitterly, "Hunger ist ein tolles Tier / [...], beißt und kratzt, das glaube mir" (Hunger is a crazy animal / ..., bites and scratches, believe me) (1.3). These people understand the witch better than they would like to admit; and this is the language Harris employs to characterize the deserters, especially Grutas.

The Essonne where Grutas lives in his boat is one marsh, but the more interesting marsh is the formalin tank in which the cadavers of the anatomy class, taught by professor Dumas, are kept. Hannibal is not in charge of the tank, given the professor's authority, and we might add that he is not in charge of the action of the novel, which is a classic revenge novel that in the name of the professor admits its debts to *The Count of Monte Cristo*. Nevertheless, in the tank Hannibal maintains a collection, to which he adds Milko when the man attacks him. Stapleton dies, if he does die, offstage in the Great Grimpen Mire; Milko dies in the tank, "bumping against the lid like a lobster in a pot" (261).

Three times the action of the novel insists that Hannibal is unreadable. The psychiatrist Rufin finds him "perfectly opaque" (86). Toward the end of the novel, in a nice pun, Hannibal asserts to Popil, "Inspector, you will never know anything about my taste" (281), and the inspector agrees. "For lack of a better word, we'll call him a monster" (283). These passages represent a valiant effort on Harris's part to redeem this Hannibal and return to the Hannibal of the first two books, but it won't do. As Anthony

Lane says, Hannibal's monstrosity, "native to him alone," has been "squandered by the uncovering of his past" (94).

Nevertheless, at the end of the novel he is not rising upon his stepaunt's bridge of dreams but descending into his proper inscrutability. And on its last page the narrator, in a telling indirect quotation, assures the reader that Lecter shall fulfill his name as he reads and reads and reads the faces of Americans (323). And we readers, no matter how much is squandered, continue to follow his lead.

V. Conclusion

What are we to make of these stories? Have we collected them for our mere titillation? Holmes had boasted, "Before tomorrow tonight [Stapleton] will be fluttering in our net as helpless as one of his own butterflies. A pin, a cork, and a card, and we add him to the Baker Street collection" (13; 880). It is an easy irony, but Holmes is a collector of rare crimes, abetted by his animus Watson; the Baker Street collection has its own titillations, and so does a reader. Where is the animus of these stories? What is escaping us? The Lecter tetralogy depends upon the works that preceded it but also escapes their inertia. Hannibal remains an original and compelling creation; and thus we are distressed when Harris seems to trespass Lecter's integrity, allowing him to achieve genital mastery only after he kneels to Starling's breast (483).

Despite her victory as he kneels, she does not escape. An important reason for her capture is the complex character of Harris's antagonists. Through the relation of the lower middle-class Clegg and the upper-class Miranda we can see that the master-slave relationship is active internally in the Lecter trilogy. The master, attempting to establish a self, "finds that something has come about quite different from an independent consciousness. It is ... a dependent consciousness that he has achieved. He is thus not assured of self-existence as his truth.... The truth of the independent consciousness [such as the mastering impulse imagines] is accordingly the consciousness of the [slave]" (Hegel 236–37). The mastering impulse finds that it is a mask for the impulse of the slave. The impulse of the slave, however, achieves an independence over the master after having felt through the master "the fear of death, the sovereign master," which makes it experience a "complete perturbation of its entire substance" (237). Each of Harris's antagonists insists upon his mastery, but each is driven by impulses upon which he depends for his life. Dolarhyde aspires to be the Red Dragon, but draws his energy from the castration traumas of his childhood. Gumb yearns for his transformation into a woman, but is energized and betrayed by a mother-fixation that the narrator relates with some irony, as though in the critical voice of Lecter (329–30). Mason, who appears so much in control because of his inherited wealth, is absolutely dependent upon his bodyguards and his sister, whom as a child he abused and at whose hands he dies, his precious eel stuffed into his mouth; further, his dependence upon an amyl popper and the goodwill of his psychoanalyst, Lecter, belie his independence. Emblems of social dependence surround Grutas and Kolnas. And Lecter, despite the several gestures he makes toward aesthetic and cultural mastery is nevertheless energized and driven by his utter dependence, no matter what his blood pressure may be, on devouring human flesh. The assertion and contradiction of the self endure incessant rehearsal in these books

Ambivalence is in the nature of the myth. The figure of the Minotaur, Minos and bull, man and beast, contains the butterfly and the hound, for the Minotaur's half-sister is Ariadne, who connives at his murder — shades of Mason and his sister. In Ariadne we find the possibility of escape rendered both in her desertion and death and in her marriage to Dionysus. Death, whether transforming or not, awaits the soul at its birth.

Works Consulted

Bachofen, Johann Jakob. *Das Mutterrecht: Eine Untersuchung über die Gynaikokratie der alten Welt nach ihrer religiösen und rechtlichen Natur,* ed. Hans-Jürgen Heinrichs. Frankfurt a. M.: Suhrkamp, 1975.

Browning, Robert. *The Complete Poetic and Dramatic Works.* Boston: Houghton Mifflin, 1895.

Butler, Diana. "Lolita Lepidoptera," in Phyllis A. Roth (ed.), *Critical Essays on Vladimir Nabokov.* Critical Essays on American Literature. Boston: G.K. Hall, 1984.

Dante Alighieri. *La Divina Commedia,* ed. E. Moore. London: Oxford University Press, 1900.

Doyle, Sir Arthur Conan. *The Complete Sherlock Holmes.* Garden City, N.Y.: Garden City Books, 1930.

Fowler, Douglas. "The Aesthete as Serial Killer: Dr. Lecter." *Notes on Contemporary Literature,* vol. 25, no. 1 (January 1995).

Fowles, John. *The Collector.* Boston: Little, Brown, 1963.

Gilbert, W.S. *The Complete Plays of Gilbert and Sullivan.* Ill. W.S. Gilbert. Garden City, N.Y.: Garden City, 1938.

Graves, Robert. *The Greek Myths.* 2 vols. Baltimore: Penguin Books, Pelican, 1955.

Harris, Thomas. *Hannibal.* New York: Delacourte, 1999.

_____. *Hannibal Rising.* New York: Delacourte, 2006.

_____. *Red Dragon.* New York: G.P. Putnam's Sons, 1981.

_____. *The Silence of the Lambs.* New York: St. Martin's Press, 1989.

Hegel, G.W.F. *The Phenomenology of Mind,* trans. J.B. Baillie. 2nd ed. London: Allen and Unwin, 1949.

Hoffman, Daniel. *Poe Poe Poe Poe Poe Poe Poe.* Garden City, N.Y.: Doubleday, 1972.

Humperdinck, Engelbert, and Wette, Adelheide. *Hänsel und Grete,* ed. Wolfram Humperdinck. Stuttgart: Reclam, 1952.

Lane, Anthony. "First Bite: What's Eating Hannibal Lecter?" *The New Yorker,* 18 Dec. 2006.

Lindsay, Vachel. *Collected Poems.* New York: Macmillan, 1946.

Magistrale, Tony. "Transmogrified Gothic: The Novels of Thomas Harris, " in Tony Magistrale and Michael A. Morrison (eds.), *A Dark Night's Dreaming: Contemporary American Horror Fiction.* Columbia: University of South Carolina Press, 1996.

Nabokov, Vladimir. *Conclusive Evidence.* New York: Harper, 1952.

___. *Lolita.* New York: Putnam's, 1955.

Neumann, Erich. *The Origins and History of Consciousness,* trans. R.F.C. Hull. Bollingen Series 47. Princeton: Princeton University Press, 1970.

Poe, Edgar Allen. *Collected Works,* ed. Thomas Olive Mabbott. Vol. 3. New York: Bantam, 1982.

Shakespeare, William. *The Norton Shakespeare,* ed. Stephen Greenblatt. New York: Norton, 1997.

Van, Thomas A. "The Dionysian Horrific in Thomas Harris's Novel, *The Silence of the Lambs.*" *Kentucky Philological Review,* vol. 13 (March 1998).

5

This Is the Blind Leading the Blind

Noir, Horror and Reality in Thomas Harris's Red Dragon

DAVIDE MANA

> "No. I know I'm not smarter than you are."
> "Then how did you catch me, Will?"
> "You had disadvantages."
> "What disadvantages?"
> "Passion. And you're insane."
>
> —*Red Dragon* 40

Published in 1981, Thomas Harris's second novel (after the more conventional *Black Sunday*, 1975), *Red Dragon*, was one of the first to use the serial killer theme soon after the adoption, in 1978, of the expression "serial killer" as part of the official criminal taxonomy, to indicate a sexually related murderer of three or more, following a discernible pattern or scheme in the choice of victim and execution.

In this sense, *Red Dragon* not only marks an important divide in the narrative field, but also acts as an essential connection between the eminently industrial phenomenon of the serial murder with the fundamentally modern, post-industrial sensitivity represented by noir; by adopting the newly coded and taxonomically defined "serial killer" as the mover of a fictional investigation still close to the traditional canon, *Red Dragon* recalls, re-uses and updates the classical themes of noir, heralding the birth of what will be called, at the end of the twentieth century, neo-noir.

I. Worlds of Darkness — Serial Killer and Noir Defined

His activities on record only from the second half of the nineteenth century (thanks to Jack the Ripper, the patron saint of modern murderers), the serial killer belongs to the industrial world — perhaps unsurprisingly: the serial production of infinite equal replicas is one of the basic traits of the industrial process, and the serial killer can therefore be regarded as a sort of "industrial killer," taking full advantage of the new media to give wide echo to his activities and bringing the horror, if you will, home to the client.

While offering ample opportunities for the amplification, through the media, of the murderer's acts, thus leading to a form of secondary, narcissistic gratification, modern society reduces drastically the opportunities for the "healthy" (or at least socially acceptable and state-sanctioned) exercise of extreme violence — to wit, war in its most primitive, personal, man-to-man, one-on-one form. And the absence of socially acceptable releases for extreme violence might indeed be connected with the fact that the few earlier cases of serial murder on record, from the pre-industrial world, normally deal with characters whose personal circumstances, social status or gender prevented them from riding off to war or taking to the highway as robbers and marauders; Elizabeth Bathory, the aristocrat "vampire" whose blood fetish and possibly homosexually related crimes are well documented and the subject of much popular fascination, being a case in point.[1]

Further, as in the case of that other twentieth century classic monster, the mass murderer, the modern industrial world provides the works of Einstein, Darwin and Freud as keys to the interpretation of the killer's actions, as inspiration for his crimes, and as tools for the writer seeking inspiration. With the new century, the murderer can cast a philosophical meaning to his action, claiming some legitimacy thanks to a misguided reference to the work of a great thinker of the recent past: from Einstein's principle of relativity, the serial killer takes his moral ambiguity, his random striking and, later, will act as a metaphor for the greatest mass murderer of them all, the atomic bomb; from watered-down and badly digested Darwinian thinking comes the serial killer's role of social predator, the modern world equivalent of the sabre-toothed tiger — randomly weeding out the "unfit, asserting the right of the strong over the weak. And from Freudian analysis the serial killer extracts his most obvious trait, the sexual obsession driving him to murder, his narcisistic need to be the focus of the public attention, violence as a surrogate for gratifications he can't achieve otherwise.

Thus codified and equipped, the serial killer exercises a strong pull on some of the darker strings of the human imagination: like a modern bogeyman, he is basically faceless, one with the crowd on the streets of the big industrial city. He is the realistic alternative to Mr. Hyde, a believable werewolf for a world that has no longer faith in the supernatural but still feels the fear of the unknown.[2]

The serial killer choosing his victims according to a twisted, deranged logic, further provokes fear in the public, as anyone, anywhere becomes a potential victim; but at the same time, he releases the victim from any form of moral guilt — the serial killer does not act out of revenge or retribution, he does not set straight the wrongs of the past. The serial killer is crazy but not a raving lunatic, he is smart but unpredictable, he merges in the crowd and cannot be found by normal means, unless the code of his insanity is cracked.

The seriality and the facelessness of the serial killer add an element of true horror (as in "horror fiction") to the mix, crossing the cerebral investigation of the classic mystery with rougher, more basic sadistic thrillers such as the venerable *The Cat and the Canary*; as noted by Ben Harper in his overview of what might be called the "serial killer sub-genre," we are dealing with "a character that is simultaneously cunning and crazed — methodical and rational in his planning, but overwhelmed by an impulse towards unrestrained violence during the actual commission of his crimes.... A killer who is frustratingly logical and efficient in his modus operandi ... yet utterly irrational in his motive" (Harper 234).

What better character, argues Harper, than a serial killer to revive a genre, the police procedural or mystery novel, that so easily slips into a repetition of basic clichés?

Now it can be argued that anyone willingly committing a homicide has left sanity behind and entered his own personal world, governed by his own rules. In this sense, the deranged killer is not a new feature of mystery novels — being a distinctive element, for instance, of many plots of Ellery Queen novels in which the game played by the authors with the reader consists in decoding the personal set of rules by which the killer navigates reality in order to identify the murderer himself. The serial killer goes one step beyond — for one thing, upping the ante, piling bodies on bodies, widening the area of menace to the whole city, state or nation, and secondly by adding the element of true horror, almost in a Lovecraftian sense. What are H.P. Lovecraft's faceless, indifferent deities whose essentially random acts against humanity lack any true hostility, if not serial killers on a cosmic scale? And what is a serial killer, down in his deepest core, but a man who has cast himself in the role of indifferent deity, in a very Lovecraftian sense?

As such, the serial killer genre that is being established as *Red Dragon* hits the shelves in the early eighties is a true cross-genre character, straddling the line that separates mystery and horror fiction, crossing *Black Mask* with *Weird Tales*.

The same bridging of reality-based mystery thriller and fantasy fiction is to be found in the "genre" that is normally defined as "noir."[3] While often regarded as a generic synonym of "hard boiled," noir is in fact a special instance of hard-boiled fiction — and indeed, noir can be better described as a mode than as a genre (Erickson, 313): we can have noir thrillers, noir westerns, noir comedy. The "noir" element is an extra ingredient that, by being added to the basic recipe of a given genre, generates a result that is more than the sum of the parts. And if hard-boiled is essentially a realistic form of mystery, and was indeed hailed as such by his earlier theorist, Raymond Chandler, in 1945, noir is hard-boiled through a dark filter, through a lens which twists and deforms reality giving it an evil, almost neurotic bias; noir thriller is hard-boiled with a self-conscious attention to elements derived from psychoanalysis and the world of the unconscious, set in a fantasy world which is very close to our own, but in which our worst nightmares can, and probably already have become reality. Unsurprisingly, noir will have its greatest success in the visual media, where twisted, darkened images can readily convey the twisted, darkened atmosphere of the story.

> It is no wonder that psychoanalysis, dreams and sexual interplay in all its varieties take on such a prominent role in the noir city. The labyrinths of dreams and sexual fantasy overlap, interconnect and merge in each individual within the greater labyrinth of the physical city — which itself is a catalyst of dreams and fantasies [Christopher, 154].

The world in which noir action takes place is familiar but different, the everyday reality of the mentally disturbed, of the alienated and the melancholic, of the junkie and the alcoholic, of the individual disaffected with positivist representations of the world. Once again, the noir world is a Lovecraftian world, minus the supernatural.

Robert Bloch, literary father of the first iconic serial killer of the modern world, with *Psycho*, was a *Weird Tales* alumnus and Lovecraft correspondent. And the fact that one of the earliest collections of Weird Tales stories was actually edited by hard-boiled mystery icon and *Black Mask* stalwart Dashiell Hammett is also telling of the close ties between the genres.

The deranged criminal has been part of the nightmare noir world from day one, well before the FBI or anyone else defined and coded the phenotype of the "serial killer"— psychos and "sickos" have been lurking on the pages of *Black Mask* or *Gold Medal* paperback originals decades before the real world, let alone traditional thriller, noticed their presence: twisted gangsters, sadistic masterminds, homicidal hitchhikers, repressed housewives extracting a bloody vengeance on their spouses, sexually ambiguous thrill-killers and vengeful hoodlums, all have been a staple of the noir genre, both high and low, both literate and trashy. As an example, it can be argued that all characters in the novels of noir icon David Good's are somewhat deranged, and live in a world that borders on the hallucination.

As a straight, self-contained "genre," noir extends between 1929 and 1960 (O'Brien, 177). During this interval, while style remains consistent — with a strong emphasis on dark moods, feelings of alienation and disaffection, anti-heroic characters and a disquieting undercurrent of repressed sexuality — the themes shift to adapt to the contemporary panorama of crime and underworld culture. The gangsters of the thirties are replaced by the grifters and adventurers of the forties, and finally by the youth gangs and dope-fiends of the fifties and the rebel teenagers of the sixties. It is therefore unsurprising that, with the arrival of the late seventies and early eighties, noir, as a mood-defined genre, should appropriate the new phenomenon, making the serial killer a denizen of its darkened alleys, as if by default.

With *Red Dragon*, the crossing of the genres, the heady mix of realistic fiction and wild dark fantasy, is not a simple hybridization, but a true merger, with old rules respected, and new rules established.

II. "You're Insane"— Smart Madmen and Alienated Gumshoes

[*Red Dragon*] was a good noir, maybe too modern for the sensibilities of the time, but certainly of high literary weight, and with a plot as tight and precise as Swiss clockwork [Carlotto 3].

> Using the narrative conventions of the crime thriller — the honorable hoodlum, the crooked cop, the femme fatale, the untrustworthy pal, illicit sex, and sexy violence — noir presents the dark side of the American soul [Meyer, 1].

David Meyer's noir video book, a small catalog for noir aficionados haunting the darkest corners of their local video-shop, does include a wealth of condensed information on the noir formula — useful reference for the following paragraphs, where we will try and see how, in Red Dragon, the "narrative conventions of the crime thriller" are respected and referenced, while being subtly distorted and modified: most of the cliché characters of standard noir and hard-boiled fiction appear in Red Dragon, apparently unchanged from their central casting type, in fact subtly and often ironically twisted.

A special agent — belonging to FBI, the organization that has classified and therefore forever "trapped" the serial killer archetype — Will Graham is a former "cop" running from a traumatic past, and finding refuge in a simple, solid, down-to-earth existence as a family man. He is not a "crooked cop" in the sense of corrupt, but he is a damaged, twisted character. And as a more classic crooked cop, he is willing (despite all his claims to the contrary) to strike a deal with the criminal element, the (not so) "honourable hoodlum" Hannibal Lecter, who acts as an untrustworthy pal to Graham, and proves to be the same for the Tooth Fairy, too.

Both Crawford and Graham think they can rely on Lecter's honor — he's been defeated, he's bound to collaborate, if unwillingly. Likewise, the Tooth Fairy perceives Lecter as a friend and compatriot, the only person capable of understanding him. In fact, Lecter is a solipsist character, self-centered like a gyroscope and basically unable to relate in any way with other characters, if not by seeking their corruption, destruction or consummation.

But untrustworthy pals seem to be a dime a dozen in Red Dragon. Will Graham is an untrustworthy friend for sleazy Freddy Lounds, which he uses as a tool. And Lounds' attitude towards his collaboration with Graham, on the other hand, is absolutely self-serving. And what of ape-like, ruthless Crawford? Is the sanity of his friend Graham a price he's willing to pay in order to solve the case? With friends like these....

The noir character is, archetypically, a victim to his own neuroses.

Unwilling to participate in the community of his fellow men and progressively engulfed by the darkness seeping through the novel, Will Graham, the former Special Agent called back from retirement for one last case he alone is likely to crack, carries the weight of being the noir "hero" in *Red Dragon* on his shoulders, as Marlowe and Spade did before him, but without the moral crutch of being his own man. Like most noir characters, Graham is, at the start of the novel, running from a traumatic past. His course will bring him, as we can anticipate from the earliest paragraphs, on a head-on collision with those same traumas he is trying to avoid, forget, exorcise.

And exorcism is not a bad word for what he will be doing through the novel — confronting his personal demon and somehow escaping alive from the trap his nemesis has set.

> The story is this man's adventure in search of a hidden truth, and it would be no adventure if it did not happen to a man fit for adventure. He has a range of awareness that startles you, but it belongs to him by right, because it belongs to the world he lives in. If there were enough like him, the world would be a very safe place to live in, without becoming too dull to be worth living in [Chandler 7].

Will Graham, just like Phil Marlowe before him, gropes his way through the novel, displaying much technical prowess but basically failing to solve the mystery — that, just like in Chandler's *The Big Sleep*, fifty years earlier, will sort of solve itself, leaving both investigator and reader baffled and hurt. Like supernaturally endowed The Shadow, the quasi-psychic Graham knows the evil that lurks in the heart of men, but unlike The Shadow, he is too busy coming to term with his own slice of darkness to fully concentrate on the case at hand. He craves the tranquility of a domestic life and a nine-to-five job, but might be also feeling the shackles of such a sedated life — and so, as soon as he can, he finds an excuse goes back to face that past he's supposedly trying to escape, setting up a meeting with Hannibal Lecter.

In his confrontation with Hannibal Lecter, Graham faces the darkest recesses of his mind and, like all good noir heroes before him, faces the challenge of overcoming that darkness to emerge victorious, and sane, from the match. This is the essence of the novel, and that is all there is to say about noir, if you will — set in a corrupt world and facing his own dark side, the hero must strive not to succumb. From this simple core, one can derive any noir plot — and Harris himself will use this device as the unifying core of his three Lecter novels.

The face-off between Graham and Lecter in *Red Dragon* anticipates the confrontations between Sterling and Lecter in *Silence of the Lambs*, and the various attempts at riding the wave of the serial killer "phenomenon" on the part of various characters in *Hannibal*. As noticed by Luisa Mariani Valerio in her thorough and highly perceptive critique of the

"Hannibal trilogy," while the scenes involving Lecter and Clarice Sterling are tightly integrated in the economy of the novel, the scene involving Will Graham and Lecter seems to be gratuitous and somewhat "tacked on," the author missing the opportunity to better amalgamate the action with his narrative.

> In the novel (*Red Dragon*) Lecter silently exits the scene, excluding a few later moments, after his confrontation with the detective, a simple tool, therefore, useful not to the evolution of the plot but to explain the psychology of the detective, his fears, his nightmares. It is singular that in the novel often defined as the "prologue" of the trilogy, the "Lecter File" is closed for good already, definitively filed away. The criminal is already in jail, even better, in a mental institution; mention is made, of course, of the homicides of which he was the author, and of the aggression to Graham himself, but these happened years before, in a time past that is not the time of the novel [Mariani Valerio].

According to Mariani Valerio, therefore, Lecter is not a true character in the story, but more of a personification of Graham's personal problems — a plot device, a much darker and involved variation of the classic crutches of the noir character.

What Mariani Valerio is probably missing is that in *Silence of the Lambs* Lecter has still to break into Clarice's mind, while in *Red Dragon* he already has the keys to Graham's unconscious, if not a proper foothold there. He needs therefore less time on screen, so to speak, to do his job.

Also, in *Red Dragon* most of the important bits about Lecter are dispersed through the narrative, hiding in plain sight — waiting for the reader's own investigation to piece them together. Consider the simple revelation that Lecter, as a practicing psychologist, used to see his patients only on Sunday — and compare this with his penchant for playing god, already clear in the novel as he maneuvers and plots to unleash the Tooth Fairy against Graham's family, or with Francis Dolarhyde's role as a "Pilgrim" in his relation with Lecter. And remember what we said about serial killer fiction being the same as the old "indifferent gods" narrative so dear to Lovecraft.

There is much deceptive subtlety at work in *Red Dragon*: maybe Harris was not planning a trilogy in 1981, but for sure he was at his most elegant and crafty when establishing the character of Hannibal Lecter, a plot device to some, but certainly not a secondary character.

Passingly, it is worth mentioning that Lecter, a true noir character (and a heir to such mastermind icons as Moriarty and Dr. Fu Manchu) is no true serial killer as defined by the rules described early in this paper. We do not know the details and the motives behind his earlier crimes, but all his actions in the Harris novels lack the randomness and facelessness of the serial murder; Hannibal knows those who he is going to kill, and has a good reason for killing them. His attack on Graham and his family, in *Red Dragon*, while unusual in terms of means, is a personal affair motivated by anger, revenge and hostility. One is almost tempted to read Lecter as a thrill-killer, using serial murders to attract brilliant investigators, who are his real intended victims; he probably resents their intelligence and their ability to fit in — which are mutually exclusive as far as his life is concerned.

Noir tropes appear again concerning the character of Freddy Lounds, a sleazy journalist that's too good for the trashy job he's doing, Lounds is burned by ambition and by desire for vindication in front of those colleagues that look down upon his tabloid-related work. Everything in the character of Lounds, from his disregard for truth masquerading as desire to serve the public, down to his stripper girl-friend, comes straight from the rain-soaked and neon-lighted alleys of a generic 1950s noir downtown, and Freddy Lounds is certainly the most traditional noir character in the novel.

> Reba McClane was guilty of liking Francis Dolarhyde. Demonstrably guilty [Harris 173].

With her cold control over her predicament and the penchant for strong drink (perhaps a way to "loosen up" and give in to her darker side), Reba McClane is a femme fatale in the most literal sense — she'll prove fatal to Dolarhyde and almost as fatal to Will Graham. Far from being traditional like Freddy Lounds is, she is also an ironic twist on some classic noir elements, and Harris almost spells it out for the reader: Reba is blind and aggressively sensual at the same time, going against general expectations and the popular cliché.

Times have changed indeed — in a 1940s noir like *High Sierra*, Velma, the physically challenged girl who is Bogart's damaged gangster's ideal of purity, had to undergo an operation, getting rid of her handicap, in order for the transformation from innocent country girl into whiskey-slinging wanton urban hussy to take place. In the eighties, the innocent (but self-reliant) girl next door can turn into a sexual predator at will, staying firmly in control, freely showing her animal instincts.

But in the end, the results are the same — both the nightmare-haunted gangster of High Sierra and the serial killer of *Red Dragon* will emerge shattered from their confrontation with the unexpected sexual hungers of their dream girl.[4]

III. Fear and Rut, and Anger at the Fear — The Noir World of Red Dragon

But probably Harris's strongest and most complete adherence to the noir sensibility is in his passing portrayal of humanity at large in the background of the main action, as a series of vignettes in which hostility, anger, greed and the other basest human instincts are at play. It is a dark world in which Will Graham is trying to make a living and in which Francis Dolarhyde is trying to come to terms with his own traumas.

> The Atlanta FBI office had booked him into an absurd hotel near the city's new Peachtree Center. It had glass elevators shaped like milkweed pods to let him know he was really in town now. Graham rode up to his room with two conventioneers wearing name tags with the printed greeting "Hi!" They held to the rail and looked over the lobby as they ascended. "Looka yonder by the desk — that's Wilma and them just now coming in," the larger one said. "God damn, I'd love to tear off a piece of that." "Fuck her till her nose bleeds," the other one said. Fear and rut, and anger at the fear. "Say, you know why a woman has legs?" "Why?" "So she won't leave a trail like a snail." The elevator doors opened. "Is this it? This is it," the larger one said. He lurched against the facing as he got off. "This is the blind leading the blind," the other one said [*Red Dragon* 11].

Francis Dolarhyde's own traumatic experiences, to which Harris devotes a large portion of the novel and an attention which echoes the attention given to technical details in the investigation chapters, has two functions in the economy of the novel. The most obvious is providing reason and explanation, if not justification, to the killings of the Tooth Fairy, thus complementing those technical details already mentioned and reinforcing the realism of the narrative — a witness of the fact that the serial killer has left the plastic, hazy, undefined "water margin" of the generic irrational, to become a scientifically investigated and thus understood natural phenomenon.

But Dolarhyde's nightmare youth, a veritable piling of negative experience upon negative experience also acts as a counterpoint to Will Graham's equally negative everyday world.

> The diner was bright and clean. Graham's hands trembled and he slopped coffee in his saucer. He saw Crawford's cigarette smoke bothering a couple in the next booth. The couple ate in a peptic silence, their resentment hanging in the smoke. Two women, apparently mother and daughter, argued at a table near the door. They spoke in low voices, anger ugly in their faces. Graham could feel their anger on his face and neck [*Red Dragon*, 20].

And really, it would be tempting to consider this emphasis on the negative an effect of the biased point of view of cynical and damaged characters like Graham or Dolarhyde, a grim updating of Marlowe's cynical wise-cracking, the interface through which the character comes to terms with an unpleasant reality. This feeling is accentuated by Harris cutting from Graham's point of view to Dolarhyde's obviously deranged perception of what's going on. But as we get deeper into the novel, the mood of angry disillusionment with human feelings persists as we meet minor characters — such as Niles Jacobi and the almost comedic H.G. Parsons. In further vignettes, a general view of a humanity sets in, a humanity that no longer has to be nice.

> The newsstand operator squatted in front of his shelves arranging the Tribunes. He had enough else to do. The day guys never did their share of straightening. A pair of black zippered boots came into the corner of his vision. A browser. No, the boots were pointed at him. Somebody wanted some damn thing. The newsie wanted to finish arranging his Tribunes but the insistent attention made the back of his head prickle. His trade was transient. He didn't have to be nice. "What is it?" he said to the knees [*Red Dragon*, 101].

Not even Graham's family escapes the darkness hanging over the world of the novel — Molly can't or won't come to terms with Graham's choices, unable to understand her man's search for redemption and self-destructive search for another confrontation with Lecter; Willy is torn between his new father and his grandparents, egoistically trying to seduce him away. The situation is further aggravated by Graham's need to teach Molly how to defend herself. While in the end this will prove critical for the resolution of the novel, and while the gun enters Molly and Will's relationship for an eminently good reason, the woman's resentment mirrors the man's guilt after the protracted and precisely described shooting range scene. From here on, Will and Molly's apparently healthy relationship, based on a clear feelings and a strong physical element, will enter a crisis from which it will probably never recover.

> Two policemen cleared a path for Wendy through the crowd of curiosity-seekers outside the gate. One of the gawkers wore a printed T-shirt reading "The Tooth Fairy Is a One-Night Stand." He whistled at Wendy. The woman beside him slapped his face [*Red Dragon*, 141].

In the end, and not without irony, only Wendy, Freddy Lounds's stripper girlfriend, comes out of the whole story with her dignity intact, a sane, strong person, capable of simple acts of tenderness and fueled in her relationship by a clean sexuality that comes unburdened by dark undertones, a woman full of quiet self-reliance in face her pain. But still people will catcall after her at her man's funeral.

Graham perceives the quiet toughness of this woman, and in his simple empathizing with her we have the final proof that we have not been watching a straight world through Graham's twisted perspective — the banality of evil is indeed endemic in the world surrounding him, and Graham's perception is painfully clear. The meeting with Wendy establishes once and for all Graham as an objective observer, as a reliable point of view — and damns his world.

Dolarhyde and Graham are therefore inhabiting the same reality, the weight of their respective traumas the same, their perception of the evil at large accurate. One of them is the hunter, the other is the prey (but who's hunting who?) and they are both victims after their own fashion: Dolarhyde's perception of reality is further darkened and twisted by his traumas and his folly, but stripped of those filters, the world in which *Red Dragon*'s action is set, seen through Will Graham's eyes, is indeed a dark, unpleasant place peopled with hostile individuals trying bluntly to give vent to their personal frustrations.

With this twist, with this implicit declaration of objectiveness on the part of the narrator, Red Dragon leaves behind forever the simple fields of the thriller, in which our reality is basically neutral, and we project our personal fears and hopes on it, and enters steadily and definitively the fantasy land of noir — a world in which "no good deed goes unpunished..., character determines fate..., alienation rules" [Meyer 15–16]. It is a world that will be sinisterly familiar to the readers of the eighties.

IV. Bad Juju — A Noir Decade and the Madman as Superhero

Mysteries and thrillers serve a social function, both reinforcing the status quo (crime is punished, order is restored) and criticizing it (crime is an option, order is fragile) by pointing out weaknesses and contradictions, providing with their heroes a role model for those perceptive enough to see the cracks in the system, and connected enough to care and look for a solution (Mandel 63–65).

The same is true for the noir hero, in which disillusionment replaces preoccupation for social integrity, and the painful knowledge that there is not much order to be restored goes hand-in-hand with the certainty the little order remaining is probably poisoned by corruption anyway. The only way to go is to follow one's role to the obvious end, doing the right thing (or the wrong thing, in fact) because doing anything else would mean losing one's own identity.

As a neo-noir character, Will Graham continues this tradition: the little he has to fight for is up close and personal, and by saving it he will probably lose it, and yet there is little else to do; becoming lost in the inner darkness (Lecter acting as the gateway and the gatekeeper) is tempting, but rationally it is not feasible as a solution — Dolarhyde will embrace it, and will pay for it, but he can avail himself of the privilege of being crazy.

But undeniably, Dolarhyde represents the other hero of the novel, almost a mirror image of Graham, and therefore an alternative role model for those, among the readers, willing to admit the novel is pointing out some cracks in our real, everyday world.

The nineteen eighties are a good template for noir — the world is going through a new cold war, that might go suddenly and definitively hot any minute: books, movies and songs about nuclear war and the cancellation of our civilization will grow in number and frequency as the decade wears on. Shuttle *Challenger* blows up (1986) as the space program that gave us a New Frontier for three decades undergoes severe cuts, to the advantage of military expenditures. The early signs of heavy environmental disruption become evident, coupled with man-made disasters like the *Exxon Valdez* oil spill (1989) and the Chernobyl (1987) explosion, literally raining heavy water on the head of Europeans. While we still do not know if the Beatles were really more popular than God, both the Pope (1981) and John Lennon (1980) are shot.

The dangers of HIV become public knowledge, putting an end to the free love of the sixties and the randy, good-natured promiscuity promoted by the media in the seventies, making sexual repression good for your health.

At the same time, politics and economics seem to come closer than ever, intertwined in a sinister dance that suggests corruption and the predominance of private interests over matters of public import, while foreign companies buy out national industries and thousands are laid off. And as it normally happens in times of crisis, a general move towards solidarity and collaboration are being counterbalanced by the emergence of the "me culture" — egoism and isolationism as an escape from problems.

Dog eats dog. Crime, fear, sexual repression. The loss of everyday certainties and basic securities: The time is ripe for the re-emergence of noir.

We know serial killers will become the main attraction in most thrillers and horror novels of the eighties — a true sign that fictional characters, at least, have embraced the alternative solution provided by Harris's other hero — trying to get things straight their way, not Marlowe's, embracing chaos instead of fighting it.

In Harris's following novels, Hannibal Lecter — the author's strongest contribution to neo-noir — will become an even more overbearing and charismatic character, casting his shadow on the "good guys" and attracting a cult following among readers, becoming the spokesman of a true alternative response to the progressive breaking up of the social structure which the novels might seem to underscore.

Compared to Dolarhyde, Lecter will come across as stronger, more charming, almost superhuman, triumphing at last over selected enemies through mental manipulation, violence, and ruthlessness so absolute to be like a new religion. A true dark messiah, Dr. Lecter, using the mask of the serial killer (which he is not — not exactly, at least) to preach to the masses.

Will somebody follow his lead? Certainly, nobody prints t-shirts about Will Graham.

Notes

1. The limited number of female serial killers is, incidentally, the reason why in this work we will use the male pronoun when speaking of a generic serial killer. No sexual discrimination is intended.

2. The werewolf angle is so strong that the Italian language edition of *Red Dragon* (Mondadori, 1984, translation by Marco Amante) was called "Il Delitto della Terza Luna" (The Third Moon Murder), and the early codename for the serial killer was changed from "Tooth Fairy" to "the werewolf," incidentally sacrificing an undertone of sexual mockery that is important (if not paramount) in the novel for the sake of reinforcing and exploiting the unconscious serial killer-werewolf parallel.

3. Used today mainly as a term in movie criticism, "noir" was originally a term coined by European critics describing the works of American novelists like Raymond Chandler, Dashiell Hammett, Jim Thompson and David Goodis (Deleuze 44–46).

4. It is interesting (and we leave it as an exercise for the reader) to compare the character of Ralph Mandy, Reba's somewhat unpleasant "other man" and Dolarhyde's last victim, and Velma's sleazy, mambo-dancing new paramour in High Sierra. Based on the little we are provided by author and director respectively, it can't be disputed that we are dealing with basically the same character, and the effect of seeing their ideal woman with "that man" is the same on both Roy and Francis, leading them to a final crime spree, a hopeless escape and ultimately to self-destruction. If women have changed in forty years, men seem to have stuck to type.

Works Consulted

Carlotto, Massimo. "Hannibal, un cannibale da salotto." *Il Manifesto*, Roma, 5 Oct. 1999.
Chandler, Raymond. "The Simple Art of Murder." *The Atlantic Monthly*, Nov. 1945.
Christopher, Nicholas. *Somewhere in the Night: Film Noir and the American City*. New York: Owl Books, 1997.
Deleuze, Gilles. "The Philosophy of the Serié Noire," in M. Fabbri and E. Resegotti (eds.), *I Colori del Nero*. Milano: Ubulibri, 1989.

Erickson, Todd. "Kill Me Again: Movement Becomes Genre," in A. Silver and J. Ursini (eds.), *Film Noir Reader*. New York: Limelight Editions, 1997.

Harper, Brian. "Serial Killers: A Motive for Murder," in E. Gorman et al. (eds.), *The Fine Art of Murder*. New York, Carrol and Graf, 1993.

Harris, Thomas. *Red Dragon*. New York, Bantam Books, 1981.

_____. *The Silence of the Lambs*. New York, Bantam Books, 1988.

Mandel, Ernest. *Delitti per Diletto: Storia Sociale del Romanzo Poliziesco*. Milano: Interno Giallo, 1990.

Mariani Valerio, Luisa. "Thomas Harris: Storia di una trilogia mancata." *Cinemastudio Magazine*, 1998. . Accessed 2 Dec. 2007.

Meyer, David N. *A Girl and a Gun*. New York: Avon Books, 1998.

O'Brien, Geoffrey. *Hardboiled America: Lurid Paperbacks and the Masters of Noir*. New York: Da Capo Press, 1997.

Silver, Alain, and Ward, Elizabeth. *Film Noir: An Encyclopedic Reference to the American Style*. New York: Overlook Press, 1992.

6

From *Red Dragon* to *Manhunter*

TONY WILLIAMS

As the first novel in a series focusing upon the sinister, yet attractive, figure of Dr. Hannibal Lecter, *Red Dragon* (1981) displays an archetypal pattern which reoccurs in its successors. This involves a traumatized investigator (Will Graham, Clarice Starling), inspired by Lecter's perverse influence, tracing the activities of a brutal serial killer. These novels also develop the theme of the symbiotic relationship between the searcher and his prey well-known in American literary and cinematic traditions such as Charles Brockden Brown's *Edgar Huntly* (1787), Robert Montgomery Bird's *Nick of the Wood* (1837), Herman Melville's *Moby Dick* (1856), to the 1950s Anthony Mann Westerns starring James Stewart and Gary Cooper, John Ford's *The Searchers* (1956) and countless American horror films. *Red Dragon* bears the same relationship to the rest of Harris's novels that Budd Boetticher's *Seven Men from Now* (1956) has to the Ranown cycle, a series of Westerns from *Decision at Sundown* (1957) to *Comanche Station* (1960). It represents a master text which its author will refine and elaborate in the succeeding novels *The Silence of the Lambs* (1988), *Hannibal* (1999), and the forthcoming prequel.

Whether initially retired (Will Graham in *Red Dragon*) or beginning a career (Clarice Starling of *The Silence of the Lambs*), the investigator has been psychologically affected by an incident in their past either caused or used by the Mephistopheles figure of an incarcerated Dr. Hannibal Lecter. Graham and Starling represent Faustian victims forced to make a bargain with the Devil. If they do not sell their souls, they are compelled to confront dark images from their past which may threaten to send them over the edge. Will Graham narrowly avoids this fate at the end of *Red Dragon*. But he is so emotionally and physically scarred (for the second time in his life) that doubt exists in the reader's mind as to whether he may not become another Francis Dolarhyde by finally succumbing to the dark temptations of Lecter. In *The Silence of the Lambs*, Clarice Starling is not as traumatically affected as Will Graham. But, by making her confront disturbing elements in a past she has repressed, Lecter initiates a process of blurring boundaries which he began with Will Graham so that she will eventually participate in his version of a blasphemous Eucharist at the end of *Hannibal*. The master succeeds in dominating his chosen disciple. So Clarice becomes a cannibalistic "Bride of Christ" in the same manner as those demure heroines infected by the bite of Count Dracula in Britain's Hammer horror series of films.

Harris's writing style is bare and rudimentary. The reader should not expect any evidence of rhetorical flourishes and distinctive touches which would make his work recognizable on the auteur level of literary criticism. Harris writes in a basic manner derived from his former profession as a journalist. But his chosen style of writing should not deceive the reader into thinking that his technique is banal and mundane. These very clinical qualities display a deliberate choice of style designed to evoke the reader into making connections and forming patterns from the evidence in the same way as police investigators have to do both in real life and the various *Law and Order* television franchises. The aftermath of the crime is brutal and ugly. But the evidence often unveils revealingly malignant patterns repressed in everyday life. The Lecter series may be regarded as manipulative pulp fiction designed for an undiscriminating audience. But its very popularity and developing cult in literature and film should alert us to the fact that it may be another example of the popular realm echoing and reworking the darker aspects of contemporary life.

Like past and present companions within the field of Gothic fiction, *Red Dragon* embodies that familiar trait of duality. But, unlike its employment the hands of a lesser writer, familiarity here does not breed contempt. The novel represents an intuitive contemporary reworking of traditional themes. *Red Dragon* opens with three quotations. Alphonse Bertillon comments that "One can only see what one observes, and one observes only things which are in the mind," a comment hinting at the damned sense of predestination haunting both Graham and Dolarhyde. Similarly, the contrasting lines from William Blake's *Songs of Innocence and Songs of Experience* reproduce not only traditional dualistic patterns of love and cruelty but also psychologically warring forces existing within the divided selves of Graham and Dolarhyde which have material rather than spiritual origins. Graham's scars result from his early encounter with Lecter in which he narrowly escaped becoming another meal. Dolarhyde has suffered from a long history of child abuse and social alienation. Both men seek escape. Graham wishes to reside securely within the bosom of a surrogate family represented by Molly and her son. Dolarhyde's dark nocturnal activities represent his desires for the family security and maternal contact lacking throughout his entire life. But try as they must, both men can never escape damnation.

In the novel, Dolarhyde's vicious family super-ego speaks to him at the moment he thinks he has achieved salvation. Jack Crawford and Hannibal Lecter are also competing super-egos. They represent different forms of power mechanisms wishing to return Graham to the disturbing worlds he has rejected. While Lecter wishes Graham to understand a dark "inner self" existing inside him, Jack Crawford battles with Molly to bring Graham back into a FBI legalistic fraternal brotherhood by playing on his sense of responsibility despite the fact that this might have serious consequences for his sanity. By denying Lecter, Graham evokes his satanic father's wrath. Lecter then attempts to use another surrogate to exert vengeance against a prodigal son who, in his view, refuses recognize the dark emotional bonds linking them together. Dolarhyde's attempt to escape his pathological destiny by seeking solace in the arms of Reba McClane evokes the return of a powerful super-ego responsible for a lifetime personal misery and violence. At the end of *Red Dragon*, one son dies. But the other will remain infected by the same alienation and loneliness that initiated the dark violent odyssey of his now-deceased blood brother. The style of *Red Dragon* is as appropriately as bleak as its subject matter.

Red Dragon opens with FBI agent Jack Crawford manipulating Will Graham to return to investigate a recent outbreak of serial killings. Like Lecter, Crawford begins to stir up feelings Graham wished to forget in his supposedly secure Florida domestic retirement sanctuary. He does this in a manner similar to Lecter consciously recognizing that Graham is dominated by forces beyond his own control.

> Jack Crawford heard the rhythm and syntax of his own speech in Graham's voice. He had heard Graham do that before, with other people. Often in intense conversation Graham took on the other person's speech patterns. At first, Crawford had thought he was doing it deliberately, that it was a gimmick to get the back-and-forth rhythm going.
>
> Later Crawford realized that Graham did it involuntarily, that sometimes he tried to stop and couldn't [Sammon 34].

Despite Molly's reservations, Crawford entices Will back into the hunt for a serial killer who has already claimed family victims in Alabama and Atlanta. Crawford recognizes the symbiotic nature of the qualities of imagination and projection haunting Will Graham so important for this quest. At the same time, Crawford promises her that Will does not have to get "too close" since "it would kill him to have to fight" (7). The climax of the novel will reveal this promise as a lie. Graham becomes little better than dead. He finally accepts Lecter's philosophy that an inhumane universe governs the whole of human existence, a fact he previously attempted to deny. When Graham arrives at the Leeds home in Atlanta, the contamination he experienced from Lecter in their last encounter returns. "Sitting in the dark, he sensed madness like a bloodhound sniffs a shirt" (10). He relives the slaughter of the Leeds family as well as recognizing his morbidly intense fascination with the maternal figure of Mrs. Leeds. This haunts him as he later wakes up in his Atlanta hotel.

> He woke in an hour, rigid and sweating, seeing the other pillow silhouetted against the bathroom light and it was Mrs. Leeds lying beside him bitten and torn, mirrored eyes and blood like the legs of spectacles over her temples and ears. He could not turn his head to face her [16].

Dolarhyde wishes his image reflected in a maternal gaze denied to him throughout his life. Similarly, Graham desires emotional security from Molly. He attempts to fulfill the role of father with a stepson, significantly named Willy, thus "adopting" a family like Dolarhyde. Graham imagines Dolarhyde arranging the slaughtered Leeds children so that they can view his macabre ritual, "They were watching a performance starring the madman and the body of Mrs. Leeds, besides Mr. Leeds in the bed" (17). He is too close to Dolarhyde. By contrast, his role as husband and stepfather appears perfunctory. The different attempts Graham and Dolarhyde make to perform family roles are doomed to failure. As Graham investigates the Atlanta Leeds home in detail, he phones Molly in Florida, snaps at her reference to his "criminal mind." He begins to find her interest in him "largely inexplicable" (41) and begins to experience Dolarhyde's feelings of low self-esteem. Graham begins his emotional return to the traumatic damnation planted inside him by Lecter many years ago.

This becomes clear when he visits Lecter at Dr. Chilton's Baltimore asylum. He wishes Lecter to remain asleep allowing him time to prepare himself. "If he felt Lecter's madness in his head, he had to contain it quickly, like a spill" (58). But, as if conscious of his reluctant apprentice's wishes, the devious sorcerer wakes up five seconds after Graham stares at him through the bars. Although Graham gains his co-operation in the hunt for Dolarhyde, Lecter not only has the last word in their conversation but reawakens those traumatic mechanisms he has induced in the past. "The reason you caught me is that we're *just alike*" (62). After Graham leaves, Lecter obtains his Florida address which he will later deliver to Dolarhyde. Chapter nine introduces us to Dolarhyde and supplies information about his Missouri background. He lives in his grandparents' house which still contains their clothes as well as his grandmother's false teeth, the significance of which becomes apparent later in the novel. The *Psycho* associations of the dark house are obvious. Harris also introduces Dolarhyde's fascination with the print of William Blake's *The Great Red Dragon and the Woman Clothed with the Sun* and his movie projection of the Leeds family, where he becomes a family participant in a dark performance of his own. He wishes to be an all-powerful Father figure to compensate for his failed sense of masculinity, Dolarhyde sees himself as Blake's Red Dragon standing above the woman who symbolizes the feminine side of himself he wishes to subdue. But these repressed emotional drives return with a vengeance in the form of the castrating super-ego of his abusive grandmother seeking punitive control even after death.

Graham travels to Birmingham Alabama where Dolarhyde has already selected more "fellow performers" (74) for his dark ritual. He is now dubbed the "Tooth Fairy" due to bites inflicted on his maternal victims, a term popularized in the *National Tattler* article written by Freddy Lounds. Dolarhyde also wishes recognition by Lecter, whom he regards as a John the Baptist figure. Like the son in a dark Freudian family melodrama he wishes to kill the Father while Graham seeks to deny his influence. Dolarhyde not only desires unification with the maternal body. He also wants immersion within the "strength of the Dragon" (89). Yet he is also oblivious of the fact that Lecter has already "baptized" another chosen figure, namely Will Graham. During their last encounter, Lecter sunk his teeth into Graham infecting him with a dark version of a "holy spirit" that has since haunted him. Dolarhyde also bites his chosen victims, re-enacting a form of family abuse he has suffered from so long ago. Lecter, Graham, and Dolarhyde embody dark reflections of a pathological family. Lecter is the Kronos figure who seeks to devour his chosen sons in more ways than one. Graham and Dolarhyde are also victims and beloved sons in whom the Father may be well pleased — assuming they follow his ways.

While investigating the death of the Jacobi family in Birmingham, Graham contacts Niles Jacobi, the deceased father's son by his first marriage. He discovers Niles's homosexuality and involvement in a "rough trade" relationship with his older partner Randy and similar family history to Dolarhyde. Randy was abandoned by his father at the age of three. His mother refused her former spouse access to him. It was not until he visited his son at a correctional center and offered to help him attend college that the two finally met. Niles also suffered from maternal abuse and also resents his deceased stepmother. Graham's earlier experiences with Lecter represent another form of rough trade repeated in his final encounter with Dolarhyde. Dolarhyde's grandmother ensured that he would never enjoy a normal psychological development and family life. Lecter later attempts to destroy Graham's new family relationship by supplying Dolarhyde with the Florida address. Dolarhyde also engages in his own type of rough trade by punishing Freddy Lounds. He begins with a cannibalistic kiss, a tactic resembling Lecter's own techniques. Graham uses Lounds to try to trap Dolarhyde, making the journalist a sacrificial victim. Whether conscious of this or not, Graham does manipulates Lounds for his own ends. Lecter also attempts to use Dolarhyde for his own murderous ends. By removing Graham's family, Lecter hopes that his "prodigal son" will recognize his real inner self and "return home."

Molly decides to stay with Willie's grandparents as the quest continues. They are the parents of her former husband and are hostile towards Graham A process of gradual alienation begins making Graham as isolated as Dolarhyde. This becomes explicit as he emotionally reacts to Mollie's final words to him, "Be careful, darling" (184):

> She had never called him darling before. He didn't care for it. He didn't care for new names; darling, Red Dragon [185].

Separation brings him closer to his prey. But it will have detrimental effects ensuring permanent isolation and damnation.

> But to begin to understand the dragon, to hear the cold drips in his darkness, to watch the world through his red haze, Graham would have had to see things he could never see, and he would have had to fly through time [186].

Later chapters document the family history of Francis Dolarhyde, from his birth in 1938, abandonment by his mother, "rescue" from an orphanage by his grandmother, early low self-esteem resulting from a childhood peer group who jeer at his cleft-palate condition, verbal and physical abuse by his grandmother who threatens him with castration when he only desires maternal comfort, the beginning of his attacks on animals, and further abuse inflicted on him by his stepbrother and -sister following his reluctant adoption after his grandmother's mental collapse. The family roots of a serial killer are firmly in place. Although there is no indication that Graham intuitively witnesses these events, these chapters significantly follow the above quotation concluding the previous chapter. They symbiotically link both hunter and hunted so that they appear more like psychological blood brothers similar to Edgar Huntly and Clithero in Charles Brockden Brown's novel and Ethan Edwards and Scar in *The Searchers*. This becomes apparent in the three brief paragraphs beginning the next chapter. There the description of the open grave of Freddy Lounds leads to brief passages whose very proximity link Graham and Dolarhyde. Both bear responsibility for his death. Another dark link in *Red Dragon*'s symbiotic chain develops.

Dolarhyde views another family movie featuring the Shermans, the next victims whom he desires to "crawl in between" (211) to achieve the closeness his grandmother originally denied him. The following brief reference to his earlier attempt at comfort explains his motivations. "Crawling across her in the dark and under the covers, warm against her now" (194). Denied access to a child's normal desires for maternal love and regarded as a monster throughout his entire life, Dolarhyde plans his own type of powerful transformation. He desires rebirth within the body of Blake's Red Dragon that stands triumphant over a woman symbolizing the maternal realm that humiliated him throughout his entire life.

> There is no sense of vengeance in him, only Love and thoughts of the Glory to come; hearts becoming faint and fast, like footsteps fleeing into silence. Him rampant, Him rampant, filled with Love, the Shermans opening to him, The past does not occur to him at all; only the Glory to come. He does not think of his mother's house. In fact, his conscious memories of that time are remarkably few and indistinct [211].

After serving in the army during the late '50s, specializing in darkroom operations, viewing medical films on trauma, and enjoying " R 'n R" in the decadent environments of Hong Kong and Kowloon, Dolarhyde returns home to discover his chosen mission after seeing a color photography of Blake's influential image. He returns to Hong Kong to remove his own teeth so he will use his grandmother's dentures on his deadly missions. Dolarhyde integrates her former controlling mechanisms of castration into his own persona. The victim will now become a deadly victimizer in his own family drama.

Dolarhyde's brief encounter with his blind co-worker Reba McClane appears to offer salvation. He takes her to a zoo and sees her fearlessly stroking a sedated tiger. When the zoo director applies his stethoscope to her ears, he finds that "she was filled with the tiger heart's bright thunder"

(246). Reba senses Dolarhyde's feelings becoming "perfectly aware that it had excited him to see her with the tiger; he had shuddered like a horse when she took his arm leaving the treatment room" (247). Two revealing factors explaining the psychological history of Dolarhyde occur in this sentence. Reba positively responds to a tiger resembling the one in Blake's poem "burning bright." The reference to the horse recalls the traumatized youth of Peter Schaffer's *Equus* who also had a deep bonding with horses. The play also featured a symbiotic relationship between a psychiatrist and patient paralleling those existing between Lecter, Graham and Dolarhyde in *Red Dragon*. Before his grandmother's stroke, Dolarhyde considered killing a mule. Horses might have followed. His step-siblings blame him for losing their ponies after their father experiences financial problems. These references anticipate a later incident when Graham learns that Willy's grandfather has bought him a pony in Oregon and that "Molly hadn't mentioned it" (278). This suggests the beginning of the end of their relationship. Young orphan Clarice Starling also has her own type of bonding with horses in *The Silence of the Lambs*.

Dolarhyde believes that he has found his soul mate in Reba. He hopes that the Dragon may be cured by "the presence of a living woman" (251). Dolarhyde now gains the warmth he vainly sought many years in the past. He experiences Reba's "startling live moments of acceptance in Grandmother's bed" (255). He returns to an Edenic world from which he was earlier expelled from by a grandmother threatening him with castration. But it is not to last.

Graham receives a letter from Lecter taunting him about killing a dangerous psychopath in the past and congratulating him for setting up Lounds. This stirs up dark feelings within his psyche similar to those which will affect Dolarhyde:

> Graham knew that Lecter was dead wrong about Hobbs, but for a half-second he wondered if Lecter might be a little bit right in the case of Freddy Lounds. The enemy inside Graham agreed with any accusation [260].

At the same time, Dolarhyde's dark side re-emerges. His malevolent super-ego humiliates him by speaking in the voice of his grandmother in imagery indebted to "Mrs. Bates" in Alfred Hitchcock's *Psycho* (1960). It again threatens him with castration, turns him against Reba, and reaffirms his mission of destruction. Dolarhyde experiences his own version of agony at Gethsemane. But his internalized dark spirits, representing past abuse inflicted on him by grandmother and his childhood peer group, will not allow this cup to pass away from him. Although Dolarhyde makes one last attempt to control his murderous energies by swallowing the rare print of *The Great Red Dragon and the Woman Clothed with the Sun*, his action is futile. Graham senses the presence of Dolarhyde. Dolarhyde recognizes this. "Graham knew. The son of a bitch was a monster" (299). Dolarhyde's dark super-ego now moves into action. The last act of a deadly drama begins which will contaminate everyone.

Believing that Reba has betrayed him, Dolarhyde kidnaps her. But, his real object is Will Graham. Unlike *Manhunter* (1986), *Red Dragon* moves toward a different confrontation between two symbiotic adversaries. Dolarhyde fakes his suicide, allowing Reba to live to tell her version of events. Graham attempts to reassure Reba that she should not blame herself for Dolarhyde's attraction to her. But as he leaves her, "he couldn't be sure" (319). She has also suffered emotional damage. Michael Mann possibly altered the novel's climax due to its affinities to the shock endings typified by Brian DePalma's *Carrie* (1976) and those prolific, lesser versions represented by the "Friday the 13th" series and others. But Thomas Harris's reasons for depicting his final confrontation are valid. It must occur in Graham's supposedly secure home in Florida where Molly and Willie await his arrival.

Molly, ironically, greets him as Graham brushes mosquitoes away from his face. "What you ought to do is come on in the house before you get eaten up" (326). But, after discovering that their relationship can never be the same again, Graham experiences another version of his earlier attack by Lecter. If he is not "eaten up," the facial and bodily injuries he receives from Dolarhyde return him to an intensive care unit where he once recovered from Lecter's assault. Molly kills Dolarhyde by shooting him in the thigh and face after he has knifed Graham in the chest and face. The killer ironically dies receiving final punishment from a woman whose gender parallels his own mother and grandmother who psychologically devastated him throughout his entire life. Molly's son witnesses this. He may also suffer trauma.

Red Dragon concludes bleakly. Awaking in hospital, Graham sees Crawford and Molly. She ironically compliments Crawford on his appearance and suggests he give Graham a face transplant. Her comment evokes Dolarhyde's facial condition at birth. Graham receives a letter from Lecter who wishes him a speedy convalescence expressing the hope that he "won't be very ugly" (335). This line echoes Dolarhyde's appearance. After learning that Willie is now back in Oregon with his grandparents, Graham understands that his normal family life is over. Following an injection of Demerol he drifts away and thinks about his visit to Shiloh, the scene of one of the bloodiest Civil War battles. Graham finally accepts Lecter's philosophy concerning the indifferent nature of a beautiful, yet hostile, universe. Alone, like Dolarhyde, he now understands the deep bonding with Lecter that he once, hopelessly, attempted to deny:

> Graham knew too well that he contained all the elements to make murder; perhaps mercy too. He understood murder uncomfortably well, though [339].

Manhunter also contains parallels between Graham and Dolarhyde (spelled with two l's in the film, while Lecter appears as Lektor; I will follow Harris's spellings here except when different versions occur in quotations) but moves toward a different climax. Although Molly (Kim Griest) resents the intrusion of Jack Crawford (Dennis Farina) into their Florida home to pressure her already traumatized husband back into service, the film ends on a positive note with Graham (William Peterson) peacefully reconciled with Molly and his actual son Kevin against the Florida landscape. *Manhunter* drops the shock ending of the novel. It chooses to depict the climactic encounter between Graham and Dolarhyde in a more cinematic manner. Graham jumps through the window of Dolarhyde's home to confront him for the first and only time in the film. Mann also omits passages concerning the family history of Dolarhyde and incidents such as Graham's various encounters with Atlanta and Alabama officials, Atlanta meter reader Hoyt Lewis, Graham's meeting with Dr. Chilton prior to his first contact with Lecter, and Niles Jacobi. They work better in the novel but would be merely redundant in a film version.

Manhunter instead chooses to emphasize the novel's symbiotic relationships between Graham, Lecter, and Dolarhyde by visual techniques and screen acting where subtlety plays a key role. Shots of Dolarhyde overpowering Freddie Lounds with chloroform and depictions of Lounds's charred body were cut. Dolarhyde is appropriately seen for the first time in the film in his own home dominating his terrified victim in a low angle shot. Lounds's incinerated body is best left to the imagination. William Peterson's performance as Graham intuitively depicts a traumatic victim. There is little need for unnecessary explanation here. Although Mann omits the novel's background information about Dolarhyde's abusive upbringing, Tom Noonan's performance as Dolarhyde intuitively depicts someone both monster and victim. It also needs little verbal explanation. Dolarhyde's brief salvation with Reba (Joan Allen) and his mistaken feelings of betrayal represent exemplary examples of understated screen acting where less means more. Noonan's techniques of facial expression eliminate the need for superfluous dialogue. The *Psycho* super-ego voice-overs Harris uses in *Red Dragon* to explain Dolarhyde's motivations are unnecessary. Although Anthony Hopkins now overshadows Brian Cox in popular memory, the first Hannibal still remains impressive. Although limited in screen time in contrast to Hopkins's star appearances in the unnecessary remake *Red Dragon* (2004), Cox subtly depicts the incarcerated doctor as a low-key, but still, dangerous, figure. He avoids those melodramatic acting techniques later employed by Anthony Hopkins which unfortunately resemble John Carradine thespian mannerisms. *Manhunter* displays superior screen acting where understatement works much better. Every performance smoothly integrates into a highly accomplished visual structure significantly indebted to Michael Mann's direction and Dante Spinotti's cinematography. Spinotti uses particular colors to emphasize dark emotional moods often contrasting green, purple, violent, and magenta in certain scenes involving Dolarhyde and Lecter. When Graham looks inside Lecter's white cell, discordant colors of green, purple, and violet appear as the camera pans subjectively. They trigger the mental collapse Graham experiences outside the hospital envisioned by blurred grass seen through a prism lens. Spinotti also uses deep romantic blue colors bathed in moonlight to show Graham and Molly in bed together before he leaves home. Dolarhyde's activities also occur during the full moon.

Manhunter has appeared in three different versions, the first of which no longer exists except in the form of stills of deleted and alternate scenes in the 2003 Anchor Bay DVD version of the film. This also contains director's commentary and is advertised as the restored director's cut (Lucas, Sammon). The running time is three minutes longer than the previously released 2000 DVD Anchor Bay version containing interviews with Dante Spinotti, William Petersen, Joan Allen, Brian Cox, and Tom Noonan which do not appear in the 2003 DVD. Based upon Michael Mann's screenplay available on DVD-ROM in the 2003 version, the original running time of the rough cut probably was some 131 minutes and contained more references to the "Red Dragon" motif of Thomas Harris's novel. Mann decided to eliminate these elements since they work better on the page rather than the cinema screen. Mann instead emphasizes more subtle and indirect visual elements. The theatrical version of *Manhunter* originally ran nearly 120 minutes.

Harris's novel emphasizes the fact that Dolarhyde wishes to merge his personality with the powerful figure of the Red Dragon. Traces of this exist in the theatrical version and the longer cable version on which Mann based his restored director's cut. Dolarhyde shows a slide of Blake's painting to Freddie Lounds (Stephen Lang) after the kidnapping. The image also appears after Dolarhyde's dinner with Reba at his home. Some extra dialogue contained in Mann's final screenplay revealed Dolarhyde explaining his final transformation into Blake's Red Dragon to Reba when she is a captive in his home. "Francis tried to keep me off you, but he was wrong." An alternate version of the scene where Dolarhyde reveals himself to the kidnapped Freddie Lounds showed the killer with a red dragon tattoo covering his chest and back. He extended his arms in the manner of Blake's monstrous being. This scene followed the description given in Harris's novel where Dolarhyde drops his kimono to reveal the tattoo to Lounds. Former vice-president of special promotions for the now defunct DeLaurentiis Entertainment Group (which originally produced the film) Paul Sammon believes these deleted segments "clarified Dolarhyde's delusional quest to become the Red Dragon of Blake's painting."[3] He thinks their removal obscured key elements deriving from the original novel that would have elucidated the nature of the killer's psychopathology to the audience.

However, Sammon also recognizes that Mann may have intended a much more subtle approach for Dolarhyde's psychic condition as well as the symbiotic nature of Will Graham's talent as a manhunter. Graham describes the nature of these feelings to his son Kevin in some lines cut from the supermarket scene which did not appear in either the theatrical and 2000 DVD version. They were restored to the 2003 Restored Director's Cut version based upon the Showtime cable television version of 1989. There Graham explains his fears to Kevin concerning knowledge of the killer's motivations as well as feelings of having more in common with Lecter than he wishes. However, William Petersen's performance in the earlier versions needs no special dialogue to emphasize what exactly is going on in his mind. From the moment Jack Crawford makes an unwelcome visit to his Florida home to call him back into service, his traumatic feelings are obvious. When Lecter first attacked Graham, he left his mark emotionally and physically. A scene deleted from the theatrical print, but restored to the other versions, showed Graham standing naked in front of a hotel window when Molly makes a brief conjugal visit to his hotel room. His reflection appears in the glass showing the scar Lecter left on him, a scar familiar to readers of the novel as well as alert viewers who recognize the visual reference to the attack he suffered from the evil doctor earlier in the film. Such references are cinematic and need no explanatory dialogue. Both image and performance silently evoke the required meaning.

However, as Mann explains on the DVD audio-commentary, his Francis Dolarhyde owes little to the Dolarhyde of Thomas Harris's novel.

He is instead based upon a serial killer the director knew over a period of years whose favorite song was Iron Butterfly's "In-A-Gadda-Da-Vida," which occurs during Dolarhyde's last stand in the film. This musical reference does not occur in Thomas Harris's *Red Dragon*. William Blake's *Red Dragon* is a central component of the original novel but it is not crucial to *Manhunter*. Instead, it is just one of many elements contributing to the psychotic nature of Francis Dolarhyde in the director's reworking of the original novel. Yet despite Mann's decision to remove the tattoo from Tom Noonan's body, the Red Dragon motif does occupy a role in the film. But it is now less a leading player and more one of the elements influencing Dolarhyde. A huge photograph of the lunar landscape appears in his apartment as does a television set whose vertical control is deliberately distorted. Dolarhyde is a serial lunar killer and a victim of child abuse as Graham recognizes. However, Blake's Red Dragon imagery does occurs in two key sequences in Manhunter. But it operates on more implicit levels than in Harris's novel.

The first of these occurs the morning after the lovemaking between Dolarhyde and Reba (Joan Allen). She is the first woman before whom he does not feel insecure as opposed to his second appearance in the film when he negatively reacts to the touch of the attractive technician Eileen. His reaction suggests a dark, history of maternal abuse which indelibly colors his feelings toward the opposite sex. The fact that Reba is blind certainly helps. Dolarhyde feels insecure because of a hare lip which is not as bad as he imagines. In an earlier scene derived from the novel, Reba's caressing of the sleeping tiger evokes sexual feelings within Dolarhyde. He sees that a woman can also appreciate the qualities in another type of animal celebrated by William Blake in his immortal poem "Tyger, Tyger, Burning Bright." Dolarhyde feels closeness toward a woman who can react positively to this beast's fearful symmetry. He encounters a live, caring, and warm female who can accept him as a human being rather than the dead mothers he seeks maternal recognition from. As they lie in bed together, Dolarhyde places Reba's hand over his hare lip as if finally understanding that his facial scar is not as bad as he once believed. Mann originally shot the scene with Reba's hand over the tattooed body of Dolarhyde. But he changed this to show a bare-chested Dolarhyde finally gaining the affection he has craved for so long and revealing the potential of becoming a different human being rather than the powerful monster he once wished to be. When Dolarhyde later sees Reba outside basking in the rising sun, featured in one of the most beautiful shots in the film in which Mann expresses his pride during his director's audio-commentary, he tells her that she "should stay outside...' cause you look so good in the sun." As Tim Lucas points out, for viewers aware of Blake's painting, "the dialogue reveals that Dolarhyde has not only allowed Reba into his heart, but into the painting that rules his fantasy. He now sees her as 'The Woman Clothed with the Rays of the Sun,' raising her arms in adoration of the Red Dragon" (Lucas 35).

However, his salvation is short-lived. Outside Reba's apartment, Dolarhyde imagines that she betrays him with Ralph Mandy. After shooting Mandy, he knocks on Reba's door telling her that Francis is no more. He removes her to his house where he intends to make her another sacrificial victim. Mann also mentions in the 2003 DVD audio-commentary the reason for the racked vertical images on the television set in Dolarhyde's apartment. Some psychotics believe that the carrier frequencies glimpsed on television signals between frames reveal the clue to their identities. So Dolarhyde racks the television's vertical focus in his desire to control another visual gaze. Before Dolarhyde slaughters Reba, Graham jumps through the apartment window. He smashes the glass and also receives a facial wound from a fragment from the bathroom mirror Dolarhyde intended to use on Reba. After Graham shoots Dolarhyde we see two images of the dead body displayed to reveal other indirect visual references to Blake's imagery.

Dolarhyde lies flat on his back in a pool of blood. His arms are spread wide. They evoke not only the wings of Blake's Dragon but also the fearful display of arms Dolarhyde earlier revealed to Lounds, an image more explicit in the scene showing his tattooed body in the earlier version of the film. His prone position now resembles the woman clothed with the rays of the sun as if exhibiting the feminine side of his personality as well as the maternal realm he has sought acceptance from throughout his life. Tim Lucas suggests that Dolarhyde's body might indicate the final dominance "of The Tooth Fairy's own feminine side (i.e. homosexual principle) which Dolarhyde violently protests to Lounds and others throughout the picture" (Williams 9). But it is equally possible that Dolarhyde has finally managed to reconcile the warring parts of his personality in death. He has achieved autonomy free from his personal demons and gains an acceptance in death that he has vainly sought since the moment of his birth.

Manhunter operates significantly on visual realms of meaning. Mann challenges his viewers to *see,* rather than read, clues unlike the manner of a detective novel and the different type of literary meanings contained in *Red Dragon.* When Graham experiences his own type of epiphany in the

Leeds bedroom, he sees Dolarhyde's vision of the deceased Mrs. Leeds looking at him with mirrors in her eyes and mouth. "I see myself accepted and loved in the silver mirror of your eyes." He finally understands the particular dimensions of Dolarhyde's psychotic power involving his pathological desires to be united with, and accepted by, a maternal body denied to him from the moment of birth. The clinical nature of the Leeds family's antiseptic white bedroom also visually links Graham to the environment of Hannibal Lecter's cell. Graham recognizes that Dolarhyde's primary sense is vision involving the seeing and reflecting of images. He immediately understands that Dolarhyde has also been seeing the home movies he has been constantly watching. After tracing the films to the St. Louis photo laboratory where Dolarhyde works, Graham moves toward a final confrontation, hoping to destroy his own inner demons personified by Dolarhyde and Lecter.

Mann's Dolarhyde is a killer who aims less at the desired autonomy of his counterpart in Thomas Harris's novel. He is rather one seeking acceptance by the maternal figure within the Lacanian mirror gaze prior to the necessary separation of mother and child. He is still trapped within the mirror phase due to his lack of normal personal development. As a serial killer trapped within a repetition-compulsion scenario, he is doomed to re-enact that brief moment of acceptance by the mother's body some unknown event in the past denied to him from at a traumatically early age. *Manhunter* constantly employs windows, mirrors, and the cinematic gaze. Molly and Crawford sit on separate sides of a room looking at Will Graham below through a window. During a brief conjugal visit, Molly and Will embrace before a window, their images reflected in the glass. Dolarhyde engages in perverse performances within family relationship which he also films. "Selecting his victims from home movies, Dolarhyde creates his family, cinematically inserting himself in a scene of dead family centered on mother. He dances and reaffirms his presence within her gaze like a child within the Lacanian scenario"[5] When Graham first visits Lecter in his prison cell, the horizontal and vertical presence of the bars creates a "fearful symmetry" between both men hinting at the intuitive nature of the deadly identity they both share. But, unlike his damned counterpart in Harris's novel, Graham returns to his family in Florida. He discovers that the net he constructed to guard baby turtles before he left on his mission from marauding crabs has saved "most of them." That is all he can expect.

Before his return, Mann restores Graham's visit to the Sherman family to his director's cut. They were Dolarhyde's next intended victims.

This sequence did not appear in either the theatrical or the DVD version released in 2000. Mrs. Sherman (Patricia Charbonneau) now appears as a living person in the film as opposed to being just a visual image on the home movie footage that Dolarhyde had viewed. Graham refuses her offer of a drink stating awkwardly that he "just dropped by to see you. That's all." As he walks away, the shot uses slow motion before cutting abruptly to Graham's return to his own family in Florida. The restored Sherman scene is not redundant. It is crucial toward understanding the salvation of Mann's Will Graham. Like Dolarhyde, he has constantly watched the same home movies. But he now sees a real, living person with her family, as opposed to the artificial image on a cinema screen who will become a dead object in Dolarhyde's deadly game. The novel ends with Graham's bleak isolation. But the film moves towards a more positive ending that is not entirely neo-conservative.[6] Graham not only needs to inform the Shermans that they no longer face any danger. He also has to assure himself that his *gaze* on the next intended victims of Dolarhyde has no dark, psychic implications. After reassuring himself, he does not want to push his luck. So he refuses offers to stay and have coffee. He can now quickly return home. Thus Mann employs an abrupt cut (and not a dissolve) to the final sequence. Graham has definitely escaped from the past. *Manhunter* ends with a freeze frame. Graham and his family look at the ocean in a daylight contrasting with the concluding scene of the film's first sequence. There Molly and Crawford looked through the window at the twilight bathing the ocean. The twilight's red hues suggestively foreshadowed the dawn "clothing" Reba with the opening rays of a sun that so affected Dolarhyde. Michael Mann now, humanely, restores Will Graham to the family whose love saves him. He is more fortunate than his doomed counterpart in the original novel forever permanently affected by the inhumanity represented by Hannibal Lecter.

Works Consulted

Harris, Thomas. *Red Dragon.* New York: G.P. Puttnam's Sons, 1981.

Lucas, Tim. "Michael Mann's *Manhunter:* Spread Your Wings and Learn to Die." *Video Watchdog,* no. 13 (1992).

Sammon, Paul M. "The Unseen *Manhunter:* The Slaying of *Red Dragon.*" *Video Watchdog,* no. 13 (1992).

Williams, Tony. "Through a Dark Mirror: *Red Dragon's* Gaze." *Notes on Contemporary Literature,* vol. 25, no. 1 (1995).

7

Suspense vs. Horror

The Case of Thomas Harris

S.T. Joshi

The exact line of demarcation between, on the one hand, the mystery or suspense story and, on the other hand, the horror story (what I, following Lovecraft, prefer to call the weird tale) can sometimes be nebulous to the point of vanishment. L.P. Hartley, a master of both the psychological and the supernatural ghost story, famously wrote in 1955:

> Even the most impassioned devotee of the ghost story would admit that the taste for it is slightly abnormal, a survival, perhaps, from adolescence, a disease of deficiency suffered by those whose lives and imaginations do not react satisfactorily to normal experience and require an extra thrill. Detective-story writers give this thrill by exploiting the resources of the *possible;* however improbable the happenings in a detective story, they can and must be explained in terms that satisfy the reason. But in a ghost story, where natural laws are dispensed with, the whole point is that the happenings cannot be so explained. A ghost story that is capable of a rational explanation is as much an anomaly as a detective story that isn't [vi–viii].

Lovecraft expressed very much this sentiment in a letter written more than twenty years earlier. Discussing William Faulkner's grim story of necrophilia, "A Rose for Emily," Lovecraft wrote:

> Manifestly, this is a dark and horrible thing which *could happen,* whereas the crux of a *weird* tale is something which *could not possibly happen.* If any unexpected advance of physics, chemistry, or biology were to indicate the

118

possibility of any phenomena related by the weird tale, that particular set of phenomena would cease to be *weird* in the ultimate sense because it would become surrounded by a different set of emotions. It would no longer represent imaginative liberation, because it would no longer indicate a suspension or violation of the natural laws against whose universal dominance our fancies rebel [*Selected Letters 1929–1931* 434].

It is possible that Lovecraft's bias toward what he called "cosmic horror" made him undervalue the horrific potential in some literary works that do not involve the supernatural, but can nevertheless generate a substantial emotion of horror within the reader. Even if, as Lovecraft would maintain, this emotion — what might be termed "psychological horror," the horror engendered by an awareness of the depths of perversity to which humanity can descend — is of a different order from "supernatural horror," or the perception of a "suspense or violation of ... natural laws," there nonetheless seems to be an impressive body of literature, especially of recent vintage, that can legitimately be placed within the subcategory of the weird tale labeled "psychological horror."

There is no denying that there is a very broad area of overlap between the mystery, suspense, or even detective story on the one hand and the weird tale on the other, insofar as both employ such elements as suspense, concealment of the nature or identity of the criminal or weird manifestation, and a climax that is at once a revelation (an appeal to the intellect) and a dénouement (an appeal to the emotions). It would of course be simplistic — and, in fact, false — to say that in the mystery story the resolution is natural while in the weird tale it is supernatural: firstly, this dichotomy ignores the non-supernatural weird tale, which is exactly what is under discussion here, and secondly, in a supernatural tale there is very frequently not a *full* revelation (we do not, in the end, know the exact nature of the entity or entities in Lovecraft's "The Colour out of Space"), something that would be intolerable in the formal detective story.

The relation between the mystery story and the weird tale is of very long standing. We do not need to be told that Edgar Allan Poe initiated both forms, virtually inventing the detective story out of whole cloth and rescuing the weird tale from the staleness of the later Gothic tradition by investing it with a psychological realism that has rarely been equaled in subsequent literature. Joseph Sheridan Le Fanu, amidst the plethora of his supernatural work, short and long, wrote a superb mystery-suspense tale, "The Room in the Dragon Volant" (1872), which, if it were better known, would be of great significance in being one of the earliest modern works of what I call the *pseudo-supernatural,* in which seemingly supernatural manifestations are ultimately explained away naturally. This device was, of course, utilized in a significant body of Gothic fiction (most of the works of Ann Radcliffe and Charles Brockden Brown), but Le Fanu's work (and later work of its kind) is different if only for the skill with which the pseudo-supernatural is suggested and the highly satisfying way in which it is resolved naturalistically.

Many detective stories, indeed, function on this premise, and it is worth examining a few of them briefly to see how closely the mystery or detective tale can approach weird fiction. John Dickson Carr (1906–1977) was a master of the pseudo-supernatural while being the most orthodox of "fair play" detective writers. In some cases Carr merely used the pseudo-supernatural as atmosphere, as when he metamorphosed the country manor-house of the conventional British detective story into a neo-Gothic castle in *Hag's Nook* (1933). In other works — I think in particular of *The Man Who Could Not Shudder* (1940) — Carr concocts so bizarre a method of murder that only the supernatural could seem to account for it, until by some sleight-of-hand the crime is finally explained, usually as some elaborate contrivance on the part of an especially fiendish and cunning murderer. It is because Carr used the pseudo-supernatural in his early novels so extensively that he could pull off such a tour de force as *The Burning Court* (1937), where a murder is first explained naturalistically and then, in a stunning appendix, as the product of witchcraft. Since we are reading what we imagine to be an orthodox detective story which appears on the surface to be merely pseudo-supernatural (the suggestion that one of the characters is a witch), we expect the matter to be resolved naturalistically, and so it appears to be until we read that appendix and slowly and horrifically come to realize the true state of affairs. What this novel really does is to play tricks with genre, working upon and confounding our expectations of what a detective story is and of how it differs from a weird tale.

Later mystery writers continue in this tradition, with increasing subtlety of execution and psychological analysis. The psychological mystery has become a distinct subgenre of the mystery story, and writers like Margaret Millar and Ruth Rendell are its masters. Their works are very close to the works of psychological horror that I shall shortly study precisely because a disturbed personality is under examination. Such of Millar's work as *The Iron Gates* (1945) and *Beast in View* (1955) can virtually be considered weird in their acute depiction of madness and their cumulative atmosphere of foreboding. Millar's masterwork of this type is perhaps *A Stranger in My Grave* (1960), an enormously rich and complex work that is pseudo-supernatural both in the Carrian manner (brooding atmosphere, events that seemingly cannot be explained save by supernatural means) and in the very close psychological portrayal that itself almost generates a sense of horror. Ruth Rendell's novelette *Heartstones* (1987) is also of this sort.

The rationale for including the psychological horror tale as a subset of the weird tale rests upon the very obvious notion that, just as we do not know everything about the universe, we similarly do not know everything about the workings of the mind. Lovecraft's memorable pronouncement in "Supernatural Horror in Literature"—"The oldest and strongest emotion of mankind is fear, and the oldest and strongest kind of fear is fear of the unknown" (21)—is nearly as valid a justification for works dealing with aberrant psychological states as for those dealing with unknown forces in the external world. I say "nearly as valid" because there is a real sense in which psychological horror seems metaphysically subordinate to supernatural horror: no matter how extreme the mental aberration, it is difficult to see how this embodies Lovecraft's "violation of natural law," something he felt to be a critical component of the weird tale.

The psychological horror tale perhaps has roots in the psychological ghost story, where the seemingly spectral phenomena are ultimately explained away as the product of a disturbed mind; such writers as Walter de la Mare and Oliver Onions excelled in the form. In these stories, however (as, of course, in what is perhaps the prototype of them all, Henry James's *The Turn of the Screw*), there is frequently doubt, maintained (and intended to be maintained) to the end of the tale, as to whether the events — or, rather, the seemingly weird component of them — are "external" or "internal": whether the specific weird manifestation is postulated as actually occurring in the real world (supernatural horror) or merely in the mind of a disturbed individual (psychological horror). Ambrose Bierce wrote a good number of tales in which the weird is fairly clearly internal, but he had few followers, and his work was in any case very close to the *comte cruel*. Shirley Jackson frequently provides no explicit hints one way or the other; indeed, one of the many distinctive features of her work is the suggestion that the "supernatural" events are simultaneously external and internal.

If, then, the mystery story and the weird tale can be so closely related, what are the distinctions? How are we to decide whether a tale belongs in one class or the other? Kenneth Clark's definition of civilization —"What is civilization? I don't know. I can't define it in abstract terms — yet. But I think I can recognize it when I see it" (1)—has been ridiculed for apparently being rather nebulous and perhaps even a little philistine, but it seems to me not a bad way to distinguish between the two fields in question. Much of the difficulty is, I believe, caused by the very use of the term "horror," a term I now find more and more repulsive or, at the very least, unwieldy. Horror literature is not necessarily a literature where horrible things happen. Horrible things happen in *Oedipus Rex,* but it is not a work of horror. In the end it may be merely a matter of emphasis. Let us return to Poe: loathsome things certainly happen in "The Murders in the Rue Morgue," but since the emphasis is on the solution of the case, there is no opportunity for horror to emerge; the fundamental intellectualism of the formal detective tale prevents us from experiencing emotions such as horror.

Perhaps the prototypical work of psychological horror in our time is Robert Bloch's *Psycho* (1959). It is difficult to treat of *Psycho,* just as it is now difficult to read it, without reference to Alfred Hitchcock's film, but we must try to do so, for the novel reveals subtleties and moments of chilling terror that even the film has not captured. One of the many details the film fails to convey is the degree to which, at the outset, Norman Bates's symbiotic, love-hate relationship with his (dead) mother is elaborated. By a transparent projection, Bates imagines that it is his mother who is mentally ill and ought to be locked away in an asylum; in a brilliant updating of the Jekyll and Hyde syndrome, Bates on occasion wholly adopts the personality of his mother and then, regaining his own personality, professes horror at what his "mother" has committed. But Bates is by no means wholly unaware of his condition, and at one point comes dangerously close to realizing it:

> It was like being two people, really—the child and the adult. Whenever he thought about Mother, he became a child again, with a child's vocabulary, frames of reference, and emotional reactions. But when he was by himself— not actually by himself, but off in a book—he was a mature individual. Mature enough to understand that he might even be the victim of a mild form of schizophrenia, most likely some form of borderline neurosis [83–84].

What makes *Psycho* a genuine weird tale is not primarily—or, rather, not *initially*—our awareness of Bates's profound mother fixation, which has led him to deny the fact of his mother's death, extract her body from her grave, place it in his home, and imagine her alive once more: all this we learn only toward the end of the novel, and we can now only imagine what an impact this revelation would have had on its first readers. What has laid the groundwork for the weirdness of this conclusion is, firstly, the *apparent* lack of mystery as to the deaths that occur at the Bates motel—

they are, we believe, clearly the work of Bates's mother — and, secondly, some exceptionally fine touches of the pseudo-supernatural. The revelation that Bates's mother is actually dead comes about two-thirds through the novel; shortly thereafter we learn that the private detective Arbogast had told Lila Crane, sister of the murdered Mary Crane, that he saw Bates's mother (actually Bates dressed as his mother) as he drove into the motel. At this point the sheriff, who knows Bates's mother is dead, remarks: "Maybe he saw her ghost sitting in the window" (120). And indeed, it is momentarily conceivable to a reader that Bates's mother is in fact a ghost and has killed Mary and Arbogast, although most ghosts in standard weird fiction do not wield knives. Another pseudo-supernatural touch occurs when Bates sees Lila come to the motel and thinks it is Mary who has come out of the swamp where he dumped her (125).

The episode in which Lila boldly enters Bates's home in order to find out the truth of the matter is the most horrific scene in the novel. The pseudo-supernatural here functions on several levels. This entire episode is an adaptation and subtilization of the conventional haunted-house story in which a protagonist explores some centuried and cobwebbed dwelling where a sheeted figure may emerge at any moment; and Bloch's use of language simultaneously enhances and subverts this convention. Lila, examining the musty and archaic surroundings, uses such terms as "ghastly" and "horrors" to describe her aesthetic response to the furnishings ("There was a bureau over in the corner ... one of those antique horrors" [142]), but we as readers are led to connote them very differently. Lila then enters Bates's mother's room (Bates has taken his mother's corpse down to the fruit cellar), and although she notes that all the items in it are some fifty years old, the room was *"still alive"* (144): again a double meaning is intended here, suggesting both that the mother's spirit lives because of the meticulous way in which the room has been kept and that Bates is attempting to keep his mother alive in a bodily manner. Finally, Lila, becoming increasingly affected by the eerie atmosphere of the house, repeats to herself harriedly, *"There are no ghosts"* (144, 145): here again this brings to mind the conventional haunted-house character's attempts to reassure himself in the presence of the supernatural, but in fact Lila is right — there are no ghosts here but only Bates's twisted mind. The enormous skill with which this chapter, and the entire novel, is written must place it at the pinnacle of Bloch's output.

All this may perhaps be a somewhat roundabout way of approaching a discussion of the works of Thomas Harris, but it seems to be a necessary prelude in order to determine his precise place as a genre writer. In his two best and most representative novels, Harris straddles — or, at least, is thought by some to straddle — the thin boundary between suspense and horror, but to my mind he ultimately lands in the former domain. No one is likely to claim that there is anything genuinely supernatural in any of Harris's four novels, but the critical question is whether any of them contain sufficient elements of psychological terror to classify them within the realm of the weird tale. In my judgment they do not, although this is by no means a reflection on their status as independent literary works.

Black Sunday (1975) is a mere potboiler, with a preposterous premise — terrorists wish to blow up the Super Bowl from a blimp — and stereotypical characters (Dahlia Iyad, the fanatical Palestinian terrorist; Michael Lander, the embittered Vietnam War vet who seeks nothing but death and destruction; David Kabakov, the ruthless Israeli secret service agent who foils the plot) representative of popular fiction. It has only one point of interest: early on a portion of a chapter is devoted to a psychological history of Lander from infancy onward, supplying the inner motives for his actions and desires. It is written in a clinical, almost emotionless manner, but it nevertheless provides the necessary psychological motivation for the entire novel.

Harris developed this idea in an ingenious way in *Red Dragon* (1981). The premise of this novel is the attempt by Will Graham, a semi-retired FBI agent, to hunt down a serial killer by adopting the mindset of the criminal. Graham has an unusual sensitivity to other people's minds (it must be emphasized that this idea is not presented as in any way supernatural or occult, and Graham is far from the "psychic detectives" who lumber implausibly through some of the work of Algernon Blackwood, William Hope Hodgson, and others), and the FBI, stumped in the matter, feel that this may be the only way to capture the killer.

This premise is, as I say, ingenious, but I wonder whether in fact it is actually carried out. That is to say, does Graham really solve the case, or any part of it, by entering the criminal's mind? It seems that what Graham really does is simply to interpret the physical evidence more thoroughly, sensitively, and keenly than others have. Graham states his purported principles to his wife:

> Molly, an intelligent psychopath — particularly a sadist — is hard to catch for several reasons. First, there's no traceable motive. So you can't go that way. And most of the time you won't have any help from informants. See, there's a lot more stooling than sleuthing behind most arrests, but in a case like this there won't *be* any informants. *He* may not even know that he's doing it. So you have to take whatever evidence you have and extrapolate. You try to reconstruct his thinking. You try to find patterns [18].

This is all well and good, but let us now examine a particularly vivid example of Graham's psychological insight, as he examines a murder scene and notes that the murdered children of a family have been brought down to the bedroom where the parents have been killed:

> *Why did you move them again? Why didn't you leave them that way?* Graham asked. *There's something you don't want me to know about you. Why, there's something you're ashamed of. Or is it something you can't afford for me to know?*
> *Did you open their eyes?*
> *Mrs. Leeds was lovely, wasn't she? You turned on the light after you cut his throat so Mrs. Leeds could watch him flop, didn't you? It was maddening to have to wear gloves when you touched her, wasn't it?*
> There was talcum on her leg.
> There was no talcum in the bathroom.
> Someone else seemed to speak those two facts in a flat voice.
> *You took off your gloves, didn't you? The powder came out of a rubber glove as you pulled it off to touch her, DIDN'T IT, YOU SON OF A BITCH? You touched her with your bare hands and then you put the gloves back on and you wiped her down. But while the gloves were off, DID YOU OPEN THEIR EYES?* [29–30].

The murderer perversely wanted the dead children to watch the killing of the parents. All this is rather effective, but there does not seem to be any conclusion here that has not been arrived at by anything other than very acute deduction from the evidence. If Harris or his supporters think that he has invented some "new" form of detection, then he and they had better think again.

But this is not what I wish to study here. What (if anything) makes this a horror novel? Chet Williamson, both a sharp commentator and a gifted weird fictionist, has written of this novel that it is "quite simply, the most frightening book I have ever read" (184). I suppose I cannot quarrel with Williamson on what he finds frightening, and it is, I trust, not because I am exceptionally hardened that I did not find anything particularly frightening in this book. The work is highly compelling, but it is a work of detection and suspense and not horror. Much of the novel is given over to a very careful forensic analysis of evidence, until finally sufficient clues are found to identify the murderer. Harris, with unusual restraint for a popular writer, has not even peppered this novel with much overt violence: the murders have already occurred at the start of the book, and we can only infer their loathsomeness from the gradual accumulation of evidence.

It is, presumably, this whole notion of trying to enter the twisted mind of a serial killer that is supposed to generate horror in this work, and there are occasions when Harris attempts to invest this action with portentous shudders. Graham's great triumph is the capture of Dr. Hannibal Lecter, a highly learned but fiercely cynical and misanthropic psychiatrist who sports the charming soubriquet of "Hannibal the Cannibal." Graham actually seeks Lecter's advice on the serial killings, and Lecter delivers a parting shot: "The reason you caught me is that we're *just alike*" (73).

This sets the stage for a psychological history of the killer very much like that in *Black Sunday;* and it is here that the parallels to *Psycho* become striking. The killer, Francis Dolarhyde, was an orphan who was raised by a hideous and tyrannical grandmother who made fun of his speech impediment and who once threatened to cut off his penis with scissors when she found him as a young boy exposing himself to a little girl. Although Dolarhyde certainly does not resurrect his grandmother's body like Norman Bates, he seems to have preserved her false teeth (one suddenly thinks of Poe's "Berenice"), and he pretends to have self-tormenting conversations with his grandmother very similar to Bates's; Dolarhyde fancies that it is the grandmother who is urging him to kill a young blind woman, Reba McClane, who has taken a romantic interest in him: "'YOU MAY PUT AWAY MY TEETH. YOU PITIFUL LITTLE HARELIP, YOU'D KEEP YOUR LITTLE BUDDY FROM ME, WOULD YOU? I'LL TEAR HER APART AND RUB THE PIECES IN YOUR UGLY FACE. I'LL HANG YOU WITH HER LARGE INTESTINE IF YOU OPPOSE ME. YOU KNOW I CAN" (275). The parallels with Norman Bates's unacknowledged attraction to Mary Crane, and his "mother's" murder of her in order that the bond between Bates and his mother can be preserved, are striking. But Dolarhyde is tracked down, Reba is saved, and Lecter's plot to have Graham's wife killed is foiled.

The Silence of the Lambs (1988) has now exceeded the acclaim of *Red Dragon,* largely as a result of the success of the 1990 film version, one of the most faithful adaptations of a literary work in years. If *Silence* lacks the gripping and monomaniacal intensity of its predecessor, it is overall a finer work—in fullness of characterization, in intricacy of plot, and in cumulative suspense. But it, too, is not a weird tale. Once again much of the action revolves around the mechanics of tracking down the serial killer; and here the evidence ranges from death's-head moths (found in the victims' throats) to anomalous triangular markings found on the back of one victim. As in *Red Dragon,* several of the murders have already occurred, and much attention is given to rescuing the killer's latest victim, who has been abducted but is not murdered immediately.

Dr. Hannibal Lecter, who was merely a sort of sardonic commentator in *Red Dragon,* plays a much larger role in *The Silence of the Lambs,* virtually orchestrating the events even though he spends much of the novel behind bars. (It is interesting that Harris has never given a full account of Will Graham's capture of Lecter, or even of Lecter's own crimes; perhaps a future novel will deal with this rich issue.) Lecter really is one of the more delightfully evil figures in recent literature, and his knowledge of psychiatry allows him to play the most exquisite games of mental torture upon his various targets. While there is something of the Gothic villain in Lecter, he could just as well be considered a Moriarty figure. In this case, however, the Sherlock Holmes figure is not Will Graham but Clarice M. Starling, a trainee in the FBI Academy. She has been chosen to interrogate Lecter so as to produce a psychological profile of serial killers, but — because she finds that Lecter appears to know much about the serial killer known as Buffalo Bill — she becomes enmeshed in one case and ultimately helps to solve it. The sensitive portrayal of Starling is one of the quiet triumphs of this novel.

The gripping mental battle between Lecter and Starling actually ends up relegating the actual murderer to the background, and we learn relatively little about the motivations of Buffalo Bill, who is ultimately identified as one Jame Gumb. This is unfortunate, for had such a psychological history been supplied, a much better case could have been made for the weirdness of *The Silence of the Lambs.* It turns out that Gumb is profoundly confused sexually: he is not homosexual, nor does he truly fit the psychological model of the transsexual; for that reason he has been turned down for a sex change operation, and so he resorts to killing women. Why? He wishes to make an entire suit *out of women's skin,* since this will be the closest he will ever come to being a woman. So he takes various pieces of skin from each of his victims: the back from one, the thighs from another, and so on. This, certainly, is exceptionally perverse, but Harris's presentation of it is so indirect (this, in fact, is the clue to the killings, and so it cannot be fully revealed until the end) as to rob it of potential horror. This is not a criticism: it only confirms that Harris's *prime* goal in the novel is detection, not horror.

What is interesting is that the film version of *The Silence of the Lambs* is actually much more horrifying (and, accordingly, much less of a detective story) than the novel. An early scene, in which Starling must confront Lecter in his heavily guarded cell in a madhouse, is presented in the film as something out of *Melmoth the Wanderer:* we seem suddenly transported out of the present and into the horrors of the Inquisition. There is nothing like this in the novel. Jame Gumb's home in the film is a Gothic castle with a stone-encircled well in which he keeps his hapless victim; one wonders whether the director of the film was thinking of the climactic scene in Lovecraft's *The Case of Charles Dexter Ward;* Harris certainly wasn't. I am not saying that the film is unfaithful to the novel in these and other particulars; perhaps it is merely drawing out hints that were only implicit in Harris's work. Nevertheless, it is not paradoxical to say that the film *The Silence of the Lambs* is horrific whereas the novel is not.

Harris's next novel, *Hannibal* (1999), was an avowed sequel to *The Silence of the Lambs,* and it featured many characters familiar from its predecessor. Dr. Hannibal Lecter was a shadowy figure in Harris's two previous novels, but is very much at center stage in this one; so is Clarice Starling. *Hannibal* opens superbly, with a gripping confrontation between Starling and some drug dealers in Washington, D.C.; the resulting loss of life, fueled by biased press reports, causes Starling to be vilified, even though she acted in self-defense. After years of silence, Lecter writes to her, urging her to resist her superiors, who are seeking to make her a scapegoat. We ultimately learn that Lecter is living well in Florence, Italy, disguised as a museum curator.

About a quarter of the way through the novel, however, things start to go downhill. We learn that the wealthy Mason Verger — one of Lecter's first victims (he survived, although much of his face was eaten away by the hungry villain) — has offered a $3 million reward for the capture of Lecter alive; Verger naturally wishes to exact some particularly loathsome revenge on his nemesis. Accordingly, an unscrupulous Italian police officer strives to catch Lecter, whose disguise he has seen through; but he ends up being Hannibal's next victim. This entire Florence segment reads rather like an overenthusiastic travelogue: Harris cannot resist including every possible bit of information he has soaked up about Italy, going well beyond the bounds of verisimilitude and sounding on occasion like an encyclopedia.

But if the first half of *Hannibal* is somewhat of a disappointment to those who admired Harris's two previous works, the second half plummets into realms of dreadfulness not seen since the heyday of Harold Robbins and Irving Wallace. Several flashbacks portray Lecter's childhood in Lithuania; and we are asked to believe that he became a serial-killer-cum-cannibal because he saw his sister caught, killed, and eaten by starving looters in World War II. This may be bathetic enough, but the ending of the novel is worse still. It was only to be expected that Verger's cohorts would suffer the very fate — being eaten by a herd of man-eating wild pigs — they had envisioned for Lecter; but Harris goes on and destroys the uneasy relationship between Lecter and Starling that lent such vivid tension to *The Silence of the Lambs.* Lecter, it appears, sees in Starling a kind of replacement for his devoured sister, and so he rescues both himself and her from Verger, drugs her, and hypnotizes her so that she becomes his companion (and presumable lover). At the conclusion of the novel we see them enjoying an opera in Buenos Aires.

All this is really too preposterous. Would Starling be so amenable to hypnotic control? And could Harris really have thought that this conclusion would prove satisfying to the readers of his previous novels? It has become obvious that Harris himself has, after a fashion, fallen in love with Lecter: he takes care to portray Hannibal's enemies as even more repulsive, hypocritical, and avaricious than Hannibal himself; and of course they lack his elegance, refinement (the first thing Lecter does after he settles in Virginia is to purchase a clavichord), courage, and psychological fortitude. And then there is an absurd and irrelevant subplot involving Mason Verger's sister, a lesbian bodybuilder who is so determined to bear a child that she secures some of her brother's sperm and promptly kills him.

Harris's latest novel, *Hannibal Rising* (2006), appears to have engendered widely divergent judgments among early reviewers and readers. To be sure, it does not come close to the level of *Red Dragon* or *The Silence of the Lambs,* but in some ways it is superior to *Hannibal*— more, perhaps, for what it lacks than for what it actually contains.

The central theme of the novel is the issue of moral responsibility. Harris provides a much more detailed account of Hannibal's youth: the novel starts when Hannibal is eight years old and ends when he is about eighteen or twenty. We learn that he and his family are forced to leave their castle in Lithuania in the face of the Nazi blitzkrieg early in World War II. During the Germans' retreat in 1944–45, the family manages to reoccupy the castle, but all its members, with the exception of Hannibal and his beloved younger sister Mischa, are killed before Hannibal's eyes: throughout the novel he is plagued by visions of his mother dying by fire. But the worst is to come: a gang of looters, led by one Vladis Grutas, takes over the castle, imprisoning and brutalizing Hannibal and his sister; desperate for food, they decide to eat Mischa, and he can never forget her pleas as she is taken away.

We move to a period just after the war. The Lecter castle has been turned into an orphanage, and Hannibal, now thirteen, is a resident there. Presently his uncle, Robert Lecter (who has married a Japanese woman, Murasaki), comes to take him away to his chateau in France. It is at this point that Harris begins to engage in the issue of moral responsibility.

Hannibal had already exhibited some violent tendencies at the orphanage, chiefly in response to bullying by other boys. But now, in France, he performs his first murder: he pummels a butcher who had directed some lewd remarks to Murasaki. Later, Robert accosts the butcher, but in so doing he dies of a heart attack. Hannibal now confronts the butcher and brutally kills him. The body is later found, with the head missing; still later, when the head turns up, it is lacking its cheeks — and we are immediately meant to recall what the Lecter family cook told Hannibal a short while before: "The best morsels of fish are the cheeks. That is true of many creatures" (107).

In spite of this instance of cannibalism, we are led to sympathize with Hannibal and to believe that the butcher has received his just desserts — and this scenario is repeated throughout the novel, which is largely engaged in recounting how Hannibal systematically hunts down and kills the other looters who had eaten his sister. Given that most of the erstwhile looters have since entered a life of crime, we can scarcely waste any sympathy upon them. In any event, Hannibal reveals himself to be both intellectually brilliant (he is the youngest man ever to be admitted to medical school in France) and culturally sophisticated (perhaps, indeed, a bit more so than his creator: Harris commits such gaffes as leaving the accent off of "Place de l'Opéra" [165] and "Île de la Cité" [169] and noting Hannibal's listening to a "Bach string quartet" [176], although the string quartet as a musical form did not exist in Bach's time), so that it becomes easy to root for him in his vigilantism.

Hannibal is, indeed, careful not to harm anyone except the specific individuals he is pursuing. One of these, a man named Kolnas, has a wife and two children. At one point Hannibal confronts him, tossing at him a blood-stained bag that he suggests contains portions of his family. Although Kolnas had given one of his children a bracelet that had been worn by Mischa, this fact in itself does not confer moral guilt upon the child, and we are momentarily outraged that Hannibal could have committed such an act of wanton murder; but in fact the bag contains only a "beef roast" (292), and was therefore designed merely to taunt Kolnas with his own former cannibalism.

Harris, however, does suggest that there is nonetheless something anomalous, perhaps even inhuman, about Hannibal. After the death of his sister, he apparently lost his power of speech for years, not regaining it until his uncle's death. Hannibal subsequently exhibits incredible powers of coolness under pressure: he passes a polygraph test given by the police after the death of the butcher (the polygrapher remarks that Hannibal has "a monstrous amount of self-control" [120]); when waiting to kill the ringleader of the looters, Vladis Grutas, Harris notes: "Hannibal was calm. His pulse was 72" (298). A police detective, fully aware that Hannibal is engaging on a murderous rampage, delivers a telling comment:

> The little boy Hannibal died in 1945 out there in the snow trying to save his sister. His heart died with Mischa. What is he now? There's not a word for it yet. For lack of a better word, we'll call him a monster [283].

But this is one of the few moments of reflection and analysis that we find in the novel. The greatest failing of *Hannibal Rising* is its author's unwillingness — one can hardly call it an inability, given his past work — to engage in a psychological portrait of Hannibal. Harris evidently wishes the reader to infer Hannibal's overall mental and psychological condition merely from the events of the novel; and while there is some plausibility in this exercise (adhering as it does to the standard writer's advice to show rather than to tell), the novel ends up being nothing but a flat succession of incidents. A little more of the author's ruminations on the significance of Hannibal's actions would have been welcome: is Hannibal truly justified in his murderous onslaught, or has he now already become a "monster"?

As it is, Harris is in danger of becoming so enraptured with the figure of Hannibal that he loses his manifest skill as a writer of suspense novels. Hannibal Lecter has indeed become an icon of popular culture, but there is only so much aesthetic nourishment that Harris can squeeze out of him. Harris is clearly relying on the heavy overtones of horror and evil that the figure of Hannibal brings to any work in which he appears; taken by themselves, *Hannibal* and *Hannibal Rising* are quite undistinguished as novels, and even Hannibal's "star quality" cannot carry them. Long ago, H. P. Lovecraft warned of the dangers of the serial character:

> Now this is manifestly inartistic. To write to order, and to drag one figure through a series of artificial episodes, involves the violation of all that spontaneity and singleness of impression that should characterise short story work. It reduces the unhappy author from art to the commonplace level of mechanical and unimaginative hack-work [*Selected Letters 1911–1924*, 158].

Harris has, to be sure, not quite reached the level of "unimaginative hack-work," but one suspects that the figure of Hannibal Lecter may now be something of an albatross whom he would be well advised to throw overboard.

But our evaluation of Thomas Harris must rest on his best, not his poorest, work. Even if *Red Dragon* and *The Silence of the Lambs* cannot be considered genuinely weird, they are certainly among the more successful works of popular fiction in recent years. I am trying not to say this condescendingly, although it is a fact that Harris tends to succumb to various conventions of popular fiction — abundance of dialogue, stereotypical conflict of good and evil, occasionally contrived plot twists, an abundance of technical knowledge of certain matters (especially forensics) that is meant to impress the reader — although he at least avoids certain other conventions such as sentimentality, slipshod or colloquial style, and a complete resolution of all plot threads at the end. I am not sure how aware of the weird tradition Harris is; but if he is working in the field that Robert Bloch termed "psychological suspense," then he gives equal emphasis to both halves of that compound, and perhaps even a little more to the latter.

Works Consulted

Bloch, Robert. *Psycho.* 1959. Reprint. Greenwich, Conn.: Fawcett Crest, 1960.

Clark, Kenneth. *Civilisation: A Personal View.* London: British Broadcasting Corporation/John Murray, 1969.

Harris, Thomas. *Black Sunday.* New York: Putnam's, 1975.

_____. *Hannibal.* New York: Delacorte Press, 1999.

_____. *Hannibal Rising.* New York: Delacorte Press, 2006.

_____. *Red Dragon.* New York: Putnam's, 1981.

_____. *The Silence of the Lambs.* New York: St. Martin's Press, 1988. Reprint. (paperback). New York: St. Martin's Press, 1989.

Hartley, L.P. "Introduction." *The Third Ghost Book,* ed. Cynthia Asquith. 1955. Reprint. New York: Beagle Books, 1970.

Lovecraft, H.P. *The Annotated Supernatural Horror in Literature,* ed. S.T. Joshi. New York: Hippocampus Press, 2000.

_____. Letter to Frank Belknap Long (8 October 1921). In August Derleth and Donald Wandrei (eds.), *Selected Letters 1911–1924.* Sauk City, Wis.: Arkham House, 1965.

_____. Letter to August Derleth (20 November 1931). In August Derleth and Donald Wandrei (eds.), *Selected Letters 1929–1931.* Sauk City, Wis.: Arkham House, 1971.

Williamson, Chet. "*Red Dragon* by Thomas Harris," in Stephen Jones and Kim Newman (eds.), *Horror: 100 Best Books.* New York: Carroll and Graf, 1988.

8

Transmogrified Gothic

The Novels of Thomas Harris

TONY MAGISTRALE

... when the Male & Female
Appropriate Individuality, they become an Eternal Death.
Hermaphroditic worshippers of a God of cruelty & law!
— William Blake, *Jerusalem*

In his intriguing study of Gothic film and literature, *Dreadful Plea-sures: An Anatomy of Modern Horror* (1987), James Twitchell argues that our attraction to the art of terror is essentially psychosexual: "Horror has little to do with fright; it has more to do with laying down the rules of socialization and extrapolating a hidden code of sexual behavior" (66). Twitchell's thesis is very helpful in providing a Freudian model for viewing the genre, particularly in understanding its relevance to an adolescent audience engaged in the complicated and sometimes terrifying transition to adulthood. Perhaps the most provocative corollary to terrifying analysis, however, occurs late in his book when Twitchell addresses the structural prototypes of Gothic art. In his chapter on Stevenson's *Dr. Jekyll and Mr. Hyde*, Twitchell postulates that the horror genre has always revolved around concepts and images of transformation and shape changing — whether psychological, physical, or both. Mr. Hyde, the Frankenstein creature, the Wolfman, and the vampire all share a common lineage: the acting out of taboo behavior once the polite, socially acceptable human being has been displaced by the monster.

Thomas Harris's three novels — *Black Sunday* (1975), *Red Dragon* (1981), and *The Silence of the Lambs* (1988) — are all in keeping with the Gothic tradition Twitchell defines; they are each, to lesser or greater degrees, books that highlight characters undergoing identity transitions and transmogrifications. And like the Jekyll-Hyde paradigm, the characters in Harris who are most involved with physical transformation also view their change in self-transcendent terms. Jekyll comes to recognize that the Hyde part of his personality is not only more physically dominant, but more psychologically compelling. In *Black Sunday*, the Black September terrorists are willing to sacrifice individual lives — their own included — for the sake of a political cause that has consumed them; the death of thousands at the Super Bowl becomes a radical but necessary prerequisite toward transforming society. Similarly, in the stripping away of former selves, to be replaced by some new physical being perhaps imagined but never actualized, Francis Dolarhyde in *Red Dragon* and Jame Gumb in *The Silence of the Lambs* may be likened to the Black September group insofar as they all seek liberation in violence against an indifferent society. These characters share a philosophy of obsession: for them, Twitchell's "projection of repressed desire" (241), whether it serves a personal or political agenda, can only occur through the violent imposition of one will over another.

I. Red Dragon

William Blake's painting *The Great Red Dragon and the Woman Clothed with the Sun* is the dominant symbol for Dolarhyde's process of "becoming" in the novel *Red Dragon*. As is often the case in Blake's watercolors, the painting highlights the emergence of the man-God (a vision of the imagination made tangible and direct). Dolarhyde writes to Hannibal Lecter hoping the incarcerated psychiatrist will recognize the visionary dimension of Dolarhyde's "becoming." In this correspondence he refers to himself as "Pilgrim," indicating his acute self-awareness of his role as an explorer engaged in a transcendant journey. Like Blake's conception of the artist, Dolarhyde views himself as a man pressing, with the full power of his aroused creativity, against the walls of obedience and restraint.

Dolarhyde's first exposure to a reproduction of Blake's painting initiates a personal identification with the figure of the demonic dragon hovering over the figure of a terrified woman: "He carried the picture with him for days, photographed and enlarged it in the darkroom late at night.... With the fervor of conversion he saw that if he worked at it, if he followed

the true urges he had kept down for so long — cultivated them as the inspi-
rations they truly were — he could Become" (223–24). At least half of *Red
Dragon* concerns the gradual unfolding of exactly what Dolarhyde wishes
to become; Blake's watercolor, which Dolarhyde eventually eats in an effort
to subsume the painting's potency, appears to connect directly with
Dolarhyde's transformative urge to assume the role of masculine avenger.
As Stevenson's Hyde assumes and abuses the privileges of patriarchal control and physical dominance, so does Francis Dolarhyde view the process
of his own "becoming" (the "hyde" of Dolarhyde perhaps a direct allusion
to Stevenson's earlier creature). Blake's painting portrays "the Man-Dragon
rampant over the prostrate pleading woman caught in a coil of his tail"
(296); correspondingly, Dolarhyde's metamorphosis revolves around the
accumulation of power at the expense of women. He appears to measure
the level of his "becoming" by forcing women the simultaneous roles of
adoring spectators and sacrificial victims.

His own self-delusions notwithstanding, Dolarhyde's obsessive need
to become something else — a Blakean concept beyond traditional moral
codes, societal restraints, or even human recognition — suggests the extent
of his own self-hatred. True to the romantic code of art born of human
anguish, Blake's paintings and poetry frequently juxtapose suffering a transcendant consciousness. As Mario Praz argues in *The Romantic Agony*, "For
the Romantics beauty was enhanced by exactly those qualities which seem
to deny it, by those objects which produce horror: the sadder, the more
painful it was, the more intensely they relished it" (21). Born into a world
where he has known only exclusion and humiliation, Dolarhyde punishes
women at the same time as he seeks their veneration Women are an incessant reminder, in their sexual rejection, of his is own physical deformity
and, equally as important, of the childhood abandonment by his mother.
His violence can be seen, in part, as violence against himself, or at least
against that part of himself that he is desperate to forsake. This is why
Dolarhyde is interested only in women victims (he virtually ignores their
husbands and children). Female eyes that once averted their gaze and
mouths that once uttered patronizing words are now filled with, and project, the emerging physical images of Dolarhyde's "becoming." The dead
women are at the center of a ritualized ceremony; they assume the role of
the prostrate female in Blake's painting or of a participant in the numi-
nous experience: blinded by the dragon-god's emergence and struck dumb
in transfixed awe.

Blake wrote and drew from a fathomless inner window through which
he attempted to discover radical insights. As Alfred Kazin observes, "Blake

then used the thing created — the poem, the picture, joined in their double vision — as a window in itself, through which to look to what was still beyond" (21). "I look through the eye," Blake said in words that would have meant everything to Francis Dolarhyde, "not with it." Like Blake's Satan in *The Marriage of Heaven and Hell*, Dolarhyde lives to destroy individual lives, but he believes their destruction to be a source of energy — opening vistas to new worlds induced by transcendant transformation. As Blake acknowledged, a person's true nature could be discovered only by pursuing "the lineaments of Gratified Desire"; destruction was necessary to release the full power of a person's creative will to assert and transform. Similarly, "Dolarhyde knew the unreality of the people who die to help you in these things — understood that they are not flesh, but light and air and color and quick sounds quickly ended when you change them.... Dolarhyde bore screams as a sculptor bears dust from the beaten stone" (96). Most importantly, Dolarhyde's ritualized actions put him in contact with a beautiful, although dead, female audience no longer capable of rejecting him. The fact that his ritual is highly choreographed, and then scrupulously critiqued during his later reviews of the videotape, indicates that Dolarhyde is obsessed with his new emergent identity; the act of watching his own "becoming" reveals his essential link to the protean energies inherent in Blake's creation myths.

The irony ultimately inherent in Dolarhyde's quest is that he reduces Blake's evocative symbols of the visionary human imagination to mere acts of degrading butchery; his dragon-man alter ego revels in attacking helpless women and children who are asleep. A more sophisticated and accurate response to Blake, including his many endeavors to contrapose gender stereotyping, opposes what Dolarhyde interprets from his work. As Mary Lynn Johnson argues, most of Blake's poems and watercolors "present an unsparing critique of a male-dominated world order and an androcentric value system" (61). Blake's art epitomizes the positive attributes of breaking free from the oppressive social veneers of everyday life. In his need to tyrannize others in order to achieve his own sense of freedom, Dolarhyde certainly misapprehends Blake, but nowhere in the novel does Harris acknowledge this misapprehension. Is this because the writer is reluctant to become an intrusive presence in the narrative by balancing the reductive thinking of his unbalanced character? Or does Harris mean to indict Blake by twisting and critiquing the naive and destructive potential inherent in the romantic urge to recreate the self? I would suggest that the latter is the more compelling of these two speculations; moreover, its self-encoded explanation represents the essential separation between

Gothicism and romantic optimism. Whereas Blake and other romantics understood that freedom from social, political, and ethical codes of conduct would produce individuals capable of realizing their divine potential, the Gothic romance marked a shift from faith in human nature to moral skepticism. The Gothic, and here the fiction of Thomas Harris would seem to concur most completely, has always challenged humankind's capacity for balancing forces of good and evil — further suggesting that when their impulses remained unchecked, humans were more likely to perform acts of perversity than poetry.

II. The Silence of the Lambs

It is crucial to keep in mind Dolarhyde's inimitable desire-aversion conflict in his attitude toward women if we are to understand the similar psychology at work in *The Silence of the Lambs*. Like *Red Dragon*, *The Silence of the Lambs* is about the evolutionary process of "becoming." Although Jame Gumb shares with Dolarhyde a definition of the self engaged in a glorious transition, his metamorphosis is no less monstrous. The serial killers in each book require the ritualized slaying of women to enact their respective changes. Dolarhyde appears to be interested in securing some level of homage or acceptance from the women he selects, while Jame Gumb (known as Buffalo Bill) sees women only as "its": physical beings selected purely for the quality of their skins. Dolarhyde thinks himself to be the apotheosis of masculinity, while Gumb identifies with the feminine. In addition to adhering to stereotypical, one-dimensional gender definitions, both suffer from severe mother fixations and complexes. Dolarhyde desires to transform his female victims into mother-surrogates exulting in the birth of a beautiful son, while Gumb actually seeks to recreate the image of his own mother in himself.

The biological advance of the death's-head moth — from larva, to pupa, to emerging adult — is a metaphor for Jame Gumb's transmogrification from male into female. Early on we learn, for example, that the moth is clearly linked to Gumb's stalking; there are some moths who live entirely on "the tears of large land mammals, about our size. The old definition of moth was 'anything that gradually, silently eats, consumes, or wastes any other thing.' It was a verb for destruction too" (96). Buffalo Bill not only feasts on the wasted "tears" of his victims who must be destroyed for their "pelts," but he is also crying for himself. his own tears of pain and frustration over years of entrapment in a male body. His victims, like Dolarhyde's, are necessary, though expendable, elements leading to the realization of a new self.

Gumb's journey to femininity descends into the realm of the grotesque. He believes that becoming female is merely a matter of physiological disguising (or assuming the form). Of course, the issue of what it means to be female is as much spiritual and psychological as it is physical. As statistics on serial killers confirm, men commit these acts; women do not systematically murder and skin other human beings. Jame Gumb's quest to become a female is ironically thwarted by his misogyny: the male brain that continues to operate underneath layers of makeup and stolen feminine flesh.

Buffalo Bill is not the only individual undergoing transformation in this book. All the characters appear in a state of "becoming"; it is just that their transitions are less radical — more psychological than physiological — and viewed more positively by Harris. The death of his wife, Bella, has challenged Jack Crawford's personal outlook on the world; her loss has deeply affected the human being underneath the exterior of the Federal Bureau of Investigation bureaucrat. Hannibal Lecter deludes the authorities and escapes by wearing the face of the policeman he has just murdered. And he departs the novel about to undergo radical facial surgery to become someone else. In spite of his obsessive need to control the dynamics of their relationship, the doctor also seems to have been affected by his contact with Clarice Starling. In his final letter to her, he acknowledges the degree to which she has influenced him: "I have no plans to call on you, Clarice, the world being more interesting with you in it" (337).

His psychopathic cruelty notwithstanding, Lecter is Harris's most compelling character to date. He embodies what film theorist Robin Wood has labeled the "ambivalence of the horror Monster," at once "horrifying us with his evil and delighting us with his intellect, his art, his audacity; while our moral sense is appalled by his outrages, another part of us gleefully identifies with him" (80). Amoral and unemotional, Lecter is a pure intellect and consummate gamesplayer. But he is also intensely human — an empathic therapist as well as a brilliant scholar. His love of Bach and "a window with a view" begin to suggest the complexities of his nature. An angel with horns, the doctor fascinates us with his dualities: both a paragon of civilized man and a connoisseur of human flesh. Yet Lecter's cannibalism is never just about eating. As when Dolarhyde ingests Blake's watercolor, Lecter's selections in dining reveal the essence of his personality; for him, cannibalism is a means of exerting absolute domination over another person. Moreover, his worldly sophistication is present even in what he chooses to eat — only the organs that constitute the "sweet meats." Lecter's proclivity toward consuming human body parts also helps to explain his success as a psychoanalyst. His occupation employs a kind of psychic cannibalism in the transference of one individual's feelings, thoughts, and wishes to another. The psychiatrist is attracted to Starling because of her physical beauty, but he also comes to savor her for other reasons: Lecter wants the details of Starling's tragic adolescence so that he can digest her anguish and make it his own. Her personal pain — the screams of the lambs — becomes his pain, and this is why he dines on lamb chops after listening to Starling's narrative about the spring slaughtering. It is Starling's simultaneous vulnerability and strength in the face of her lingering childhood memories that establishes whatever respect Lecter is capable of summoning toward another human being — particularly one he does not intend to eat.

Harris's novels, like the work of so many writers in the Gothic tradition (from Mary Shelley to Stephen King), highlight the conflict between forces of rationality and human civilization and the irrational, destructive acts of individuals who have suffered severe rejection from the society they now seek to destroy symbolically. Certainly a main reason for Hannibal Lecter's attractiveness to readers is that he fully embodies this dialectic within his own personality: the cannibal is never far removed from the scholar. Harris's "monsters" are social outcasts; similar to Mary Shelley's monster, Jame Gumb and Francis Dolarhyde were not born monster, but were created by society's reductive definitions of gender, parenting, normalcy, and acceptability. Likewise, Lander and the members of the radical terrorist group in *Black Sunday* are the cyclical product, of historical violence and political betrayals. For all these characters, rebellion against personal codes of conduct, gender definitions, political hegemony, and morality itself must be seen as the consequence of social repression and abuse.

These individuals are, on the other hand, out of control; their social torment has transformed them into society's torturers. Consequently, Harris's sympathy for their plights is necessarily limited. True to the detective genre that has influenced Harris as much as the Gothic, there is a need to control them and to reestablish some palpable order to counterbalance the terror Black September, Gumb, Dolarhyde, and Lecter have unleashed upon the world. Harris's detectives — Major David Kabakov, Will Graham, Jack Crawford, and Clarice Starling — are the heroes and heroine of *Black Sunday*, *Red Dragon*, and *The Silence of the Lambs*, respectively. They place themselves in opposition to the destruction and madness that are the consequences of psychopathic behavior. Graham and Starling, in particular, are compelled into bonding with the female victims in *Red Dragon* and *The Silence of the Lambs*. These detectives are committed to restoring the individuality and human dignity that Dolarhyde and Jame Gumb strip from their female victims in the transformative process of objectifying all women into grandmother-mother surrogates.

In spite of their unwavering dedication to an essentially moral vision of life, Harris's detectives are nonetheless deeply shaken by their close contact with evil. In *Red Dragon*, Graham often appears on the verge of insanity. Lecter is acutely aware of Graham's susceptibility and enjoys taunting him with this prospect. On several occasions, Dr. Lecter suggests an affinity between himself and the detective, and this parallel so unnerves Graham that he must conscientiously work to repel its implications (67–68). Only Graham's contact with his wife and stepchild separates him from the realm of madness he is forced to endure each time he must track severely disturbed men such as Lecter and Dolarhyde.

In *The Silence of the Lambs*, Clarice Starling has no family to counterbalance her own descent into hell. Perhaps this initial vulnerability helps to explain why she emerges as the individual most transformed by her experiences. From the beginning of the book, we are made aware of Clarice as a woman operating in a male domain. On her way to visit Lecter in prison, she is verbally assaulted by insults from the male prisoners and by Dr. Chilton's patronizing commentary. As she approaches Lecter's cell, she "knew her heels announced her" (12). Once she is in front of the doctor, he proceeds to examine intimate facets of her person — from her choice of perfume to the quality of her handbag and shoes. Why does Harris underscore so much gender consciousness so early in the novel? Most obviously, because this is a book that will center, at least in part, around women — particularly those gender traits that distinguish women from men. Perhaps more important, these opening scenes call attention to Starling as a female, and do so in order to illustrate that women in this culture are subject to constant linguistic, as well as physical, violations and intrusions by men. Moreover, if Starling hopes to capture the man who preys on women, she must somehow transform the daily anger and outrage she feels as a woman into something useful: "The proximity of madmen — the thought of Catherine Martin bound and alone, with one of them snuffling her, patting his pockets for his tools — braced Starling for her job. But she needed more than resolution. She needed to be calm, to be still, to be the keenest instrument. She had to use patience in the face of the awful need to hurry" (129).

Any discussion of *The Silence of the Lambs* must include at least a brief mention of the enormous popularity this book has garnered, especially in light of the successful film adaptation that won several Academy Awards. *The Silence of the Lambs* catapulted Thomas Harris into national prominence. Its mass appeal notwithstanding, several groups, most notably those objecting to the negative image of homosexuality (represented by the psychotic transsexual) and the graphic level of violence perpetuated against women, were very vocal in their protest against book and film. Detective novelist Sara Paretsky, in an article written for the opinion-editorial section of the *New York Times*, expressed her dissatisfaction with both Harris's work and those women readers who tacitly support his portrayal of violence against women by purchasing his novel: "So why should I be surprised that women are paying to read about a man flaying women alive and stripping off their skins? Or a man releasing starving rats inside a woman's vagina? That's what we're doing. And we're doing it enough to make *The Silence of the Lambs* and *American Psycho* best sellers.... Why do women as well as men want to read about these exploits in vivid detail that seeks to re-create the pain and humiliation of the attack?" (17).

The Silence of the Lambs is much more than just another tale of misogyny and violent titillation. In fact, in the end it has more in common with the heroic quest — to create a world of greater security and beauty where women need not be afraid — than it does with the recreation of pain and humiliation. Paretsky ignores the major contribution Clarice Starling makes to this novel, thereby overlooking an answer to her own rhetorical questions: women readers are drawn to Harris's novel because they strongly identify with Starling. Indeed, she is ironically similar to Paretsky's own female detective — if not a sister of V. I. Warshawski, then at least a close cousin. Like Warshawski, Starling is a woman who does battle against the patriarchy, in all of its violent and oppressive manifestation, and the commitment to her (feminist) work is ultimately its own reward.

Starling is "toughened" by her contact with men. As a result, she comes to know the men in this book better than they — even the one who wishes to become female — ever learn to know women. And, of course, she is angered and frustrated by what she learns. Hannibal Lecter asks her, "how do you manage your rage?" — a question that becomes as important to Clarice as it is to the officious psychiatrist (155). For the better part of the novel, Clarice is surrounded by men who either patronize women or murder them: Lecter, Buffalo Bill, Crawford, Chilton, and the male-dominated bureaucracy of the FBI itself (her status as a woman is underscored by her other "subordinate" role as student agent who must operate under the constant threat of being "recycled"). Without a conscious effort to exercise self-control and discipline, contact with these men and their patriarchal institutions might have produced a woman overwhelmed by her rage against male sexism and aggression. But this is not what happens. The importance of the final scene in the novel, curiously left undeveloped in the film version (where Starling shares a "deep and sweet" bed with the noble Pilcher), suggests that she certainly has not given in to the urge to reject males, or to place them into the sexist categories that the men in this book assign to her and the other women characters.

Harris's book is not only about the screaming of lambs; it is also about their silencing. Starling must somehow silence the anger she feels toward men. But the silence she finds does not come from repression, sublimation, or contribution to the madness by becoming a crazed anti-male revenger who seeks to punish men for their random carnage. Instead, Starling assumes, control over her anger by pursuing what she can change — in herself as well as in the world. By focusing her emotions and energies, Buffalo Bill becomes a symbol for the perversity that men perpetuate upon women — behavior that Starling understands intimately and translates into an empathetic bond with Bill's female victims.

If *Red Dragon* operates in an essentially male-centered universe, *The Silence of the Lambs* is female-centered. The narrative action of *Red Dragon* is completely male-generated: the main characters are all men, while the novel's female characters appear as parallel models to Blake's feminine representation in his *Red Dragon* painting: terrified, supplicant, and victimized. *The Silence of the Lambs*, on the other hand, embodies an altogether different gender perspective; the women in this book are not isolated victims. In fact, they band together to fight both their isolation and victimization. Catherine Martin, the last intended addition to Gumb's collection, makes her own rescue possible because she actively helps herself. Instead of assuming the role of sacrificial lamb in his ritualized slaughter, Catherine's refusal to panic allows her to outwit Gumb and gain more time. A similar level of inner strength characterizes Starling's roommate, Ardelia Mapp. While the latter does not participate in the action of the narrative, her presence subtly shapes the way Starling views other women — and eventually herself: "Of the two brightest people Starling knew, one [Mapp] was also the steadiest person she knew and the other [Lecter] was the most frightening. Starling hoped that gave her some balance in her acquaintance" (252). Clarice and Mapp share a noncompetetive, mutually respectful relationship that serves as a balance to counterpoint the fierce misogyny and spiritual anguish that threatens to engulf whatever is life affirming in this novel. In those moments Starling is made to feel the weight of what appears to be a male collusion against her, Mapp offers crucial support and counsel.

As Starling learns to discipline herself, she comes to trust deeply in what is scorned and coveted by the men in this book: her femininity. She tells Crawford that "The victims are all women and there aren't any women working on this. I can walk into a woman's room and know three times as much about her as a man would know" (274). It is the woman in Starling who makes the discovery of Buffalo Bill possible. Only a female would interest Lecter sufficiently to gain his trust and help. A female would be more likely to recognize the sewing link between Fredrica Bimmel and Gumb. And only another female would be capable of identifying so completely with Gumb's victims that she becomes as obsessed with his capture as he is with the skins of his captives. Starling translates feminist theory into reality, and does so without ever compromising her humanity.

Although Gumb believes that the resolution to his own inner warfare between masculine and feminine — what Carl Jung has called animus and anima — rests in completing his transformation into a woman, we have seen that his journey results not in psychic integration, but in its opposite — disintergration. Only Starling is able to integrate harmoniously the opposing parts of herself. To achieve this level of integration we must "become conscious that within ourselves we have combined opposites and need no longer project our personal devil onto others" (39). As he is intimately involved in uncovering her "personal devil" throughout the novel, Hannibal Lecter puts Starling into contact with her shadow — the "negative aide of her personality" (147). He challenges Clarice to acknowledge her unconscious or repressed self and the unresolved hostility she still harbors toward her childhood: specifically her memory of abandonment and victimization symbolized in her identification with the endangered lambs and the horse, Hannah. Contact with the shadow instructs her in how to integrate the positive characteristic with the negative. As Neumann asserts, "Only by making friends with the shadow do we gain the friendship of Self" (353). Her remembered pain, which Lecter coerces her to reexamine, becomes a measure of Starling's capacity for constructive, righteous anger and the self-discipline necessary to survive in the present. In confronting her shadow by allowing Lecter to lead her back into the darkness of her childhood, Starling discovers the positive side of what the shadow proffers and integrates into her personality. As Jung describes the process, it is a considerable moral effort: "To become conscious of it [the shadow] involves recognizing the dark aspects of the personality.... This act is the essential condition for any kind of self-knowledge" (145). Starling is able to secure what Dolarhyde and Gumb passionately, desire (yet never actually attain) from deep inside their respective gender hells: a resolution to the conflict between animus and anima that creates a psychic world of wholeness and maturation.

One of the great rewards in reading *The Silence of the Lambs* is savoring the complex set of relationships Starling establishes with Hannibal Lecter and Jack Crawford. While the two men appear to use Starling as a vehicle in their continuing mental warfare against each other, thereby deepening the novel's theme of women being exploited by men, they also occupy remarkably similar roles insofar as they emerge as competing father figures and teachers to Starling. Crawford instructs her about detective procedurals and, conversely, the importance of knowing when her instincts may be superior to "imposed patterns of symmetry" (70). Lecter, as I have already noted, is likewise interested in teaching Starling valuable information about the criminal psyche, but his approach is always more personal, and therefore perhaps more impressionable because it strikes to the essence of Starling's personality. In turn, Starling provides a certain measure of human dignity to Lecter, and this becomes partial explanation for his willingness to instruct her. Although the authorities acknowledge the power of his intellect and amoral will, their terror makes it impossible for them to appreciate his humanity; Lecter remains an exotic, albeit dangerous object to be studied and exploited. While Starling is always willing to exploit him, she also accords him a level of genuine respect that is, ironically, shared elsewhere only by Dolarhyde and Gumb. As Greg Garrett argues, "Whether unconsciously or consciously, Clarice, who knows what it's like to be an object, treats Lecter as human rather than object, and the lesson is not lost on him." Starling needs both her mentors to advance—personally and professionally; through their inimitable pedagogies, they teach her the same thing: the value of balancing self-trust against self-restraint, and the importance of recognizing when to apply either.

Danse Macabre, Stephen King's analytical treatment of the Gothic genre in fiction and film, provides a useful theoretical paradigm for comprehending horror art. In particular works such as Harris's, which revolve around anomalous beings who are morally and ontologically transgressive, King notes: "The horror story, beneath its fangs and fright wig, is really as conservative as an Illinois Republican in a three-piece pinstriped suit; its main purpose is to reaffirm the virtues of the norm by showing us what awful things happen to people who venture into taboo lands. Within the framework of most horror tales we find a moral code so strong it would make a Puritan smile.... [T]he horror tale generally details the outbreak of some Dionysian madness in an Apollonian existence, and the horror will continue until the Dionysian forces have been repelled and the Apollonian norm restored again" (368). Noël Carroll takes King's thesis a step further when he argues that the horror tale ends with "the norm emerging stronger than before; it has been, so to say, tested: its superiority to the abnormal is vindicated" (201). This pattern of thematic and philosophical exposition is exactly what occurs in *Black Sunday, Red Dragon,* and *The Silence of the Lambs.* Only Hannibal Lecter's escape at the end of *The Silence of the Lambs* would appear to subvert this narrative design. His reemergence into the world tends to qualify the novel's concluding restoration of "the Apollonian norm" and proves, I suspect, that the very notion of a postmodern status quo is always an endangered concept.

The fictional transformations which are at the center of Thomas Harris's art all revolve around "ventures into taboo lands." The psychopathic criminals in his world want to enact some kind of radical transformation over society and themselves. For them, power is synonymous with domination and destruction. Against their Dionysian visions, Harris's detectives are poised in a counterstruggle of their own: how does one enter the world of madness — identifying with victim and murderer alike — apprehend a killer, and emerge with sanity and humanity intact: The transformative energies which stand in opposition to Harris's detectives, and to the readers who vicariously identify with them, are psychologically terrifying. The threats they represent are an assault on the basic assumptions of personal conduct and social interaction. Thus, the reader is manipulated subtly into sharing a level of investment in the conservative worldview that Harris summons to refute these threats; for as they are encoded within the contexts of his fiction, "the virtues of the norm" are inevitably reaffirmed with a sigh of relief.

Works Consulted

Carroll, Noël. *The Philosophy of Horror, or Paradoxes of the Heart.* New York: Routledge, 1990.

Garrett, Greg. "Objecting to Objectification: Re-viewing the Feminine in *The Silence of the Lambs.*" *Journal of Popular Culture,* vol. 27 (spring 1994).

Harris, Thomas. *Red Dragon.* New York: New American Library, 1981.

_____. *The Silence of the Lambs.* New York: St. Martin's Press, 1988.

Johnson, Mary Lynn. "Feminist Approaches to Teaching Songs," in Robert F. Glecknew and Mark L. Greenberg (eds.), *Approaches to Teaching Blake's Songs of Innocence and of Experience.* New York: Modern Language Association, 1989.

Jung, Carl G. "Aion: Phenomenology of the Self." *The Portable Jung*, trans. R.F.C. Hull. New York: Viking, 1971.

Kazin, Alfred. *The Portable Blake*. New York: Viking, 1968.

King, Stephen. *Danse Macabre*. Rev. ed. New York: Berkeley, 1982.

Neumann, Erich. *The Origins and History of Consciousness*, trans. R.F.C. Hull. Princeton: Princeton University Press, 1970.

Paretsky, Sara. "Soft Spot for Serial Murderers." *New York Times,* 28 Apr. 1991.

Praz, Mario. *The Romantic Agony*. New York: Oxford University Press, 1970.

Rogers-Gardner, Barbara. *Jung and Shakespeare*. Wilmette, Ill.: Chiron Publications, 1992.

Twitchell, James. *Dreadful Pleasures: An Anatomy of Modern Horror*. New York: Oxford University Press, 1985.

Wood, Robin. *Hollwood from Vietnam to Reagan*. New York: Columbia University Press, 1986.

9

Hannibal Rising
Look Back in Anger

ALI S. KARIM

His books are very, very complex, and I think he thinks about
them for a long time before he puts a pen to paper
— Morton Janklow, Thomas Harris's Agent

The genesis for the long awaited fourth appearance of Thomas Harris's Dr Hannibal Lecter is as complex as that of his character. The first official word that there would be a fourth novel came on 28th October 2004 from William Heinemann (an imprint of The Random House Group) in the U.K. (Harris's British publisher) and simultaneously from Bantam Press in America. Then there was silence. *Behind the Mask* (the preliminary title) was not released in the Autumn of 2005, however rumors began appearing that the book was "on-hold" while the film script was being developed as plans started to formulate to release the film closely behind publication of the book. It was also mooted that the film would share the same title as that of the novel. Other working titles for the book and the film were *Behind the Mask: The Blooding of Hannibal Lecter, Hannibal 4, Hannibal IV, The Lecter Variations, The Lecter Variation: The Story of Young Hannibal Lecter, Young Hannibal, The Adventures of Young Hannibal,* and *Young Hannibal: Behind the Mask.*

I. The Lecter Variations

Prior to the December 5 release of Thomas Harris's *Hannibal Rising* many people were done talking about the book and were discussing the movie adaptation instead. Some of you may not be aware that principal photography had been completed on director Peter Webber's film version of *Hannibal Rising* prior to the novel's release. Starring Gaspard Ulliel as the young Hannibal, it was officially released in February 2007. Like anything associated with Harris, the movie was cloaked in secrecy, with the International Movie Database (IMDb) releasing only the most basic facts about the story line. In a surreal twist of fate, director Webber was also behind *Girl with a Pearl Earring* (2003), the movie made from Tracy Chevalier's novel based on the life of Dutch painter Johannes Vermeer. If you read Harris's previous book, *Hannibal* (1999), you'll no doubt recall that Vermeer's work plays a subtle part in that story's plot.

So we then knew that Lecter IV had an official title and a worldwide release date — December 5, 2006, but most importantly we had a plot outline. I received, on 24 September 2006 from William Heinemann (an imprint of the Random House Group) in the UK (Harris's British publishers), a cover image (which differs remarkably from the U.S. Bantam Dell version) and the following press release statement.

> Hannibal Lecter emerges from the nightmare of the Eastern Front, a boy in the snow, mute, with a chain around his neck. He seems utterly alone, but he has brought his demons with him.
>
> Hannibal's uncle, a noted painter, finds him in a Soviet orphanage and brings him to France, where Hannibal will live with his uncle and his uncle's beautiful and exotic wife, Lady Murasaki.
>
> Lady Murasaki helps Hannibal to heal. With her help he flourishes, becoming the youngest person ever admitted to medical school in France.
>
> But Hannibal's demons visit him and torment him. When he is old enough, he visits them in turn. He discovers he has gifts beyond the academic, and in that epiphany, Hannibal Lecter becomes death's prodigy.

So *Hannibal Rising,* as we'd all heard on the rumor mill, would feature Hannibal Lecter's childhood and what made him into the "monster." This seemed the logical choice in commercial terms because publishing is after all a business. After all the hullabaloo and build-up vis-à-vis the release of *Hannibal* on 8 July 1999, the only other fictional character who has exceeded it in terms of media interest is J.K. Rowling's Harry Potter, so it seemed somewhat apt that *Hannibal Rising* should feature the boy Lecter and that a film appear hot on the heels of the books release.

So, as December 5, 2006, approached, we started to see the true scale of the release. Motoko Rich at *The New York Times* reported in September 2006 that:

> Mr. Harris just handed in the manuscript for *Hannibal Rising* last month, and Bantam is rushing to publish the book in time for the crucial holiday sales season. It also hopes to capitalize on the February 2007 release of the movie version of the new novel, for which Mr. Harris also wrote the screenplay. The movie, which is produced by the Dino De Laurentiis Company and marketed by the Weinstein Company, stars Gaspard Ulliel, the French co-star of the 2004 film *A Very Long Engagement*, as the young Dr. Lecter.
>
> Irwyn Applebaum, publisher of Bantam, said the timing was fortuitous. "Usually even the best-selling books have an eight-week excitement cycle," he said. "But for this book, the movie excitement will hopefully be at its height just as the book goes through that cycle, so it's a very good opportunity for this book to have an extended hardcover life" [Rich].

Thus, the timing for the novel's release was intertwined with the film that had entered post-production. We also learned that Applebaum's Bantam Press planned to print a minimum of 1.5 million hardcover copies of *Hannibal Rising*, which was close to what *Hannibal*, sold in hardcover 1999. Incidentally there are now approximately 4 million copies of *Hannibal* in print in paperback, and it spent more than 15 weeks on the New York Times hardcover fiction best-seller list and more than 30 weeks on the paperback fiction list.

We also learned that Harris was going to narrate an audio abridged version of *Hannibal Rising* like he did for *Hannibal*. In the U.K. Harris released abridged narrated audio versions of *Red Dragon* and *The Silence of the Lambs*, while in the U.S. audio versions were released by Simon and Schuster narrated by Chris Sarandon and Kathy Bates, respectively.

Meanwhile, Harris's longtime agent Morton Janklow said that Harris signed an eight-figure, two-book contract for North American rights with Bantam in 2004, of which *Hannibal Rising* is the first book. This added further fuel to the rumors that *Hannibal Rising* would be the penultimate Hannibal Lecter book, and the final installment would bring the story full circle to when Lecter is an M.D. in New England and captured by Police Detective Will Graham in *Red Dragon*.

Some vocal elements in the publishing industry were concerned that the release of *Hannibal Rising* would conflict with several other "big books" slated for release in the same quarter such as Michael Crichton's *Next*, Stephen King's *Lisey's Story*, and John Grisham's *An Innocent Man* (interestingly, both Crichton and Grisham share agents with Thomas Harris with New York lawyer Morton Janklow). However Bantam Press's Applebaum was bullish about the competition in the autumn season, and stated that he was not concerned about releasing the new novel on the heels of a crammed fall publishing lineup. "It's a very crowded season," he said, "but there's nothing bigger on the fiction side than Thomas Harris."

In November I received my non-disclosure agreement from Cassie Chadderton (Publicity Director at Random House UK) and it ran to four pages — for my review copy of *Hannibal Rising*. I was advised that the review copy would only be dispatched on December 3, 2006, which meant that I would receive it one day prior to worldwide release. The worldwide embargo had serious repercussions for those who did not comply with the terms. It seems that the embargo was breached in Scandinavia reported John Sutherland in the *London Times*:

> *Hannibal Rising* has been strictly embargoed (although, amusingly, the Swedes misread the publisher's instruction and released it prematurely — prompting a small invasion of fanatic day-trippers). Bootleg copies have been available on e-bay, at vast cost. There was, however, little point in even the most devoted fan jumping the gun. The main outline of the plot of *Hannibal Rising* ("at last, the evolution of his evil is revealed") was substantially disclosed in earlier works [Sutherland].

However, there were some rather large inconsistencies between what was reported in *Hannibal Rising*'s precursors vis-à-vis Lecter's childhood, and what Harris would replay in *Hannibal Rising* (but more on that later).

Then, on November 15, 2006, an extract from *Hannibal Rising* was released via this press release, which reiterated the strict terms of the embargo:

> Random House announced today that it will release an extract from *Hannibal Rising*, the new novel by Thomas Harris, at some point on Thursday this week.
>
> This early glimpse of the most eagerly anticipated novel of the year will be available from *www.hannibalrising.co.uk*. Chapter 6 of the novel will appear both in print form and as an audio file, read by Thomas Harris.
>
> This will be the first press and public sighting of *Hannibal Rising*. Copies are to be kept strictly under wraps until the day of publication, December 5th. My dear friend the energetic writer and bookseller Maxim Jakubowski recalls his experiences in selling Thomas Harris' work as the launch date approached, stating that "we won't be opening at midnight [like he did for the release of *Hannibal*], but the Murder One staff will be wearing the notorious mask and liberally dishing out spare body parts (fingers made out of chocolate lest you are worried). Bring on the blood, brains and guts, I say" (Jakubowski).

Random House and Waterstones sent me this breakfast invite:

Hannibal's Brasserie opens at Waterstone's, 311 Oxford St, London W1 on Tuesday 5th December 2006 only.

Service from 7.30–9.30 A.M.

Join us for this event to celebrate the publication of *Hannibal Rising* by Thomas Harris (early arrival is recommended to avoid disappointment). The first 200 guests will receive a limited edition Brasserie plate and poster, and the edition purchased will contain a highly exclusive bookplate signed by Thomas Harris. The next 300 guests will receive the limited edition poster.

Proprietor: Dr. H. Lecter

MENU
Spiked Eyeballs
Benedict's Brains
Slither of Liver
Blood Shots
(Plate and signed edition limited to one copy per person. Further details: 0207 499 6100)

Best wishes,
The Random House Group Ltd.

The special treat here was the ability to purchase one of 200 signed editions of *Hannibal Rising*— as Harris had provided book plates for Waterstones. There were queues as a signed Harris book sells for vast sums due to the scarcity of Harris's signature. So on December 10 (when I was safe to avoid the penalties of defying Random House's review embargo criteria) I published my take on *Hannibal Rising* for *The Rap Sheet* and *www.shotsmag.co.uk*.

II. The Making of a Monster

After being sucked in by all the media hype surrounding Thomas Harris' new novel, *Hannibal Rising*— his fourth book to feature psychiatrist and serial killer Hannibal Lecter — I finally had a chance to read the work. And as a big follower of Harris' storytelling, I am relieved to say that my anticipation was rewarded. The novel, a sequel to the other three Hannibal outings, is a bloody tale of childhood horrors and modern retribution that could only star a sociopath.

There are a few significant points worth making about this book. It's a very different sort of work from its predecessors. The story here is much less complex and much less cerebral. *Rising* reads more like a screenplay, which isn't surprising, since a film version of the novel is already being shot, with a release planned in February of next year.

It is also a much bloodier book than I had anticipated. *Hannibal*

Rising is split into two narrative strands. The first section introduces Hannibal at age 8, living with his family in war-scarred Lithuania in 1944. The Lecter clan reside in some splendor deep within a forest. They're descendants of Hannibal the Grim — an obvious reference to the Brothers Grimm, and an appropriate one, since this section reads like a monstrous fairy tale. As readers of Harris's last book, *Hannibal* (1999), will already know, the protagonist's sister Mischa was eaten by a group of brigands in the winter, and that, coupled with the death of his family and tutor, Mr. Jakov, started to shape young Lecter's psyche. The other factor molding Hannibal's personality is his "memory palace," where he escapes (at least mentally) from the reality around him. In *Hannibal Rising*, we see the development of that refuge as Lecter — having already blanked out his sibling's horrific fate — avoids venturing into the woodlands surrounding their home. Left alone in the world, mute, and beating up bullies in an orphanage, Hannibal is finally rescued by his uncle, Robert Lecter, and his aunt, the Japanese Lady Murasaki, and transplanted to Paris.

In the novel's second section, we watch Hannibal being educated and falling in love with Lady Murasaki. That relationship becomes so strong, that, after a local butcher, Paul Momund, insults his aunt, Lecter takes his revenge in a most brutal and bloody manner. This, of course, places the boy under police scrutiny (from Detective Popil), as he advances through medical school and becomes an anatomy prodigy, thanks to the artistic talents he's developed at the side of Lady Murasaki.

Also in the second part, Harris enters Ian Fleming territory. Leaving behind the fairy-tale atmospherics, the author has young Lecter rediscovering memories of Mischa's murder and embarking on a violent trail of revenge, which sends him across Europe and North America, and eventually puts him face to face with the brigands, led by the vile psychopath Vladis Grutas. Hannibal shows no mercy as he tracks down these men who deal in prostitution, kidnapping of women, and sexual slavery, as well as post-war art smuggling (which includes their theft of the Lecter art collection).

To be honest, I don't really care what other critics have to say about *Hannibal Rising*, because for me the novel provided such a wonderful opportunity to be back in the embrace of Harris's prose and his dark, witty imagination. As expected, after it was released it became a bestseller worldwide.

III. The Perplexing Context of Hannibal Rising

It is Harris's way to give conflicting meanings and inconsistencies in his narrative. *Hannibal Rising* is no exception as it has a few perplexing ones, which reviewers like myself picked up on. In all his work you can see his use of "reportage" a common way of detecting that the writer was a former journalist. Harris also changes tense from past to present many times, often in the same paragraph — another piece of baggage that a former journalist carries. However, the most interesting lapses in consistency as well as subtext in *Hannibal Rising* are worth pointing out.

Hannibal Lecter's documented and actual birth date and age when his sister Mischa died are not consistent. It is stated that he made fabrications in order to avoid capture. This claim, however, doesn't explain why (during his flashbacks in *Hannibal*) he personally remembers being six years old when his sister died; as opposed to the "actual" age of twelve in *Hannibal Rising*.

No mention is made of Lecter's fully functional sixth finger (duplicated middle finger, termed "polydactyly"), which was mentioned in the earlier books; this sixth finger was removed surgically in South America after his escape in *The Silence of the Lambs* and is mentioned in *Hannibal*. Nor is there mention of his distinctive maroon eyes.

In *Red Dragon* it is stated that, as a child, Lecter tortured and murdered animals, a common feature in the youth of many psychopaths and serial killers, but out of character in my opinion with the sociopathic Dr Lecter. Harris did not pursue this in *Hannibal Rising* as there is no mention there of Lecter killing animals.

In *Hannibal*, Lecter recalls seeing Mischa's baby teeth in a reeking stool pit. In *Hannibal Rising*, he has similar visions, but when he later visits Mischa's remains before giving her a dignified burial, he notes that all her teeth are intact.

We are led to believe that something in Hannibal's soul has perished, as a result of seeing Mischa killed and eaten. In the final confrontation with ringleader of the Hiwi Brigands, Vladas Grutas, Grutas reveals that Lecter too had consumed his sister in broth fed to him by the soldiers. Enraged, Lecter kills him by repeatedly carving his sister's initial into his body, howling "M for Mischa" over and over. It is no wonder that Clarice Starling becomes Lecter's surrogate little sister in *The Silence of the Lambs*, and perhaps why he developed a sexual interest in Clarice at the tail-end of *Hannibal*, a relationship that many readers doubtless "switched off" as they could not cope with near-incest.

Hannibal Rising also explained how Lecter was trained to build his memory palace, a place where he could hide from the reality around him. Lecter's cerebral architecture was introduced to us in Hannibal, and was "inspired" (a useful word) by Jonathan D. Spence's *The Memory*

Palace of Matteo Ricci (1985). Ricci was the 16th-century Jesuit priest who came up with the mnemonic system into which the good doctor likes to retreat. It is Lecter's kindly Jewish tutor Mr Jakov that helps build this refuge.

Some commented that *Hannibal Rising* seemed like "Hannibal-Lite," an allusion to the screenplay-like style that is deployed in the narrative, but bear in mind that Harris wrote the screenplay (simultaneously) this probably explains why the book is written in this pared-down style. Less cerebral than its precursors, and faster flowing in terms of plot, it does resemble a screenplay in terms of narrative style.

Thomas Harris is a renowned researcher (almost pedantic), so I was amused to read that literary editor Erica Wagner in the *London Times* as well as Maxim Jakubowski at the *Guardian* both commented on Harris's French faux pas — examples from Ms. Wagner: "petites oiseaux should be petits oiseaux. There is no Gare de l'Este in Paris; there is a Gare de l'Est. 'Salad Nicoise' or, perhaps, salade niçoise. The famous car, a little Citroën, is a Deux-Chevaux" (Wagner). While Jakubowski reports that "a lengthy sequence at the heart of the book takes places in France, you see. And though Harris has visibly done his research when it comes to flora, antique paintings, weapons and other intricate elements of his plot, he regularly gets the French language and setting wrong" (Jakubowski). This is most peculiar for someone as methodical as Harris when it comes to inter-twinning fact within his fiction.

Lecter, like many of the Gothic villains (such as Stoker's Count Dracula), has an apparently Eastern European bloodline. Hannibal Lecter was born in Lithuania in 1933 to a wealthy aristocratic family (his father, simply known as Count Lecter), was a descendant of the warlord "Hannibal the Grim" (1365–1428), who defeated the Teutonic Order at the Battle of Grunwald in 1410, while his mother, Madame Simonetta Sforza, was descended from both the Visconti and Sforza families who separately ruled Milan for a total of 250 years. Hannibal is the eighth in his blood-line to bear his ancestor's forename. Lecter was also apparently descended from the 12th-century Tuscan Giuliano Bevisangue ("Bevisangue" means "Blood-Drinker"), and also from the Machiavelli bloodline. In *Hannibal*, Lecter tries to trace his heritage from the records of the Capponi Library by researching Bevisangue, but he was unable to definitively answer the question before having to flee to America. *Hannibal Rising* also asserted that Lecter was a cousin of the artist Balthus.

John Sutherland remarked in the *UK Telegraph* about Harris's literary allusions:

In the acknowledgements to *Hannibal Rising* Harris tells us, enigmatically, "As you see, I have borrowed S. T. Coleridge's dog." You may not immediately "see" it. It's in Chapter 15, where Harris writes "the mastiff bitch in her kennel stirs"— a remote allusion to "what can ail the mastiff bitch?" in Coleridge's gothic poem, *Christabel*. It doesn't end there. The boat on which the arch-villain, Grutas, gets his comeuppance is called the *Christabel* [Sutherland].

More interestingly Sutherland also noticed some similarities between *Hannibal Rising* and Lecter fan-fiction that circulates along the "damp floor of the internet." Sutherland writes about these literary allusions:

> Pull them whichever way you will, these allusions lead nowhere. Why did Harris insert them and ostentatiously point Lecterphiles in their direction? Because he's playing games with fansites such as *www.hannotations.com* which owlishly exegetise his fiction. It evidently amuses him to see his disciples scampering, pointlessly, up and down his novels looking, vainly, for "the key." Trawling through the Lecter fanfic, one comes on other tantalising parallelisms. Six years ago, for example, "Leeker17," on *www.typhoidandswans.com* posted a narrative which uncannily forecasts the opening chapters of Hannibal Rising in its detailed description of how the hero's parents and sister met their ends in 1944. So close is it that one might fancy that Leeker17 had some privileged connection with Harris. Or that Harris himself, under a nom-de-web, may be the "leaker." Or, like Blythebee, Leeker17 may just have struck lucky [Sutherland].

Writer and critic Peter Guttridge of *The Observer* also noticed some literary allusions in *Hannibal Rising*:

> Lady Murasaki[:] Harris points out in his afterword that she shares the name of the medieval Japanese writer Murasaki Shikibu, who wrote one of the first great novels, *The Tale of Genji*. Harris borrows Coleridge's dog and there is a French doctor called Dumas. There's even an ill-used Philip Larkin epigraph.
>
> At times these literary allusions add depth, at others it seems that Harris is simply having fun. Lecter as a descendant of Hannibal the Grim, ruthless medieval Lithuanian ruler, is a pretty obvious pointer to the Grimm Brothers [Guttridge].

The reference to the twisted Hansel and Gretel fairy tale is very obvious as a subtext to the novel as is the reference to Dumas, where when Will Graham meets Lecter in his cell in *Red Dragon* a copy of Alexandre Dumas's *Le Grand Dictionnaire de Cuisine* was open on his chest. It is interesting that in *Hannibal Rising* his mentor at the French medical school (Lycee) was also called Dumas, Dr. Dumas.

Writer Tibor Fischer reports that Harris is also an educationalist:

Any idea what a Hiwi is? A suzumushi? A non-sheep mouton? They are respectively the Nazis' little helpers on the Eastern Front — SS wannabes from the local population; the Japanese "sleigh bell" cricket; and part of the guillotine's mechanism. You can't say that Thomas Harris's books are without educational value [Fischer].

Writer Will Self was less generous when writing about Harris's literary allusions:

In *Hannibal*, Harris "did" the Renaissance as thoroughly as any wealthy American taking the modern Grand Tour. There was plenty of guff about beautiful palazzi and priceless daubs; clearly, he had spent a lot of time truffling in libraries. In *Hannibal Rising*, we have the fruits of seven more years' dilettantism. This time, Harris shows us that he knows a great deal about Japanese flower arranging, Lithuanian aristocracy, Paris in the aftermath of the Second World War and, naturally, enormous viscous heaps of anatomy. I won't trouble you with the rest of his murderous search for authenticity, save to say that, even when it's going well, Harris manages to hamstring your suspension of disbelief.

Thus we have references to a "Rube Goldberg contraption" (something only a U.S. readership of a certain age would comprehend), while anachronistically, given that the book is set in the 1940s, one of Lecter's hallucinations is described as being like "a hologram." Towards the end, a character is identified by his resemblance to Lawrence Welk. While the big-band leader who created "champagne music" did not become nationally famous until the mid–1950s, let's not quibble about this: the fact is that he's pretty bloody obscure, and name-checking him jibes with the rather tony impression Harris seeks to create with his blethering about haikus and Huygens's *Treatise on Light* [Self].

One of the most moving sections of *Hannibal Rising* for me, and one that haunted me, was a simple French phrase that Harris deployed. Around 1940, young Hannibal Lecter was lowered into the old stone well that served as a holding cell and torture chamber. Scratched by a dying man, a desperate question survived on the wall: "Pourquoi?" ("why"). I find in all of Harris's work a questioning of the human condition and an investigation into the nature of our own wickedness, such as the "Instruments of Torture" exhibition in *Hannibal* as well as the links to a God indifferent to human suffering. Harris was brought up a Southern Baptist, but in all his work is a questioning on why God is indifferent or perhaps even malevolent toward his creations. There is a real poke in the eye toward organized religion in all Harris's work, but the most blatant is Lecter's telephone call to Will Graham in *Red Dragon* where Lecter wonders why God would allow a church roof to collapse on a congregation groveling at his magnificence.

In *The Silence of the Lambs* Lecter pondered on the nature of God to Clarice Starling in wondering how could God create something has awful as typhoid as well as something as beautiful as swans? In *Hannibal Rising* we get a snapshot of Lecter and Mischa's happier times feeding the Swans, before the evils of war come to their door. So the French phase Harris uses to great effect, "pourquoi?" becomes even more resonant and poignant.

Lecter's relationship with his Japanese aunt, Lady Murasaki, is as complex as it is sensual. The two conduct a peculiarly unpersuasive courtly love affair, at the unsatisfying conclusion of which Hannibal becomes, we are perhaps meant to suspect, a Ronin, or a samurai without a master, but a man on a mission filled with anger as he seeks to take savage revenge on the brigands that ate his sister. As a Ronin, perhaps Mischa was his Master, Master he failed saving, and he now wishes to avenge her death.

It is interesting that the first victim of Lecter's revenge trail is Paul Momund, the butcher who insulted his aunt with a crude racial and sexual jibe. We knew he shouldn't have, because in *Hannibal*, his cell-keeper Barney remarked to Clarice Starling that Lecter would "eat the rude" and we all know that Lecter is a man of his word.

In *The Silence of the Lambs* Lecter while incarcerated tells Clarice Starling that he cannot be measured or explained away like conventional serial killers with the FBI behavioral science tools. This caused many readers to rebel against the explanations of how and why Lecter became the monster (in *Hannibal* and *Hannibal Rising*). I would take exception to this because in *Hannibal Rising* he proves that he cannot be measured by conventional means (at least). Lecter soon attracted the attention of his first lawman, Inspector Pascal Popil. Popil intuitively grasped what Lecter had become and, when Momund subsequently became Lecter's first murder victim (Lecter slashed him twice in the stomach with a katana and then beheaded him), Popil pressed him to admit his guilt. Lecter proved impenetrable, however, even passing a polygraph test. We already knew from the opening of *The Silence of the Lambs* that Lecter could control his body — even maintaining his heart-rate at 74 beats per minute when biting the tongue out of a nurse's mouth — so a lie detector test proves no match for Lecter's skills. The inspector intuits in the boy a trait stronger and stranger than homicidal brutality: a disorder we now term suffers as sociopaths. In *Hannibal Rising* Popil wants Hannibal declared insane so an asylum can study him and determine *what* he is: "For lack of a better word, we'll call him a monster." So Popil was the first policeman to detect Lecter's evil nature, but unlike Pazzi from *Hannibal*, we see Popil as competent as well as conflicted.

The concluding section has Lecter carrying his retribution in an almost James Bond manner. I was amused at this one-liner after he has drowned a man in a vat of embalming fluid: "He arrived at a solution." By the novel's finale, Lecter has become morbidly wisecracking, informing his last victim, a taxidermist: "I've come to collect a head." These lines come straight from the movie versions of Bond, and one could easily imagine either Sean Connery or Roger Moore raising their eyebrows as they polished off their opponents with such one-liners.

So if *Hannibal Rising* is an exploration in the making of a monster or even a transformation or a boy into a savage, then who is he based on? They say Hannibal Lecter is based on a composite of serial killers: part Ted Bundy (who mutilated college-aged brunettes), because Bundy was egotistic and educated and a college graduate and a law school student, part Ed Kemper, who, with an IQ of 140, is an avid reader and a lover of vintage cars like Hannibal Lecter (Kemper devoured the flesh of his victims after he cut them up), and most interestingly, part Issei Sagawa, Japanese literary scholar and gormande, who wrote a book about how he killed and cannibalized a German woman in London.

However, Harris told Cleveland librarian Ron Wise that he got the idea for Lecter from a little known serial killer called William Coyner (Laughlin). William Coyner, a student of religion and philosophy, was also an escape artist like Lecter. After Coyner escaped from an Indiana prison and went on a 1934 murdering and cannibalizing spree in Cleveland, Miss., 35 miles south of Rich (Harris's hometown), police captured him and assigned 200 armed police to guard him. After he went to the gallows, he took on mythical proportions for being superhuman. When Harris was growing up more than a decade later, Coyner was the topic of the scary stories kids told around a campfire to keep each other up all night.

So the end of *Hannibal Rising* leaves us with the young doctor coming to America to begin his residency at Johns Hopkins Hospital in Baltimore, Maryland. This of course leads up to the period just prior to where *Red Dragon* started, and we will have come full-circle. The next episode in Hannibal Lecter's life is reportedly the last work from Harris. I just hope that we don't have to wait the many years that typically precede a release from this icon in modern crime-fiction. It is likely to please his fans as it will also herald the return of Detective Will Graham, the only policeman to have captured Lecter.

But I'll leave the last line to my dear friend the writer and literary critic Mark Timlin, who summed up *Hannibal Rising* in the most apt manner, because despite all its flaws and contradiction, at times it moved me close to tears. Bravo Mr Harris.

> In the end, the story of Hannibal's early life is tinged with a great sadness as the reader comes to realise that Hannibal Lecter, the monster was created by circumstance rather than choice, and, even though his later actions are far beyond the pale, knowing what caused them, half a world away and a lifetime before, I couldn't help but feel sympathy for that little boy who so loved feeding the swans [Timlin].

Works Consulted

Fischer, Tibor. "A Taste for Cannibalism Acquired Young." *UK Telegraph,* 24 Dec. 2006. http://www.telegraph.co.uk/arts/main.jhtml?xml=/arts/2006/12/24/bohar 216.xml. Accessed 1 Dec. 2007.

Guttridge, Peter. "SoThat's Why Hannibal Eats People." *The UK Observer,* 10 Dec. 2006. http://observer.guardian.co.uk/review/story/0,,1967886,00.html. Accessed 1 Dec. 2007.

Harris, Thomas. *Hannibal Rising.* London: William Heinemann/Random House, 2006.

Jakubowski, Maxim. "*Hannibal Rising*: Bring on the Blood, Brains and Guts." *Guardian Unlimited,* 1 Dec. 2006. http://blogs.guardian.co.uk/books/2006/12/hannibal_rising_bring_on_the_b.html. Accessed 1 Dec.2007.

Laughlin, Meg. "Books Section." *Tulsa World,* vol. 32, no. 7 (15 Aug. 1999).

Rich, Motoko. "Hannibal Lecter to Drop By for Holiday Helpings." *New York Times,* 19 Sept. 2006. http://www.nytimes.com/2006/09/19/books/19harr.html?ex=13163 18400&en=55e1866854669e7b&ei=5088. Accessed 1 Dec. 2007.

Self, Will. "Senseless Evil." *UK New Statesman.* 8 Jan. 2007. http://www.newstatesman com/200701080044. Accessed 1 Dec. 2007.

Sutherland, John. "Into the Lists." *UK Telegraph,* 7 Jan. 2007. http://www.telegraph.co.uk/arts/main.jhtml?xml=/arts/2007/01/07/bolists.xml. Accessed 1 Dec. 2007.

_____. "The Monster Is Born." *London Times,* 10 Dec. 2006. http://entertainment.timesonline.co.uk/tol/arts_and_entertainment/books/article660902.ece. Accessed 1 Dec. 2007.

Timlin, Mark. "*Hannibal Rising*: Sympathy for the Devil." *The Independent on Sunday,* 10 Dec. 2006. http://enjoyment.independent.co.uk/books/reviews/article 2062658.ece. Accessed 1 Dec. 2007.

Wagner, Erica. "An Indigestible Back Story Is Hard to Swallow." *London Times,* Dec. 2006. http://entertainment.timesonline.co.uk/tol/arts_and_entertainment/books/book_reviews/article663996.ece. Accessed 1 Dec. 2007.

10

Before Her Lambs Were Silent

Reading Gender and the Feminine in Red Dragon

PHILLIP A. ELLIS

Is it possible to define day, without an understanding of night? Can we do the same for gender? Can we define masculinity, without reference to femininity, or vice versa? I believe that it is, in a sense, impossible to totally isolate aspects of either, without addressing aspects of the other. If we follow the standards of binary opposition, the presences of one must imply, at least, the absences of the other. One, essentially, defines in part the other through that other's absence. This binary opposition of masculine and feminine is not static. It evolves continually. It is part of an ongoing dialectic predicated on the basic principles that govern the binary opposition of both. That is, what is masculine can not be feminine, and so that what defines a man cannot define what makes a woman, and vice versa. It is possible, I am sure, to look at men and women in this way in real life, but what of literature? Do the same guidelines apply?

In essence, yes, although what we look for in literary characters can differ from what we look for in living people. I say this because there is strong pressure, a strong tendency, to want the literary characters to be defined as exemplars of behavior. We like to come to literature as a rehearsal, a role model for our daily lives. We can see this "desire for exemplars" in the central volume of the Hannibal Lecter series. This is not a unique novel, since *The Silence of the Lambs* is really a development and variation upon the themes, narrative and motifs of *Red Dragon*. But it is dominated by a central female character that is strong, and who defies the standard stereotypes of what makes an "ideal" American woman. There is a tendency to want that central character, Clarice Starling, to be one such an exemplar.

And, in fact, the prevalence and the strengths of Starling have led her to be read as one such feminist role-model. She has been greeted as the exemplar of what makes a strong female character, a strong feminist character, and rightfully so. Such readings have been predicated on her behavior and her character as being in defiance of common stereotypes of feminine behavior in contemporary discourses. She is, in essence, a "new" woman for a new age. In comparison with the earlier volume in the series, such a strong characterization is lacking from *Red Dragon*; there is, simply, no woman that matches the complexity and strengths of Starling in such a way. This is not to say that women are absent from *Red Dragon*. We do, in fact, find a range of females and feminine behaviors. Such a range should be of interest, as it preserves a multiplicity of viewpoints into what makes feminine behavior. We read females, possible females, not one overriding character.

As a result of the attractiveness of Starling to those interested in gender studies, particularly in relation to Thomas Harris's work, the study of the main female characters of *Red Dragon* has been neglected. This is as a result of the emphasis upon Starling as an ideal protagonist, and as an exemplary female character. We can read that Starling is clearly a hero. She is the exemplar of cultural standards. But, if we look at the earlier book, a closer examination of the characterization of that in *Red Dragon* will reveal a greater range of problematic readings. So much so that it is inherently useful to define the range of feminine responses, and compare and contrast these with their corresponding masculine representations in that earlier novel. Such a study can, and should, lead to similar studies of gender in Harris's work, and at more than just Starling herself.

Such would be an ideal, and this essay will attempt to achieve that ideal. Its main focus is, of course, the female characters, and their representation of a range of feminine behaviors. It looks at, after some general remarks upon gender, the concept of patterns of doubling and inversion between the characters. This establishes part of the structural framework for the narrative, and it enables us to see, in the characters, aspects of like and unlike. We also look at the definitions and lack of definitions of what makes good and evil women, good and evil feminine behaviors. Though

Red Dragon is a popular novel, this does not mean that it cannot attempt to consider those basic moral concepts within the compass of contemporary societal norms. Finally, we look at the concept of women as victims and as monsters. This ties into the concepts of good and evil; these, like the concepts of feminine and masculine, are binary oppositions which help create the structure of the novel and its worldview. Although studying that structure and worldview would be enlightening, and fascinating, such is beyond the aims of this essay.

But what is within those aims is a desired outcome. Ideally, we should come to an understanding of why *Red Dragon* is a fulfilling and fascinating narrative. We should come to realize the degree to which the complexity of life is echoed, however shallowly, in *Red Dragon*. It is more than just a simplistic novel: it is a rich exploration of the complexities of its outer, phenomenal, world. Part of the complexity Harris explores is gender, and gender relations. As a result, then, before addressing the novel more closely, it is instructive to consider some aspects of gender, as background, so to speak, for the wider issues in the novel.

One basic assumption of feminist scholarship is that sex is immutable, biological, whereas gender is mutable, culturally assigned. Where the verities of men and women are "eternal," their cultural manifestation changes. The study of gender has become central to such discourses, and it has rapidly increased both in importance and in sheer numbers of studies, over time. Yet we know that "As research on gender proliferates, so does the tendency to assume that the meaning of gender is unproblematic" (Hawkesworth 650). It is easy to gloss over the complexities and ambiguities of gender discourse, and it is easy to likewise forget that there is no one gender discourse, but multiple gender discourses. There is no *one* femininity, no *one* masculinity. Such a multiplicity recognizes the diversity of human reality, and it enables us to recognize that human existence is not a singular event.

In part, the range of femininities and masculinities is stratified by class. It is also divided by cultural and subcultural lines. We should not expect that the nature of gender reality for an Ohio wife to be same as for a Californian actress, let alone for an Australian poet. Simply, there is no one "ideal" behavior for, say, a woman, but there are a range of ideal positions for women. There is a multiplicity of ideals. So it is important that, in discussing gender, and in specific relation to *Red Dragon*, we must be careful to preserve "the multiplicity of meanings accorded gender in contemporary feminist scholarship" (Hawkesworth 653). Thus, although motherhood is the major role accorded to the women in *Red Dragon*, other forms of femininity exist. Most notably, for example, is that displayed by Reba.

This does not mean that it is impossible to come to some general conclusions about gender. It is possible to generalize, to a degree. We should be able to look at common characteristics that tie the lives of women, and men, together. We can consider, for example, the common characteristics of mothers, to look at what helps define them and their experiences. It is possible, also, to define what is culturally "good" and culturally "bad." We can, as a result, validly agree upon aspects of the demands placed upon characters in *Red Dragon* by gender and gender role; we can look at them, and define some as "good" mothers, for example, and others as "bad" mothers, just as we can define the characters as "heroes" and "villains." In doing so we must remember, at all times, that such are abstractions. This is the process of looking at the commonality of experiences, such as those of mothers, rather than what makes each individual, unique.

So, looking at gender, and the feminine, in *Red Dragon* we look in large part at the mothers. By far the most prevalent type of woman in *Red Dragon* is the mother. Of the main female characters, five are mothers. We have Mrs. Jacobi, Mrs. Leed, and Molly, as well as Marian, Francis's mother, and his grandmother. The other main character is Reba who, of all the main female characters, is the only one who is blind. We can see in this a significance with the importance of the visual to Francis. Let us not forget:

> He places mirrors in the eyes of his victims, so that he may see himself triumphant in their eyes. His dominant image, tattooed across his chest, is a William Blake paining [*sic*] entitled *The Great Red Dragon and the Woman Clothed with the Sun*, the Dragon rampant and exalting in its power.
> Focused almost solely on the visual, Dolarhyde chooses his victims from the home movies his photographic studio develops. He also films his intrusions, so that he may relive the atrocities over and over again... [Shaw 4].

Reba is the only significant female character to come close to Francis that has a chance of redeeming him. And it is her obviously symbolic disability that enables this possibility of redemption. Further, her disability mirrors Francis's, his harelip. In a sense, she is both the double and the inversion of Francis, and these are the next, important elements we shall look at.

Harris creates patterns of character relationships through the opposition of character doubling and character inversion. With doubling, the characters are similar, are alike. For example, Francis and Lecter are doubles because both are serial killers. Both Francis and Graham, and Lecter and Graham are doubles, through Graham's simpatico with serial killers; it is this simpatico which enabled him to apprehend Lecter, and to identify and almost apprehend Francis. Likewise both Francis and Graham are also doubles, because they are both free to move and act. This patterning between characters is also mirrored by Francis, with the development of a fissure or split between himself as Francis Dolarhyde and himself as the Red Dragon. This split is the result of involvement with Reba, when "his psyche bifurcates into Francis and the Dragon, who fight it out for the life of Reba" (Shaw 4). We must remember that the first manifestation of the Red Dragon's voice is when he awakens after sex with Reba (Harris 264).

Familial relations also see a degree of doubling. Francis, Niles Jacobi and Willy are all stepsons, for example, and Graham, Mrs Jacobi and Marian are stepparents; Molly, Mr Jacobi and Mr Vogt are also the natural parents in these families. The three can be considered as existing on a continuum. Francis is the child of the past, the natural son of the father. Niles is the child of the present, the natural son of the father. And Willy is he child of the future, the natural son, this time, of the mother. In all three families, it is the step-parent who is emphasized, the dead mothers and Graham.

As noted, Reba is the double of Francis, because of her disability and his. Their disabilities are related through the face, but it is chiefly through her eyes, not her mouth, that she is related in this way. (She is, though, also related through speech therapy: [Harris 238].) Though Francis is male, he has also been feminized in name: the epithet "cunt face" (Harris 199) that he recites to his grandmother is exactly that sort of feminization, and it accords with the later threats of castration from her. As a result, Francis overcompensates for this feminization by trying to become hypermasculine, through his acceptance of service in the armed forces and through his bodybuilding. In these, and other ways, the characters are doubled, made similar. They also lead into the other way by which characters are related in *Red Dragon*, through inversion.

Through inversion, aspects of one character are the reverse of another. Where doubling acts on "like," inversion acts on "unlike." Thus, although Francis and Lecter are doubles, because both are serial killers, they are also inverted: Francis is free, Lecter bound. Likewise, Graham is also free, again unlike Lecter. Mr Jacobi is male, Molly and Marian are both female, and Reba is, in a sense, a female "victim," whereas Francis is the male perpetrator. This gendered dialectic recurs in the following two books. For example, both Lecter and Verger are both male and the criminal foci, in *Silence of the Lambs* and *Hannibal* respectively, with Starling the female protagonist of both. In the pairing of Lecter and Starling, he is the criminal, she the law; yet both are doubles at the same time: both are united by a childhood trauma, associated with their later choice of a life-path.

These two ways that characters are related, doubling and inversion, tie the principal female characters into complex relationships. Both Mrs Leed and Mrs Jacobi are doubles, because both are Francis's victims, both are mothers, and both are dead before the narrative starts. They are both doubles, also, through details of their lives. Both are made present in the novel's narrative through the motif of the home movies. Both owned pets (although there is the inversion of cat and dog), and there is a twin emphasis upon their materiality and comfortable lifestyle. They come to represent the "safe," "normal" bourgeois existence that is threatened by Francis's very being.

They have a further importance to the narrative. They establish, through their deaths (and the deaths of their families) Francis as the killer, and as that most feared of killers, the serial killer. They are also the key for Graham to identify Francis, too. As a result, they are, in a sense, manipulated by Francis for his own ends: it is through their deaths, and the planned future deaths of the Shermans and other families, that Francis will metamorphise into the Red Dragon. In this way he is an inversion of his own grandmother. She uses Francis for her own ends on her daughter, to destroy the political career of her husband, Mr. Vogt, to stop, in a sense, Mr. Vogt from becoming politically successful.

Mrs. Leed and Mrs. Jacobi are also inversions of Molly. Whereas both are killed by Francis, Molly kills Francis. They are both, in a sense, ciphers. They are incapable of being fleshed out as the other principal female characters. Unlike Marian and Grandmother Dolarhyde and like Molly, they are both "good" mothers. Yet, unlike Molly, they are, in a sense, "bad" mothers through their clear failure to protect their young. But there is no blame assigned to them because of this; both are clearly victims of Francis. Molly, as noted, is the clear victor over him.

As we have seen, the patterns of inversion and doubling are not just tied to the female characters. For example, Arnold Lang is killed by Francis, and his face is shot. Francis, too, is killed, but by Molly, and his face is shot also. Yet, unlike Lang, whose face is shot once post mortem, the multiple shooting of his face is the primary cause of his death: we read "she shot him in the face as he slid down the door facing and she shot him in the face as he sat on the floor and she ran to him and she shot him twice in the face" (Harris 346). What Harris is doing here is tying both male and female characters into a complex web of interrelationships. These relationships are not only formal and narrative, but also familial and emotional. They help encode aspects of gender, by both setting up and confounding clear expectations of gender and gender relations. It helps develop a problematization of gender through this pattern. And, although this pattern is only partially discernible to some of the characters, and not to others, only the reader is privileged enough to be able to read the whole pattern. In doing so, only the reader is able to more fully articulate what characterizes the feminine in the characters of *Red Dragon*.

It is, of course, useful to consider what aspects of the feminine are emphasized in the characters. Notably, in looking at the main female characters, and, especially, the mothers, there is a sense of a moral dimension to their behavior, of good and bad, or good and evil. Clearly, we can see that Mrs. Jacobi, Mrs. Leed, and Molly are all examples of good mothers. They provide for their young, and protect them where able. They also have positive relationships with their partners. However, both Marian and Francis's grandmother are bad mothers. Neither has a healthy relationship with Francis, as their ward, nor with a husband. Marian comes close in this latter aspect, however, Mr. Vogt is an alcoholic (Harris 216). The presentation of both groups is not unproblematic. There is a strong degree of ambiguity in the presentation of the moral dimension of the women. Both Mrs. Jacobi and Mrs. Leed can be read, as noted, as bad mothers from their failure to protect their children. Even Molly can be criticized: she eschews traditional feminine behavior, in the protection of Willy at the novel's catastrophe. So, then, if we consider passiveness as a feminine attribute, both Mrs. Jacobi and Mrs. Leed are passive, yet this passivity is not a positive trait: both are sleeping when attacked by Francis. Molly, however, is active in killing, but this activity is positive. Reba, too, is active; she seduces Francis, but is not seduced by him (Harris 261–62). But this activity is likewise positive. Through her seduction she enables Francis to have the chance of rehabilitation and redemption. This point about the ambiguity of presentation is highlighted by the following passage about Reba: "She wondered if Dolarhyde shared the popular belief that the blind are 'purer in spirit' than most people, that they are somehow sanctified by their affliction. She smiled to herself. That one wasn't true either" (Harris 241).

To a degree, though he is a male, and traditionally expected to be active, Francis is passive, feminized. It is evident, as noted earlier, in the use of "cunt face." It is also evident in the feminized form of his name, Francis, not Frank (Maguire). As noted, he is seduced by Reba, not the seducer. He is the one threatened with castration, unlike any other male character (unlike the most recent cinematic adaptation of the novel). Further, in the childhood game of "doctors and nurses," it is his playmate who initiates the game, not he (Harris 209). (It is interesting to note that the playmate is red-haired, and that Reba's hair is the same color as the woman in the Blake painting; that is, "Her hair was a mixture of wheat and red-gold" [Harris 297, 228]. Again, as noted, Francis attempts to compensate for this feminization by his hypermasculinity. Hence the weight-lifting, as in chapter thirty-seven (Harris 276–79).

Molly, as noted, is masculinized. She attacks and kills Francis in defending Graham and Willy, for example. She learns how to shoot (Harris 136–38). As a result, it is understandable that Graham "looked like a man who had witnessed an irrevocable loss" (Harris 138). In a sense, he has just done that: Molly has clearly lost an unalloyed femininity and innocence, and this should be considered the result of being tainted by Francis's psychopathology. Her recourse to violence in the book's catastrophe also inverts the gender relations of masculine and feminine, compared to contemporary vigilante films. Whereas, in the films, "the woman suffers; the man achieves catharsis" (Fulwood 40), here it is Graham that suffers, becomes feminized as it were, and it is Molly who achieves catharsis and is masculinized. Shaw (3) reads this as a clear example of gender reversal in the novel.

It is instructive to digress momentarily here, and to consider the cinematic adaptations of the novel, in order to strengthen the importance of the book's ending. In the later adaptation, *Red Dragon*, the replacement of the catastrophe with an almost western shoot-out between Francis and Graham in the home diminishes the impact of Graham's feminization. He gets to injure Francis, and it is this "feminized" Francis that Molly shoots. Even in the earlier adaptation, *Manhunter*, both Director Michael Mann's "macho ideology, and traditional Hollywood conventions, apparently would not permit such a gender reversal" (Shaw 3). Both paradoxically highlight the problematics of the book's ending, and both of these make the book's end stronger than both their failures as film.

This makes *Red Dragon* unconventional, with Molly as the victor, not Graham as the notional protagonist. This leads into Starling as the next step in characterization, in the female protagonist of *The Silence of the Lambs*, and it could be argued that, in this way, the books lead into those that follow. As a result, *Hannibal* is the logical consequence of the developments of the sequence. And, essentially, the reaction against Starling's "defection" is a misreading of the direction that the novels took.

But returning to *Red Dragon*, we can see that the novel does not, in essence, define what makes the characters good and bad. It does not define them and their roles explicitly. It relies on basic cultural cues, rather than developing them for itself. Graham is "good" because he is an agent of the FBI, or, rather, he is an ex-agent of the FBI. Graham is also good in motivation. He acts in protection of others, which reminds us of the police motto: "to protect and serve." Yet his ability to empathies with serial killers problematises that sense of goodness.

We have "good" families, and an "evil" family. The Leeds and Jacobis are good, despite being Francis' victims. Likewise, the Graham family is good. As the "heroes," they are an inversion of the Dolarhydes. It is interesting to note how the final element of their name, *ham*, is the Old English word meaning "home," both as a place and as a dwelling. Though the *hyde*, "hide" of the Dolarhydes echoes the verb, in the sense of hidden motifs, lives and hearts, it also echoes the shelter used to "hide" hunters from being noticed by animals and birds. (It also echoes Stevenson's use of Hyde, in his *Strange Case of Dr. Jekyll and Mr. Hyde*; the parallels between the two texts deserve greater consideration.) So there is an element of the use of place to echo inhabitants: Francis lives in an old place, he lives in the past, so to speak, as Graham lives in an Edenic place that suffers the final irruption of evil. Like that earlier analogue, Stevenson's Hyde, the Dolarhydes are the inversion of the Grahams. They are the evil to the Grahams' good.

In a conventional sense the Dolarhydes are evil. Marian is evil, since it was through her that Francis was placed in a foundling home thence in an orphanage, rather than being reared by herself (Harris 197–99). The grandmother is also evil with her direct brutalization of Francis. This brutalization is made evident in both chapters twenty-six (Harris 203–5) and twenty-seven (Harris 209–10), also with the earlier use of Francis to destroy Mr. Vogt's political ambitions, in chapter twenty-five (Harris 201). Further, the children, and presumably Mr. Vogt, are also evil. The brutalization by the children is made evident in chapter twenty-seven (Harris 216–7). It is no surprise, then, that both the grandmother and the stepfamily are "coincident" with the development of Francis's killing of animals, first the chickens (Harris 211–12), then the cat (Harris 221). This part of the narrative forms the core of the novel; the narrative shuttles, as it were, from the present, back, to the past, and again to the present.

The novel also shuttles between the notional protagonist, Graham, and the notional antagonist, Francis. In this way it develops a form of balance between good and evil, with good ultimately triumphant. But Graham is not unblemished: he is not unproblematically good, as he is "tainted" by his empathy with serial killers. Just as Francis is "tainted" with good after encountering Reba. As a result, Graham becomes other than "unambiguously the protagonist" (Shaw 3; as will be discussed later). With both Graham and Francis, the consequences from their actions remains ultimately unforeseen, although, with hindsight, inevitable. The death of Lounds resulted from Graham's use of him to taunt Francis. The consumption of the Blake painting is the consequence of Francis's development of feelings for Reba. Likewise, the non-killing of the museum staff, unlike Lounds. The desired internalization of the Red Dragon, after eating the painting fails. There is no recognition of reality; the disassociation of the voice of the Red Dragon from Francis's self continues, the recognition of who the Red Dragon is continues to elude him (and in this sense he is morally and psychologically blind, in an inversion of Reba's physical blindness). Not that this posits a split from reality in Francis: he is no schizophrenic, despite the popular conception of schizophrenia as a split personality. So there is a shuttling, between Francis as himself, and Francis as the Red Dragon, as a result of his sexual union with Reba. He develops a dialogue with the Red Dragon, who is, in a sense, really a promise of a future state, rather than an embodiment of a current or past one. It echoes, in this way, Jame Gumb's desire to change in *Silence of the Lambs*. We know that this is an externalized dialogue, since the dialogue is clearly vocalized: it is heard, for example, by Reba over the phone in chapter thirty-eight, where, on hearing it she asks "My God, what was that? Is somebody with you?" (Harris 285)

As a result, the sense of a dialectic between opposing forces is important for the novel's construction. There is one axis: Graham and Francis; and there is another: Francis and the Red Dragon. Of course, there are others. We have the one between Marian and Francis' grandmother, and the Leeds and Jacobis. This binary opposition is actually more complicated than one of a simple exclusionary nature allows. We have seen this already, in the taints of Graham and of Francis. The two become akin, so that at a key point Francis can mentally articulate a truth about Graham that problematises any simplistic conception of him as wholly good; he thinks, that is, the following: "The son of a bitch was a monster" (Harris 313). We see this dialectic, this shuttling, with the women of the novel.

We see a clear shuttling between the women: first, there is Molly, then Reba, then it ends with Molly again. Likewise, the shuttling between the present and the past is reflected with the women. Molly, and Reba, alternate with Marian and Francis' grandmother. Reba belongs to the present and holds the promise of a brighter future. Francis's grandmother, and Marian, belong to the past and the specter of darkness.

There are also the associations between the genders to consider. Along with Reba association with Francis, and the grandmother's with the Red Dragon, there is the association of Molly with Graham. As a result, what may be read as a set of binary oppositions can be read as a gendered set of axes. There is the Graham/Francis/Red Dragon axis that is reflected by the Molly/Reba/grandmother axis. Both are predicated upon another, from good to evil, from, in a sense, "victims" to villains.

There is also an elementary binary opposition in crime fiction. Women are usually seen as either victims or villains. In the latter case, they are usually seen in the role of femme fatales. *Red Dragon* preserves this opposition, but at the same time it problematizes it. The victims are primarily mothers, but the villains too are not femmes fatales, but primarily mothers also. Both Mrs. Leed and Mrs. Jacobi are dead prior to the start of the narrative. The real work, so to speak, of Francis, has been committed. We do not see him kill in order that he may become the Red Dragon. Instead, all of the deaths that we read of in the narrative are very much crimes of circumstance. The murders of Lounds, Ralph Mandy, and Arnold Lang all occur in relation to Francis's attempt to either take revenge, or prevent his capture by Graham. They are not part of the pattern of Francis's psychopathology, and neither is his final attack on Graham.

Yet, though both Mrs Leed and Mrs Jacobi are, in a real sense, absent from the narrative, they are nonetheless very much present. Graham reconstructs their deaths in his walk-throughs of the crime sites, for example. And they continue to be present in the home movies, consistently reviewed by Francis. It is very much as if "I think, therefore I am," *cogito ergo sum*, has become "I am thought of, therefore I am." Both Mrs Leed and Mrs Jacobi are present in the narrative, because they are thought of, in the same way that the Red Dragon is present as a being of the thought of Francis.

As both Mrs. Leed and Mrs Jacobi are present, they are both present as victims. As a result, the boundaries between them both are, in essence, blurred. They become, like Francis's stepbrother and stepsister, something approximating a cipher, a role rather than fully fleshed characters. Yet they still serve to establish Francis's status as a serial killer. They enable us to see that he will kill again, and we see that he chooses his third intended target, the Shermans. They also serve to establish the time frame in which Graham must operate in order to prevent further bloodshed. This in turn propels the narrative momentum, creates a sense of urgency that might otherwise be lacking.

However, in their shared victimhood, both these mothers could be considered as evidence of a perceivable misogynism on the part of the author. Such a reading is both simplistic and problematic. In both cases, both women and their husbands are killed, as are the children. Likewise, when we consider the pairing of Wendy and Lounds, it is Lounds who dies, not Wendy. Ralph Mandy dies, after he is seen with Reba, and she lives, albeit to establish Francis's apparent death. And, of Molly and Graham, it is Graham who is physically injured, not Molly. So a reading that sees only women as victims, the killed and the injured, is not sustainable; not just women get injured.

Reba can also be read as a victim of the Red Dragon. Although she is almost killed, but is spared by Francis, she nonetheless loses her innocence. In essence, it is the act of lovemaking between her and Francis, and the resultant split between the Red Dragon and Francis that saves her. Yet it is also, fundamentally, her blindness that is, effectively, her salvation. Francis does not have to hide his face from her (Harris 228); she does not perceive who he is, unlike the other victims, who are killed for that knowledge. She is, further, used by Francis just as he uses his other victims. She serves to "establish" his death, as does the death of Lang, enabling him to in turn attack the vulnerable Graham. What truly distinguishes her from the other victims is that she survives by the novel's denouement, as does her inverted double, Molly, as the sole surviving example of a good mother in the text. She survives, but the cost of surviving is glossed over. We last hear of her, rather than see her, and in the end it is the mothers who dominate the novel's closing pages.

One of those mothers is Marian, mother of Francis Dolarhyde. To an extent, she is an ambiguous figure. She is, in a sense, both victim and villain. She is the victim of her own mother. She is driven out of home when she marries Michael Trevane. She fears her child, and abandons him, first to the foundling house, or orphanage. She also witnesses her second husband's career destroyed through Francis, her other children's cat killed, and Francis driven away again. As a result, she is made into a figure of scorn and pity. She sins, that is, in rejecting Francis, and is punished in turn, but in being punished a monster is born. The ambivalence with which Harris approaches her problematizes our own reactions in turn. Our ambivalence is symptomatic, in turn, of the desired reactions to others, both here, in *Red Dragon*, and elsewhere in the series. So, while Graham is the notional hero, he is an actual anti-hero. Francis himself elicits pity and horror in the sympathetic reader. Lecter, also "meant" to be hated, becomes attractive, he becomes another form of the anti hero. This last point becomes important in regard to *Hannibal*. It not only makes him the eponymous figure, as is the Red Dragon, it foreshadows the later union of Starling and Lecter, as a perverse form of "romantic" leading couple. It becomes the result of the logical developments of the narratives of the three books. And, further, it invokes the very necessary complexity of relationships in the real world. As a result, we are continually drawn back to that aspect of our lives.

The true origin of the evil here, in *Red Dragon*, is in Grandmother Dolarhyde. She banishes daughter after her daughter's marriage (Harris 197). She also uses Francis to destroy Vogt's political ambitions. Further, she serves as the castrating mother to Francis. She is, in a sense, his "real" mother, she whom Francis fears yet hopes to please at the same time. In doing so, she gives birth, metaphorically, to a monster, and he is eventually torn apart, into the binary opposition of Francis and the Red Dragon. It is, further, her lack of palpable love for her grandson which helps warp him, as does the lack shown from his mother, his fellow orphans, and his step-family. And it has been argued that, because of this lack of love that Francis's "murders are twisted expressions of a desperate need to be loved and accepted" (Shaw 4) Francis's grandmother clearly demonstrates a problematic relationship with men, with her sons-in-law, and with her grandson. She also exhibits a clearly problematic relationship with sexuality, as well as other bodily functions. Both Francis's bed-wetting and the game of doctors and nurses elicits the same response in her: the withdrawal of affection and the threat of castration (Harris 203–5, 209–10).

Harris actually implies a deeper origin for this relationship. He leaves implicit the point that Grandmother Dolarhyde's pegged and notched incisors are entirely consonant with Hutchinson's incisors, which is a symptom of congenital syphilis (Maguire). As a result, her reactions can be read as a distrust of sexuality, derived from parents; and, further, we can ask whether it was her father who was the origin of her syphilis, hence her response to men. There is, as a result of this, a clear reading of the relationship between Francis's evil and his background. As the disgust of the physical is derived from Grandmother Dolarhyde's congenital syphilis, so Francis's evil is familial, arising out of the actions and emotions of both the grandmother and both her child, Francis's mother, Marian, and Marian's stepchildren, the offspring of Marian's second husband. By implication, the grandmother is a form of *monstrum*. She is both a monster and a form of omen of Francis, requiring expiation by society.

The silence on this aetiology of Francis's evil demands that we recognize an understanding of the relevant past, in addressing the present. If we understand the past, then we understand the present, and if we understand the present, then we can predict the future. It is in the act of constructing fiction that there is enough of a selection of information for us to understand what has been happening in the narrative itself. We know what has happened, ideally, when we have the right amount of background information. This factor is clearly evident in the presentation of the initial two crimes. We gain enough to know how and why the deaths happened, not to visualize them as if they happen now, before us. So, in large part, we get enough material to draw conclusions and moral judgments about the characters. It is, though, also enough to question any of our simplistic readings of the characters. It leads us to ask questions about humanity, about ourselves: are we as much created by, as creators of, circumstance? What is nature of this evil that is so evident in Francis? Is it a presence as much as it is an absence of, say, love? Though these questions, and the questions and implications that they raise, are ultimately beyond the scope of this essay, they are still asked, and still raised, by Harris, both here and in the other books of the series. When it comes to questions of good, and of evil, here, we must be concerned to ask how these concepts affect our reading of female characters and femininity.

As we have seen, there are good women, good mothers, and bad. In general terms, the good mother is caring. She loves her children. And we see this love in Mrs Jacobi, Mrs Leed, and Molly. This love, further, is not dysfunctional. The bad mothers, however, are more problematic. Although there may be love, it is not unalloyed. Although Marian "loves Francis," that is, she accepts him after the institutionalization of Grandmother Dolarhyde (Harris 215), she still fears him, hence her initial rejection of him (Harris 196), and her response when he first appears as a growing child, at the Vogt's home (Harris 200–01); she is very much haunted by Francis. Francis's grandmother also loves him, but her love is dysfunctional. She uses him, to destroy Vogt's career (Harris 201), and she threatens him, consistently, with castration. (Her problematic relationship with physicality has already been noted.) The only major female character not a mother, Reba, is also good despite her sexuality. She is, essentially, the sexual aggressor in her relationship with Francis, not the virginal maiden. In this way she echoes the earlier playmate (Harris 208–9). Reba is also identified with the woman clothed with sun in Blake's painting (Harris 297); she is in this way set in opposition to the Red Dragon in Francis's life. Essentially, the good and the evil of the female characters are developed in relation to the figure of Francis, rather than to the notional protagonist, Graham. It is Francis, after all, and their relationship with him that really helps to define their moral standing.

As a result, Francis becomes the central figure, the real protagonist of *Red Dragon*. It is through him, remember, that the eponymous figure is manifested. He also ties all the others, particularly the women, together into a set of complex relationships. Some, like his mother and grandmother, belong to his past, as do others such as Queen Mother Bailey. Both Mrs Jacobi and Mrs Leed also belong to the past, but as his victims. Reba belongs to his present. She presents, him, further, with a dilemma, and a chance to stop his killings. It is significant, I feel, that the only murders we directly witness are those "necessary" for Francis to survive and to attempt his revenge on Graham. Finally, it is Molly who is the ultimate victor. Yet, while both Reba and Molly survive, they are both changed through their contact with Francis. Molly, for example, is implied to suffer "irrevocable lost" (Harris 138). And although there is no real expression of this for Reba, though such would be understandable, she is last seen crying, after escaping from Francis' burning house (Harris 330). It is as if the specter of Francis Dolarhyde will haunt them, just as it is Francis who is haunted by the past. He is the end product of a human environment; in the end, it is him, it is "men [who] are haunted" (Harris 354).

It is no surprise that both the family and generations are important motifs in *Red Dragon*. We can see this in the evil of the Dolarhydes, for example. We also see it in the assault that Francis represents, upon the stolid bourgeois families of both the Jacobis and the Leeds. These three belong, further, to the past, as the Grahams belong to the future. But the novel is far more complex than this simplification. It develops a richness that echoes the outer world, and this is particularly seen in the development of the female characters. We have seen this already, in the discussions on the patterns of doubling and inversion (which affect, also, the male characters), and we have seen it in the problematics of the definitions, or lack thereof, of good and evil women. Finally, we have seen it in the concepts of women as victims and villains. It is in the gender relations between male and female, masculine and feminine that the story is played out. Though Francis is the central figure, the protagonist of this novel, both *Red Dragon* and its sequel, *Silence of the Lambs*, "become powerful vehicles of popular collective expression, articulating the tensions, and reconciliation, of everyday relations between individuals and society" (Platt). It articulates a common trope of modern gothic fiction, the haunted individual. For its ultimate expression is that it is we who are haunted. We decide what makes good and bad in mothers and women, and "*we* make mercy" (Harris 354). Significantly, "We [also] make murder, and it matters only to us" (Harris 354). Is this same with good and evil?

Works Consulted

Fulwood, Neil. *One Hundred Violent Films That Changed Cinema.* London: B.T. Batsford, 2003.

Harris, Thomas. *Red Dragon.* London: Corgi, 1983.

Hawkesworth, Mary. "Confounding Gender." *Signs,* Spring 199.

Maguire, Dorothy. "Thomas Harris' Red Dragon: Chapters 1–9." http://reddragon.hannotations.com/dragon1_9.html. Accessed 8 Sept. 2006.

Platt, Len. "The Hannibal Lecter Novels: Modern/Postmodern Fables." *Americana: The Journal of American Popular Culture,* Fall 2003. http://www.americanpopular-culture.com/journal/articles/fall_2003/platt.htm. Accessed 12 Sept. 2006.

Shaw, Daniel. "The Mastery of Hannibal Lecter." http://www.lhup.edu/dshaw/Mastery.doc. Accessed 12 Sept. 2006.

11

Black Sunday, Black September

Thomas Harris's Thriller, from Novel to Film, and the Terror of Reality

SCOTT D. BRIGGS

> "U.S. intelligence doesn't think they're going to strike here at all, do they, Corley?"
>
> "No," Sam Corley said wearily. "They think the Arabs wouldn't dare."
>
> — Harris 36

The above question is asked by Thomas Harris's fascinating (if, in his novelistic form, ultimately tragic), hard-nosed, and ruthless hero, Major David Kabakov of the Israeli elite intelligence division Mossad Aliyah Beth, to his eventual close friend and ally, FBI agent Sam Corley. In a scene that comes early in Thomas Harris's first novel, *Black Sunday*, Major Kabakov asks this of Corley after a particularly frustrating, ineffectual briefing to the major figures of the American intelligence brass on a possible "Black September" Arab terrorist plot, to be perpetrated on United States soil or territories, something that even in the early-to-mid–1970s was an almost unthinkable scenario.

Any student of history — or, indeed, of modern terrorism — knows that this period was marked by an increase in Arab terrorist incidents, bombings, plane hijackings, hostage-taking, and the like, none more infamous than the following two major such events. The first unfolded on

September 5, 1972, at the Olympic Village in Munich, Germany, where a group of eight Black September terrorists ambushed and took eleven Israeli athletes hostage in the compound, resulting in the death of all the athletes and coaches as well as five of the terrorists. German military, intelligence, sharpshooters (who were inexplicably recalled at the last minute), and police negotiators all failed to gain release of the hostages, and Israel and its Mossad were completely barred politically (especially by the German government, which lacked any substantial anti-terrorism military unit) from responding to the situation directly. The second incident occurred on June 27, 1976, roughly a year after Harris's novel was published, and amazingly almost coinciding with the release of the film version of the book, when an Air France jet en route from Paris to Tel Aviv was hijacked by Wadi Haddad, an extremist Palestinian faction, and given safe haven in dictator Idi Amin's city of Entebbe, in the African country of Uganda. After much political and diplomatic debate, round-the-clock discussions and wrangling, Mossad and the Israeli army were given the go-ahead to stage a daring rescue and raid on Entebbe, resulting in almost the exact opposite of the atrocity at Munich four years earlier: all the Haddad terrorists were killed by the Israeli commandos in the raid, although three hostages also died either of natural or other causes during the ordeal. The successful raid on Entebbe has in succeeding years always been seen as a major success on the part of the Mossad and Israeli intelligence and military operations; at the time, the pressure on the Israeli government was enormous to insure that a repeat of the nightmare at the Munich airport, with all hostages lying dead on the tarmac or at the Olympic compound, did not occur. The Mossad accomplished this highly dangerous mission all within a carefully planned five minutes' time, insuring, for at least the next two decades, that Israel's new hard-line stance against terrorism was to be backed up with decisive and deadly force, and that this type of precise military and intelligence operation "came to be seen as Mossad's calling card" (Thomas 132).

Unfortunately, an operation during July 1973, in which six Mossad operatives were arrested for murder, later became known as the infamous "Lillehammer Affair," and would ultimately do as much damage to Mossad's reputation and standing in the world community as Entebbe had boosted it to an all-time high. This was the incident in which Mossad agents in Lillehammer, acting on an alleged eyewitness sighting of one of the still at-large terrorists, Ali Hassan Salameh, who was involved in the execution of the Munich kidnappings and murders of the athletes, ended up gunning down and murdering an innocent Arab waiter named Ahmed

Bouchiki, walking back home with his pregnant wife after a trip to the movies. This was one Mossad operation in which the intelligence was clearly erroneous, the execution of the plan even worse, and Mossad's policy of hard-line, public assassination of the terrorists, rather than simple capture, arrest, interrogation, or even torture-for-information of the subjects (of which the Mossad has been rumored for years to not necessarily be beneath in their zeal to accomplish their mission), would backfire in such a tragic way that perhaps the agency's reputation has still not yet fully recovered from it.

Still, none of these incidents ever took place on United States soil. Even the seemingly endless hostage ordeal in Iran, which began on November 4, 1979, and did not end until January 20, 1981, when the remaining 53 of the 66 hostages were finally released, was restricted to the Middle East. This action was overseen and encouraged by the Ayatollah Khomeini and a gang of Iranian radicals, who seized the U.S. Embassy in Tehran and took the Americans diplomats hostage. The only positive outcome of that incident was that the hostages' release was eventually successfully negotiated, albeit after a tragic, botched rescue attempt by American military forces, resulting in the loss of several lives and possibly ending the chances of then–U.S. President Jimmy Carter of being reelected in the next election, in which he was defeated by Republican conservative Ronald Reagan.

More incidents followed through the 1980s, and fundamentalist Islam and radical Arab terrorist groups and factions, including Fatah, the PLO, Hamas, Islamic Jihad, Black September, Hezbollah, and even the then-fledgling and mainly underground group al-Qaida, continued to grow in terms of financial backing and military might, with support from many of the major fundamentalist nations and governments in the Mideast.

Ultimately, it was not until 1993, roughly a year after President Bill Clinton's inauguration, that an Arab terrorist group would finally strike directly on Unites States soil. On February 26, 1993, a group of terrorists with ties to al-Qaida and followers of Egyptian cleric Umar Abd al-Rahman, who preached his radical fundamentalist doctrine in the New York City area, detonated powerful explosives hidden within a van (rented in nearby Jersey City, New Jersey) in an underground parking garage, beneath one of the World Trade Center's towers, not toppling the Twin Towers, as had been planned or hoped for, but still killing six people, injuring a thousand others, and doing severe damage to the infrastructure and parking garage lower levels of the building.

Many in the Western intelligence communities believed that al-Qaida or other such groups wouldn't dare try to attack the World Trade Center again, although after the '93 attack, the buildings were clearly a major target on the Arab terrorist list, as indeed major government or financial institutions or landmarks in the entire lower Manhattan financial center (or Manhattan, period) must have been for years, only requiring the right plan to be put into action, the right combination of agents, and the right opportunity at the right time, to present itself. On September 11, 2001, this confluence of factors resulted in the worst terrorist attack and tragedy committed on U.S. soil in history, resulting in the deaths of more than 3,000 people and the complete destruction (via hijacked commercial passenger jet airliners) of the World Trade Center towers, with concurrent deadly attacks on the Pentagon building in Washington, D.C., and an attempted attack on the heart of Washington, D.C., perhaps the White House or Capitol building. To paraphrase Harris's FBI agent Sam Corley once again, the terrorists in 1993 and 2001 had indeed "dared" to strike on U.S. soil, and indeed, had succeeded twice. The "unthinkable," after September 11, 2001, was no longer thus, and would never be again.

According to notes included with the first editions of *Black Sunday*, Thomas Harris first got the idea to write his first novel while working as a police-crime beat reporter for the Associated Press in New York City. Initially conceiving the idea for the storyline of *Black Sunday* along with two of his fellow reporters, Sam Maull and Dick Riley, and completing the research for a book on the topic of Arab terrorism with the other two, it was Harris who ultimately landed a contract to write the novel, and he quit his reporting job to finish the novel on his own.

What may very well have been a starting point for Harris, and what must be our starting point in understanding both the novel and the film, is Black September itself. The primary Black September terrorist-operative who figures in the novel is the female Lebanese-born Dahlia Iyad; her real-life namesake, Salah Khalaf "Abu Iyad," once Yasser Arafat's chief of security, was a founding member of the Fatah movement. Iyad has claimed that "Black September was never a terrorist organization; it acted as an auxiliary of the Resistance, when the Resistance was no longer in a position to fully assume its military and political tasks. Its members always insisted that they had no organic tie with Fatah or the PLO" (Iyad 98), although he has long been accused by Israel and the United States as being the founder of Black September, the actual terrorist movement, his denials notwithstanding. Iyad was ultimately assassinated in Tunis in 1991, reportedly by an Abu Nidal agent.

Elsewhere, a former senior PLO member, Mohammed Daoud Oudeh, once claimed in 1972 to the Jordanian newspaper *Al-Dustur* that "There is no such organization as Black September. Fatah announces its own operations under this name so that Fatah will not appear as the direct executor of the operation." Black September was named after events begun on September 16, 1970, when King Hussein of Jordan announced military rule after an attempt by the *fedayeen* (literally, from the Arabic, "one who sacrifices himself"), the armed Palestinian militias, who were primarily trained by the PLO and originally founded during and for the 1948 Arab-Israeli War, to take control of his kingdom, resulting in a mass expulsion of Palestinians from Jordan, many dying in the process. Black September was originally founded for the purpose of exacting revenge on King Hussein for this series of events and the treatment of the Palestinian people; allegedly the movement began with a small cell of Fatah members and recruits from other smaller such organizations.

As the original Fatah movement had started as a small political, student, and social movement and slowly gathered power and influence from the 1960s through the 1970s, so did Black September from this specialized purpose end up as the group responsible for the Munich Olympic Village Massacre — if indeed the group that took responsibility for that event in 1972 bore any relation to the original Black September Fatah splinter group and was not merely a successor that had taken on the name Black September for its own purposes.

Clearly, whatever the nature of the group or groups claiming to be, or actually operating as, Black September, during the 1970s, it is common knowledge that women as well as men were welcomed into, and utilized by, these or other splinter groups, which may seem unusual considering the traditional structure of most Arab societies and the subservient role of women in those societies. However, according to journalist John K. Cooley, Black September's hierarchy was a new and unorthodox one, and represented a "total break with the old operational and organizational methods of the *fedayeen*": "Its members operated in air-tight cells of four or more men and women. Each cell's members were kept ignorant of other cells. Leadership was exercised from outside by intermediaries and 'cut-offs' [*sic*], though there was no centralized leadership" (Cooley 1973).

This leads us to the crucial opening chapter of *Black Sunday*, which Harris sets in Beirut, Lebanon, and in which he introduces us to the beautiful but deadly Black September terrorist agent Dahlia Iyad, a woman so lovely that she can easily persuade and seduce men, but is also capable of ruthless, cold-blooded violence in the line of duty. During an earlier training mission involving three Japanese recruits for a particular terror strike at an Israeli airport, in which one of the three loses his nerve, Harris relates that she "blew his head off with a Schmeisser machine pistol," cementing for the reader her characteristic ruthlessness, while also giving us a hint of what might be in store at the novel's denouement. Dahlia's choice of weaponry, which is one of her mainstays as readers later discover, is significant from a historical point of view: the Schmeisser machine pistol is a German automatic machine gun whose manufacture dates back at least to World War I and II, and apparently has a reputation for reliability and accuracy that eclipses other such weapons such as the more commonplace Russian Kalashnikov or "AK-47<in> assault rifle, which has often enjoyed a less-than-reliable reputation among world military forces (and, perhaps, less "official" forces such as terrorist groups and militias).

As in John Frankenheimer's later film version, Dahlia arrives by cab from the airport in Beirut, to be led by various means to the terrorists' secret quarters in the Rue Jeb el-Nakhel, where she is heading for a rendezvous and debriefing with a (probably extremely rare) Black September leaders' tribunal of Hafez Najeer, Abu Ali, and Muhammad Fasil. Most of them are described by Harris as being key orchestrators of the Munich Olympic massacre; they are clearly modeled on some of their real-life counterparts, probably including Ali Salameh and others. In the novel, Dahlia must give an operative a code word, with a gun pointed at her head, before she is even allowed out of the cab and into the terrorists' quarters; in the film she is warmly welcomed, and merely walks in to join the tribunal, her identity and trustworthiness apparently not in any doubt.

Iyad is questioned by the other leaders as to her relationship with an as yet unnamed "American," and her degree of control or influence upon him, and there is also a discussion of his reliability and mental stability. Eventually Abu Ali produces a 16-millimeter film projector and screens a brief film obtained from North Vietnamese sources. The setting of the film is somewhere at a North Vietnamese POW camp, dating anywhere between 1967 and 1973. The subject of the film is one Michael Lander, who is shown standing at a lectern with an audience of other POWs and North Vietnamese officials and guards, stating for the camera:

> I am Michael J. Lander, Lieutenant Commander, U.S. Navy, captured February 10, 1967, while firebombing a civilian hospital near Ninh Binh. Though the evidence of my war crimes is unmistakable, the Democratic Republic of Vietnam has not done to me punishment, but showed me the suffering which resulted from American war crimes like those of my own and others.... I am sorry for what I have done. I am sorry we killed children [Harris 4–5].

It transpires later in the novel that Lander was held captive for six years in the POW camp; it is also revealed that his involvement in a firebombing of a civilian hospital is the purest Vietcong propaganda, invented nonsense that Lander is forced to recite for the camera to denounce both himself and his unit and commanders, in an effort by the North Vietnamese to shame and discredit all of them, and the United States forces as a whole. Lander, as Harris later reveals in several flashbacks, is actually a Navy helicopter pilot (and a decorated one) shot down during a tricky night rescue operation that goes terribly wrong, and he and his crew are captured and imprisoned by the Vietcong.

Previous to his tours of duty in Vietnam, Lander was in demand as a Navy airship/dirigible pilot, until the U.S. Navy airship program was dismantled by the early 1960s, or, more precisely, in June 1961, when the program "was ordered terminated by the Secretary of the Navy" (Vaeth 132). After Lander finds himself grounded by the program's termination, the Vietnam conflict crops up, and this is how Lander ends up enlisting as a commissioned officer for his two tours of duty, and as a POW. Here Harris's penchant for careful, diligent research reaps enormous dividends: Lander's entire back-story, including his airship and Navy military service, jibe with the real-life history of the Navy airship program, lending even more verisimilitude to Harris's storyline and characters.

Lander's filmed "confession" is pertinent both to the novel and the era in which the novel is set for many reasons, not the least of which is the very real backlash that the Vietnam War (and, later, related actions, such as air strikes and bombings in Cambodia and Laos) has engendered for many during its almost interminable duration, and even in the years directly following the final pullout of American forces in the mid–1970s. Shadows of the infamous My Lai massacre of 1968 and other such wartime atrocities, real or imagined, continue to haunt the Vietnam conflict and its considerable aftermath for both sides. Really, Lander's "confession," though in his case being invented Communist propaganda, contains kernels of truth as to the very real ancillary horrors of the Vietnam War, but of course the truth is indeed that such atrocities against innocent children, the elderly, and other civilians were perpetrated by all forces involved; they were not confined merely to the U.S. military. All this is established fact, but in terms of Lander's development from a proud, decorated Navy officer and accomplished airship and helicopter pilot into a bitter, mentally ill, angry, and suicidal would-be terrorist/anarchist, it is one of the final straws in his mental, professional, and personal unraveling.

Of course, Harris is also making a comparison here between Lander's alleged "activities" in Vietnam and the later atrocities and injustices visited upon the Palestinian and other Arab peoples before, and long after, the establishment of the state of Israel in 1947, up to and including the Black September King Hussein incident that gave the movement its name. Dahlia Iyad herself is described as a victim of this upheaval; she is born into this miserable chaos and is a direct product of it. Together, she and Lander make the oddest sort of "couple," both having survived the harshest possible human conditions as, respectively, POW camp survivor and refugee camp survivor, the only real difference being that Lander, it is slowly revealed, was mentally unstable from his earliest youth and decidedly "different," bordering on the schizophrenic to some degree, whereas Dahlia is a toughened, battle-hardened warrior who is chiefly concerned with her own survival and the aims of her people and the Black September movement in which she climbs (or battles) her way to a key position.

Harris's ultimate point here is that in all these conflicts, battles, "ethnic cleansings," holocausts, wars, and skirmishes throughout history, there are always atrocities and wrongs perpetrated by all sides; there is no true black and white in any of these situations, although of course it can also be argued that events such as the Jewish Holocaust, the massacre at My Lai, the "purging" of Stalin, the firebombing of Dresden in World War II, the atomic bombs dropped on Hiroshima and Nagasaki, or the Cambodian genocide orchestrated and carried out by the Khmer Rouge in the mid–1970s against thousands of their own people, bespeak true evil. If it is merely a matter of point of view, then of course the unspeakable terror plot later cooked up by Lander and Dahlia Iyad must be seen as a moral "necessity" for the Black September and overall Palestinian cause, and for Lander, as his justifiable (if deranged) "revenge" against the country that has disgraced and abandoned him.

To briefly summarize the remainder of the novel's plot, we can start with the events occurring in both novel and film immediately after the aforementioned "debriefing" at the terrorists' stronghold in Beirut. Unbeknownst to them, Mossad is already tipped off as to their whereabouts and in pursuit of the individuals who orchestrated the Munich massacre; accordingly, two van-loads of Mossad commandos arrive by cover of night and converge on the hideout. The two main commandos include the novel's hero, Major David Kabakov, and his assistant and comrade, Sgt. Robert Moshevsky. Dahlia has recorded a statement on cassette to be given to the authorities of the West after the terrorist plot has been carried out; the tape begs for brotherhood with their American brothers and states why this violence is necessary in light of the Palestinian-Israeli "situation," which she describes in the film version as being "unbearable for us." The speech in the novel differs from the film, but the message is ultimately the same: until the oppression stops, Americans will die by Arab hands for every Arab that dies by American hands.

The raid led by Kabakov and Moshevsky commences, and all the terrorists are murdered except a few, with Dahlia and Muhammad Fasil managing to escape unharmed. Kabakov will later live to regret his failure to kill Dahlia Iyad, finding her naked and terrified in the shower during the raid, and having no evidence or idea of her importance in the Black September movement; nor is he aware that hers is the voice on the tape recording, which he confiscates from the scene of the raid and plays for U.S. authorities a few days later. Most of the details of this raid, both in the novel and film, are clearly based on a particular Mossad post–Munich strike in Beirut on March 4, 1973, which was also part of the larger Israeli "Operation Wrath of God" (*Mivtzah Zaam Ha'el*), also known as "Operation Bayonet," a top-secret operation initiated after Munich by Prime Minister Golda Meir in the autumn of 1972, to track down and assassinate key Black September and Munich-involved agents throughout the world. The various strikes of this night, in both Beirut and Sidon, were carried out by Sayeret Matkal commandos and various Israeli support units. Several key Black September and PLO targets were eliminated in these strikes, including Youssef Al-Najjar, Kamal Adwan, and Kamal Nasser. Not only does Harris's version of the operational details of these raids in the novel conform quite closely to real events, but it is also entirely plausible that his Black September conspirators, Hafez Najeer, Abu Ali, and Muhammad Fasil, may have been based on the above three figures, or indeed others targeted or eliminated in the actual 1972 Mossad missions into Beirut.

Kabakov's mercy, he later confesses to Moshevsky, may be born of his age, experience, and perhaps his weariness of violence, war, and murder. His sparing of Dahlia's life may also be seen as commenting upon the possible differences in philosophy and mode of operation between Kabakov's side and the terrorists' side: whereas Dahlia has no mercy or time for weaklings or an agent losing his nerve, as has already been discussed, Kabakov still retains enough of his humanity to allow for some degree of mercy and compassion, although in this case it may become part of his own undoing. This may be the only chink in his armor, which otherwise, in both novel and film, is shown to be formidable indeed.

Dahlia returns to the United States, and specifically a suburban neighborhood near Lakehurst, New Jersey, where Michael Lander makes his home in accordance with his post-military career of flying the Goodyear blimps. Television network and ground crews have learned to trust and confide in Lander, who, in his role as airship pilot, is always dependable, if curmudgeonly and moody. It transpires that Dahlia had responded to Lander's contacting Black September by secret letter months before via a go-between, the ill-fated Brooklyn importer-exporter (and part-time black market smuggler) Benjamin Muzi.

Lander contacts the terrorist group because he requires a partner to help him realize his dream and act of ultimate revenge on the country and people that he now despises: a massive "suicide mission" explosive attack on the Super Bowl football game in New Orleans, utilizing the Goodyear blimp, thousands of pounds of C-4 (or the Asian equivalent thereof, which Hafez Najeer describes early in the novel as being even "more powerful" [Harris 8] than its Western-bloc equivalent) plastic explosives, and thousands of deadly "flechette" (from the French, meaning "little arrow") rifle dart projectiles, bound within the bomb itself and arranged, upon the bomb's ignition, to be projected outward in a predetermined arc toward their targets, thus causing even more casualties than even the explosives themselves.

Flechette rifle darts are actual projectiles (usually made of steel) with a sharp tip and vanes acting as flight stabilizers; they have been used in World War I and the Korean and Vietnam conflicts as primarily anti-personnel and even anti-vehicle weapons, often dropped from aircraft and capable of penetrating armor and helmets, and even reaching subsonic speeds in their descent upon their targets. The terrorists' plan is to hijack the blimp the morning of the Super Bowl, kill the crew, fly the blimp into the stadium, ignite the bomb, and release the flechette rifle darts, thus potentially killing or injuring upwards of 80,000 people. Lander cannot realize this mission by himself, since he has no access to the weapons and explosives he needs, so he is forced to seek an ally with such resources; therefore, Black September becomes his partner.

The bulk of the rest of the story involves Kabakov and Moshevsky's arrival in America, along with their hand-picked team of Mossad operatives, with Dahlia's warning tape in hand, in a desperate attempt to both warn the American authorities of the imminent threat of a major terrorist attack on U.S. soil, and also a race against time to uncover the plot, identify its players, and hopefully foil it or prevent it before whatever deadline Black September has in mind has passed with the deaths of many innocent civilian lives. In the process, the plastique C-4 explosives are successfully smuggled into America via a Turkish shipping freighter (in the unlikely form of "harmless" religious icon "Madonna" statuettes); Benjamin Muzi is gotten rid of by the terrorists via a plastique bomb hidden in his apartment refrigerator, also slightly injuring Kabakov and putting him temporarily out of action in hospital for several days, and leaving him vulnerable to a (thwarted) assassination attempt by Dahlia, disguised as a nurse (she manages almost to kill a guard, but not Kabakov, in a twist of fate); Muhammad Fasil comes to America to join Lander and Dahlia in testing a prototype of the bomb to be used in the attack, and possibly also to assist in the actual bombing, but is later detected in New Orleans by Mossad and the FBI and is apprehended and brought to justice for helping plan the Munich massacre, mirroring what actually happened, with several of the fugitive Munich operatives being tracked down and assassinated by Mossad. (One of these, Jamal Al Gashey, an alleged mastermind behind the events at Munich, is still at large, reportedly currently living somewhere in Africa with his wife and two daughters; another, Abou Daoud, is also still a fugitive to the present day, despite an outstanding German warrant for his arrest in effect for many years. Daoud was even reportedly living in the West Bank city of Ramalah for several years with Israel being fully aware of where he was living, but so far he has not been apprehended or assassinated.)

Although Lander contracts pneumonia and, by the eve of the Super Bowl, is almost unable to complete the mission, the earlier "test" of the bomb is a success, and it is now primed and ready to be hooked onto the Goodyear blimp (the "Aldrich" Company blimp in the novel, the Goodyear blimp in the film) as a *nacelle,* which resembles a small dinghy or boat-like module, and which he has been carefully constructing in his home garage over the past several winter months.

Lander recovers just enough to be able to fly the day of the mission, though exhausted and near-delirious. Dahlia injects him with stimulants to be able to fly and carry out the bombing and hijacking. Curiously, like the flechette rifle dart weapons used in the novel's Super Bowl attack, the *nacelle* has its roots in the French language from *nacele,* a suspended basket fixed beneath a hot-air balloon or dirigible, containing machinery and passengers; the English equivalent of the term is the common "gondola."

There is a small problem with their plan at the last minute: Lander has been replaced at this late stage, because of his questionable state of health, by another surrogate blimp pilot, Farley, whom Dahlia must now assassinate, early that morning at their hotel, to clear the way for Lander's piloting the airship as the last-minute replacement. This serious "problem" now out of the way, Lander takes command of the Goodyear blimp,

Dahlia goes to retrieve the bomb and truck stored in a garage nearby, and they rendezvous on the airfield and kill several of the crew or scare them away with their weapons. The two accomplices hook the bomb onto the undercarriage of the ship and hijack it; the airship takes off and heads toward the Super Bowl stadium, the match between the Washington Redskins and the Miami Dolphins already underway. As Harris comments in the novel, the authorities are completely stunned and taken by surprise, since one of the Secret Service agents who had earlier cased the Super Bowl stadium for any possible security weaknesses "never once looked up at the sky" (Harris 220).

The president of the United States is set to attend the day's football game; the Secret Service was sent along weeks earlier to make sure no threat to the president existed, but of course the president won't be dissuaded and ends up flying in for the Super Bowl and takes his place in a field-level VIP box section of the stadium, guarded as always by a detachment of Secret Service agents. Kabakov, Moshevsky, and FBI agent Sam Corley are alerted to the hijacking of the airship and race to the airfield to try to intercept the aircraft by helicopter; Moshevsky remains in the stadium as the ground agent in charge, and Kabakov and Corley take off in a helicopter in a desperate race to intercept the blimp, thus beginning perhaps one of the most unique and exciting (if, at least in the novel, sadly downbeat) final chase sequences in any action-suspense novel or film in modern memory.

In its way, the ending of both novel and film of *Black Sunday* rivals that of the famous car and subway train chase in the middle of the classic William Friedkin film *The French Connection* (1971), in which Gene Hackman's obsessive narcotics detective Popeye Doyle (modeled on the late, real-life New York City narcotics detective Eddie Egan, who appears in the film as Doyle's boss) pursues a heroin smuggler trying to escape in a subway car with hostages in tow, in a car underneath the elevated subway tracks for miles, causing mayhem and destruction along the way in his relentless pursuit; although that sequence is not the ending of that film (rather, it denotes a major turning point in the film and acts as a "pseudo"-ending or "primary" climax), both comment upon one another for sheer pulse-pounding excitement, and setting the bar in the 1970s that much higher for originality and innovation for the action/suspense film genre.

In one sense, Hackman's character Popeye Doyle mirrors Robert Shaw's portrayal of Major Kabakov in the film of *Black Sunday:* both are dedicated, driven, obsessive men who have one object in mind — to apprehend their criminal quarry at all costs. Of course, Michael Lander and

Dahlia Iyad are just as obsessive and ruthless in their own "cause," so one can interpret this as the driven pursuing the equally driven, only perhaps a different ideology or point of view (or level of madness and obsession) separating the two groups.

In purely literary terms, *Black Sunday,* although not Harris's best novel by far, often gets short shrift, or is unfairly overlooked compared to his later massive successes such as *The Silence of the Lambs.* While it can also be said that Harris has nothing, given that this was his first novel, to be ashamed of, it was in any case a critical and popular blockbuster right out of the box upon its release in 1975. Harris, as with *The Silence of the Lambs* and *Red Dragon,* gives us characters, dialogue, and action sequences, as well as psychological conflicts, that are often unforgettable. Major Kabakov is easily one of his most complex heroes, perhaps even more so than Clarice Starling in *The Silence of the Lambs,* and comes across as human and vulnerable as well as ruthless and on the verge of real violence. Dahlia Iyad makes for a fascinating villainess, reminding one of the description of one of the cyborglike, genetically engineered replicants, Pris, in the Ridley Scott film *Blade Runner* (1982), given by the police chief trying to capture and destroy her, when he remarks, "talk about beauty and the beast: she's both."

Dahlia Iyad most clearly represents the eternal concept of the banality of evil: if most of us met her on the street, we'd be entranced by her beauty and intelligence, but probably never guess her true, tough, battle-hardened, totally deadly identity. Robert Moshevsky, as Kabakov's muscular, strapping, and intimidating sidekick, impresses more with quiet brawn and menace in the novel, whereas in the film, the late actor Stephen Keats manages, as a more lanky, wiry, chain-smoking Moshevsky, to impress with passion, rage, and a clarity of purpose, even though he does not survive the film, as his character does in of the novel.

The character of Michael J. Lander gives the other, more celebrated Harris psychotic villains, including Dr. Hannibal Lecter and Francis Dolarhyde, a run for their money. Rather than merely being a post–Vietnam War exploitation movie cliché, Harris gives us flashbacks and detailed glimpses into Lander's troubled childhood, adolescence, and adulthood, including his experiences as a POW in Vietnam and events following his release. Like Dolarhyde, Lander is just short of a pitiable figure; he is deranged and set on violent revenge as a result of his troubled past, his experiences as a POW, divorce instituted by his humiliation and dressing-down after being forced to retire from the Navy, and, finally, divorce instituted by his wife Margaret, after she grew tired of his moodiness, instability, distance, apparent impotence, and even occasional flashes of minor violence. Unlike Hannibal "The Cannibal" Lecter, however, he is not motivated to violence because he enjoys it or derives a sense of power or superiority from it; unlike Dolarhyde, he is not trying to effect some kind of delusional, all-consuming spiritual transformation from his crimes.

Rather, Lander is hell-bent on revenge on the country he feels has deserted and destroyed him; as Bruce Dern, playing Lander in the film version, memorably remarks to Dahlia Iyad in a strangled, tortured voice (with dialogue not taken from the novel), "I was just going to give this whole sonofabitchin' COUNTRY something to remember me by!!" Lander is also a mechanically gifted obsessive genius, as demonstrated by his level of craftsmanship and attention to detail in constructing the bomb *nacelle* in his home garage over a period of months, and his delight at the awful results of the later testing of the bomb, wherein an innocent bystander is duped and "sacrificed" in an abandoned barn to see how well the arc of the rifle darts will conform to an expected pattern of dispersal upon detonation. The test goes horrifyingly well, and Lander almost ignores the dead victim, hapless coal company watchman, Harry Logan, on the barn floor:

> "Ground meat," Fasil said. They turned the slack body over and examined the back. Rapidly, they took pictures of the barn wall. It was bowed in and looked like a giant colander. Lander went inside the barn. Hundreds of small holes in the wall admitted points of light that freckled him as his camera clicked and clicked again. "Very successful," Fasil said [Harris 193].

Of course, in the film *Black Sunday,* Muhammad Fasil is not present for Lander's test, and does not initially protest as to its necessity (fearing an unnecessary risk is being taken) as he does in the novel, although he ultimately consents to it and his involvement in it. Also, in the film, Lander and Dahlia seem transfixed by the thousands of tiny holes in the wall of the barn the flechettes have made, the sunlight beaming through them as in some hellish anti-cathedral. Lander gloats over his "triumph" and exclaims that the darts have been dispersed in exactly the angle he intended, acting almost like some proud child in middle school who has gotten an A on his book report and is eager to share the good news.

This ghoulish scene, especially in the film, depicts Lander as even more of a psychopath than he is portrayed in the novel; the casual, detached way in which Lander and Dahlia examine the aftermath of the test, almost like a coroner going over some random dead body for a post-mortem, is casily one of the most chilling scenes in both novel and film, and brings readers back with a shock from any real sympathy they might have developed for any of these characters. Harris is reminding us that these really are murderers, terrorists, and they will stop at nothing to wreak their revenge; human life means nothing to them next to their causes.

There are many weaknesses in Harris's first novel, and several other critics have not been kind to *Black Sunday,* perhaps in some cases with good reason. Harris does demonstrate his gift for plot, action, and well-developed character histories, although some sections of *Black Sunday* tend to drag on between the more exciting action sequences, and some of his flashbacks seem to the modern reader somewhat extraneous, or unnecessarily extended, such as the long sequence in which Major Kabakov reminisces about his earlier years on the kibbutz in Tel Aviv and his and Moshevsky's involvement in the Six-Day War, and even earlier battles such as the "fight for Mitla Pass in 1956<in> (Harris 128) in the service of Israel, as well as his first meeting with later love interest Rachel Bauman, none of which makes it to John Frankenheimer's film. In the novel, at least, Harris's detailing of Kabakov's wounding in the Six-Day War and recovery in hospital, and his attending an all-night party with Rachel Bauman where a possible romance begins to bloom, serves to humanize Kabakov and show us both his sensitive side and his battle-toughened iron-clad exterior, as amply demonstrated by the remainder of both novel and film.

In the novel, all this history gives Kabakov some extra depth and makes his death at the finale all the more poignant, but since Robert Shaw's version of David Kabakov survives the film (thus sloughing off any sense of the martyr about him), it would only have slowed down the proceedings, and the decision to pare this backstory down was a wise one. Conversely, Harris's extensive delvings into Michael Lander's troubled past and psychological history don't seem to drag at all, and really provides the reader great insight into how and why Lander ends up the hell-bent terrorist he ultimately becomes. Harris would develop this type of character history in his later, much superior novels *Red Dragon* and *The Silence of the Lambs.*

Critic and scholar S.T. Joshi, in a fine, if brief, chapter on Thomas Harris in his *The Modern Weird Tale,* is fairly harsh on *Black Sunday,* and its overall standing in Harris's oeuvre: "*Black Sunday* (1975) is a mere potboiler with a preposterous premise — terrorists wish to blow up the Super Bowl from a blimp — and stereotypical characters" (Joshi 181). This condemnation of the novel is not entirely fair, and certainly it is possible that the film version of the book improves on the novel in all the above areas to a large degree. It is also possible that, in hindsight, Harris's tableau of characters seem to be somewhat stock, clichéd, or stereotypical, although at the time of writing, characters like Michael Lander had not had time to really become stereotypical. Only a few works at that time, filmic or otherwise, prominently featured troubled or psychotic Vietnam veterans, including the contemporaneous masterpiece that is Martin Scorsese's film *Taxi Driver* (1976), Hal Ashby's sensitive and devastating drama *Coming Home* (1978) (also starring Bruce Dern, once again as a wounded Vietnam veteran returning home to a less-than-receptive America), and of course Michael Cimino's somewhat muddled, confusing, and overwrought epic, *The Deer Hunter* (1978), and the much superior epic *Apocalypse Now* (1979), directed by Francis Ford Coppola. If Joshi were suggesting, however, that Harris's later characters in his next two novels (including the complex protagonists Will Graham and Clarice Starling) were less clichéd, more convincing, and possessed of markedly greater depth, his assessment would certainly be difficult to contest. As for *Black Sunday*'s plot being "preposterous," it certainly seems less so to a serious degree in light of more recent history, especially the events of September 11, 2001. The once-outlandish idea of a hijacked Goodyear blimp transformed into a deadly killing machine doesn't seem quite so outlandish after that particular aircraft-based terrorist attack, and goes some way toward vindicating Harris's decidedly somewhat "far-fetched" storyline.

Black Sunday, the novel, was a huge critical and commercial success, a near-blockbuster bestseller, and it didn't take long to be optioned by Hollywood for a major feature film, released in 1977 and directed by a master of psychologically complex, cerebral action and suspense films, John Frankenheimer. The director of such masterpieces as *The Manchurian Candidate*, *Seven Days in May*, the deeply disturbing but gripping weird fiction-meets-film-noir nightmare (and unlikely Rock Hudson vehicle) *Seconds*, and *The Train* must have jumped at the chance to direct a film of Thomas Harris's bestseller, the chance to marry his favorite themes of political conflict, suspense, and psychologically based unease and terror to a topical adventure story that would reflect the now concretized 1970s fears of terrorism, albeit (at that time) the kind of thing that happened in foreign countries. That such an unimaginable scenario as a terror plot to bomb the Super Bowl would ever occur on American *terra firma* was, in 1977, mainly an abstraction in America, and even the idea of Black September agents hijacking the Goodyear blimp to attack a football game and even the president of the United States was merely an entertainingly macabre notion for a suspense film, but nothing more than that.

Frankenheimer, producer Robert Evans, and Paramount Pictures assembled an able, talented cast and crew, and even hired brilliant composer John Williams, who was also about to make history along with George Lucas with the phenomenon that would soon become *Star Wars*, to write an equally brilliant, suspenseful, evocative, yet quite subtle score for the film. Robert Shaw portrays Major David Kabakov, Stephen Keats delivers a solid performance as Robert Moshevsky, and the durable Fritz Weaver portrays pragmatic FBI agent Sam Corley, lending him a touch more personality than is suggested by the novel, even with a small role to work with. Marte Keller, a relatively unknown actress at the time, portrays Dahlia Iyad with a strange sense of glee, although her German accent is a touch odd for the character and her diction somewhat awkward and uneven, throwing us off from the Dahlia we might have imagined from Harris's characterization. However, Keller is both attractive and even warmly (seductively might be a better term) intelligent, which does indeed fit the author's conception, so in these areas she makes a physically convincing Dahlia. When called upon to speak Arabic, as she does quite convincingly at the beginning of the film, discussing her control over Michael Lander with Najeer and her other Black September superiors, she is as three-dimensional a Dahlia Iyad as one could have hoped for.

The most spot-on casting in the film is doubtless Bruce Dern as Michael Lander; although he could be accused of playing Lander very much "over the top," he also manages, in several scenes, to bring the novel's Michael Lander to astonishing life; when he bellows through the chaos to his astonished blimp ground and TV camera crew as he is trying to hijack the airship and attach the deadly bomb nacelle, "The network wants this thing!" it is dialogue verbatim from Harris's novel, and Dern delivers it just as you would expect the character to do, making the seemingly absurd seem chillingly possible. Moments like this ring true more than most such scenes from novels adapted for films, and the crucial difference is always the screenwriting, the casting, the actors, and their delivery of the lines and feel for their character. Much of Harris's novel makes it to the big screen, and it is to the credit of everyone involved that Frankenheimer and his cast and crew get more right with *Black Sunday* than otherwise; while it is not one of Frankenheimer's finest films, it is certainly not his worst. Like Jonathan Demme's later, triumphant film version of Harris's *The Silence of the Lambs*, it remains a textbook example of the right way to adapt a novel for the big screen. Though the screenplay jettisons much of the backstory and character histories from the novel, *Black Sunday* retains the essence of the novel; key details and locations are changed, and some sequences missing, but overall the film is handled so deftly, and the cast is so convincing, that the viewer doesn't mind these deletions and changes.

The screenplay duties were shared by Ernest Lehman, Kenneth Ross, and Ivan Moffat, suggesting that a lot of care went into the collaboration to bring Harris's story to the big screen, given the general sense of deference in the film to Harris's characters and original storyline, somewhat altered as they might be.

Frankenheimer's film excises much of Harris's novel, especially the lengthy reminiscences of both Michael Lander and Major Kabakov, to make way for the primary buildup of suspense, character, and action leading up to the final hijacking scene and chase at the Super Bowl, which takes place in Miami at the Orange Bowl stadium; in the novel the climactic scenes take place in New Orleans prior to the completion of the Superdome stadium. Frankenheimer exploits the filming at the actual Super Bowl X in Miami to maximum effect, even going so far as having real-life Miami Dolphins owner Joe Robbie playing himself in the film and discussing security concerns with Kabakov on the field during the buildup to the final days before the Super Bowl.

Upon the film's initial release in April 1977, critical and public reactions were decidedly mixed, although the film was a huge commercial success, overall. *New York Times* film critic Vincent Canby apparently attended a New York City press screening (or special premiere screening) of *Black Sunday* on March 31, 1977, at the Loews State 1 theatre, and had some issues with the film, including the script, although in general he found it to be a cut above similar recent films such as the abysmal Charlton Heston and John Cassavetes vehicle *Two Minute Warning* (another suspense thriller set in a football stadium) and the formulaic, almost cardboard cut-out franchise film *Airport '77*:

> Why doesn't it work for me? I suspect it has to do with the constant awareness that the story is more important than anybody in it. The screenplay, written by Ernest Lehman, Kenneth Ross and Ivan Moffat, has the efficient manner of something hammered out — as they say in Hollywood — in a story conference. The characters don't motivate the drama in any real way. They are cut and shaped to fit it, and if the cast of "Black Sunday" were not so good, and if Mr. Frankenheimer were a less able director, the movie would be unendurably boring ... the film's best sequence has nothing to do with the action. It's the quiet recollection by Mr. Dern of his feelings when, as a prisoner of war, he received a snapshot of his wife and children and immediately realized that his wife had taken a lover [Canby 1–2].

Canby's comments are not entirely inaccurate, and this may be one of the most balanced and carefully considered reviews of his career. Although the cast is generally excellent, and the action sequences (including the final chase involving the Goodyear blimp) exciting, even given Frankenheimer's lamented shortcomings in terms of the limited budget he was apparently provided for special effects by the studio, the film, at times, either seems ultra-serious along with all the actors in a particular scene, such as the one in which Kabakov and Moshevsky play Dahlia's cassette recording to the authorities to convince them of the gravity of the situation, early in the proceedings, or the film seems just shy of self-parody or black comedy, as in the end of the scene just before Lander has to go check in at the Veterans Administration office and Dahlia shouts after him, "Michael, you won't have to kill them one at a time!" The scene comes off as almost laughable, unless this is exactly what Frankenheimer intended — for the viewer to react with a combination of horror and nervous laughter at such casual evil (and knowing of his penchant for such blackly comic moments in some of his earlier films, particularly the macabre *Seconds,* it likely was his intention); still, many of these scenes don't quite come off as well as they might have, and these are decidedly some of the film's major flaws. Canby is harsh in criticizing Marte Keller's portrayal of Dahlia Iyad, although if he had taken the time to read Harris's novel, he would have realized that "looking, as she does, as beautiful and healthy and uncomplicated as a California surfer" (Canby 2) is as it should be, since Harris describes Iyad in the novel as being extremely attractive and seductive. In fact, this is one of the major reasons she is the Black September agent chosen to go to America to respond to Michael Lander's request for assistance with his terror plot; it is no accident that they send their most beautiful, seductive operative to go seduce and, hopefully, control Lander to do their bidding. All this is only implied in the film, but is decidedly elucidated in much greater detail in Harris's novel, since the bulk of the early part of Lander and Dahlia's relationship didn't make it to the screenplay. Canby is quite right in his highlighting of Bruce Dern's wildly uneven but ultimately sensitive and moving portrayal of Michael Lander; when he is called upon to deliver a low-key line, such as the one Canby describes in his review regarding the snapshot he receives during his tenure as a POW, it becomes clear that Dern's Lander is the true center of gravity of the entire film (perhaps only matched by Robert Shaw's equally weighty and convincingly grave David Kabakov), and might have fallen apart entirely if not portrayed by an actor of such considerable skill.

It must be stated that Frankenheimer's film and its screenplay make significant alterations from the novel, although it is only necessary to detail the major changes in plot, characters, and settings here. It is to the director's credit that the film retains as much of the essence, dialogue, and major memorable action sequences from the novel as it does, even though many things have been modified, changed to different locales, or excised entirely. The most notable one is the fact that David Kabakov survives the film, while his sidekick, Moshevsky, is murdered by Dahlia halfway through, the latter taking the place of the hapless policeman at the hospital in the novel (although the policeman somehow survives the attack in the book). Letting Kabakov live allows Robert Shaw room to transform the character into a tough-as-nails hero, instead of the sadly tragic figure of the novel, who dies stopping the airship plot, along with Sam Corley and the helicopter pilot. Excising Kabakov's love interest (the not especially convincing character Rachel Bauman, so crucial in the novel as a supporting character) also allows the focus to remain on the "good guy" triumvirate of Kabakov, Moshevsky, and Corley, and overall these were all wise decisions.

Many of the settings in the film are switched from east coast to west coast, and Lander's home is not near Lakehurst, New Jersey, nor is any of the action involving smuggler-importer Benjamin Muzi set in Brooklyn or Manhattan, as in the novel. In fact,

Muzi is not even killed by a bomb hidden in his refrigerator, as in the novel, but instead survives, only to be threatened for information with a gun in his mouth by Kabakov in his office late in the film, where he is instructed, as Kabakov instructs another interrogatee in Miami in the same manner during the final chapters of the novel, "Are you ready to cooperate? Blink for yes, die for no."

Frankenheimer begins the film in Beirut, switches to Washington, D.C., and then concentrates the bulk of the Lander-Dahlia action to the West Coast — Los Angeles and environs. Probably more for opportunistic reasons than any other, the Super Bowl setting is transferred from New Orleans to Miami and the Orange Bowl Stadium (now called Miami Dolphins Stadium), along with some more of the final action, including the crucial spotting and chase of Muhammad Fasil. In the novel, Fasil meets briefly with Dahlia Iyad in Florida to discuss how the terror plot is proceeding, although Fasil is not spotted until very near the end in New Orleans, when he unwisely shows up at the helicopter airfield and is captured by Kabakov and Corley, to be brought back to Israel by Moshevsky to answer for his role in the Munich massacre. In the film, Fasil ends up being spotted during a stakeout by Kabakov, Corley, and Moshevsky in Miami, and is gunned down dead on the beach, never to be brought to justice, although at least taken out of the action as far as the Super Bowl plot is concerned.

One sequence in Harris's novel that one might have wished Franken-heimer to include in the film takes place late in the book, involving Michael Lander's ex-wife, Margaret, as she shows up unannounced at his home in New Jersey, seeking to collect some personal effects that Lander has appar-ently stored away for her nearby. Little does she know how far gone Lan-der is by this time (he is terrified that she will look in his garage and figure out what he has been up to), and the scene in the novel is filled with ten-sion and a real air of sadness that is never truly touched upon in the film. Even as the reader thinks that Lander and his ex-wife have come to some kind of understanding or reconciliation, the "real" Lander asserts himself and he sends Margaret off with free tickets to the Super Bowl for her and her new husband; Harris scores a bitter twist of events here, and it might have added to the depths of Lander's complex character in the film; but probably for time and continuity considerations, it was never filmed or considered for inclusion in the screenplay.

There are several other sequences from the novel that aren't included in the film, or vice versa, but the major ones have been detailed above. Some of the more bizarre features in the screenplay are those that are totally original to the film, such as the scene that displays Lander and Dahlia's interception and receipt of the plastic explosives shipment via power boat at night, wherein they evade a Coast Guard cutter, as in the novel (though of course in the novel this is all set in New York and New Jersey waters). Whereas in the novel it is Benjamin Muzi who is the next target to be eliminated by Fasil in the apartment bombing, because he is a liability and knows too much of their plot, in the film Lander suddenly shows up dis-guised as a Bell Telephone repairman the next day when the freighter is docked, with Kabakov, Corley and company on board questioning the Japanese captain and crew; Lander whistles away and goes unnoticed as he installs a plastique phone-receiver implanted bomb aimed at killing Muzi, the captain, or Kabakov and Moshevsky if they happen to pick up the phone receiver, or perhaps it is aimed at merely eliminating the ship's captain. In any case, this is quite a twist from the killing of Muzi in the early sections of the novel, although it is not entirely implausible, since nobody involved knows who Lander is or what he looks like at this stage of the story; even so, it is not entirely believable. This entire sequence in the film may, however, take on greater significance (and even somewhat more believability) considering that both sides in the terror "wars" follow-ing the Munich massacre, Mossad and the various Arab terrorist groups, had actually utilized such phone-based bombs in various strikes and mis-sions, the most infamous one being the attempted assassination of Dr.

Mahmoud Hamshari, the PLO representative to France (and believed to be a key Black September leader in France), who was tracked down in Paris by Mossad agents on December 8, 1972.

An undercover Mossad agent managed to lure him from his apartment, allowing another team of agents to install a bomb underneath a desk telephone, to be triggered by telephone call and detonated once it had been confirmed that Hamshari had picked up the phone receiver himself. Hamshari didn't die immediately in the ensuing blast, but he did a few weeks later of injuries sustained in the blast. Hamshari was one of the first allegedly Munich-involved Black September members to be assassinated and tracked down by Mossad as part of "Operation Wrath of God." In light of these events, and considering the sophisticated (for that era, at least) technology utilized at the time by Mossad, this scene involving Lander in the film of *Black Sunday* becomes somewhat less absurd, even though in reality any worker showing up unscheduled to an FBI-staked-out foreign freighter would likely be fully screened before he was even allowed near the site. The changes of locale and characters in this scene may not be as plausible as Muzi's Brooklyn apartment bomb assassination in the novel, but it makes for a tighter, more exciting film, which was clearly the aim of the screenwriters for this sequence. As film producer Dino De Laurentiis has recently explained in relation to a more current project written by Thomas Harris as simultaneously both a novel *and* film, *Hannibal Rising* (2007), another sequel to both The *Silence of the Lambs* and *Hannibal,* "Harris had to streamline his script ... because film plots must move faster than books" (Jacobson B4). Although Harris did not write the screenplay for *Black Sunday,* his writing, characters, and influence still permeate the film and lend it a certain air of gritty authenticity, and along with the outstanding cast and crew that Frankenheimer had to work with for his film, it managed to make a minor suspense-action classic out of a satisfactory, if flawed, source novel, and for a film that was released in 1977, *Black Sunday* manages to hold up, despite certain reservations and weaknesses, as a film that continues to entertain and compel modern audiences in a way that few modern suspense films have, sadly, managed to accomplish in the past thirty years.

Although both *Black Sunday,* the Thomas Harris novel, and *Black Sunday,* the John Frankenheimer film, both suffer to some degree by seeming somewhat dated, and retain some serious flaws and weaknesses, they are both, in the final analysis, works which continue to retain interest for modern readers and film audiences in search of intelligent, gripping and politically relevant suspense entertainment. Also, both works continue to deliver in these areas marvelously, where so many of their contemporary competitors (and even more modern works of political or psychological suspense) seem to fall short. It is still difficult for modern audiences to imagine how a work like *Black Sunday* could, so many years ago, have almost predicted (or, at least, seriously foreshadowed) the major twenty-first-century terrorist attacks perpetrated on United States soil, particularly of course the two attacks on the World Trade Center, and specifically, September 11, 2001. It is startling to realize that the allegedly "outlandish" and far-fetched plot posited by Thomas Harris's classic novel was actually, to a frighteningly accurate degree, prescient of events to come.

Whether it is an airship piloted by a deranged former Navy pilot and his Black September terrorist compatriot, or a group of real-life al-Qaida-funded and trained fanatic *fedayeen* terror cell members who learned to pilot aircraft on U.S. soil and in U.S. flight training schools and were intent on crashing jet airliners into major U.S. targets and killing thousands of innocent people in the process, the effect is the same, in both fiction and reality. These harsh, terrifying, irrefutable, and even surreal facts will continue to sustain the reputation, value, and legacy of both Thomas Harris's novel and its cinematic equivalent as more than mere reading entertainment, or more than just a gripping two hours spent at the movies or watching a DVD, and confirm *Black Sunday* as a relevant, important classic of the genre, with political implications and layers of relevance whose shock waves will be felt, especially in light of the modern terrorist "nightmare" that we all find ourselves in, and reacting to, on a daily basis, for many years to come.

Works Consulted

Black, Ian, and Morris, Benny. *Israel's Secret Wars: A History of Israel's Intelligence Services.* New York: Grove Press, 1991.

Black Sunday, dir. John Frankenheimer. DVD. Paramount Pictures, 2003. Original theatrical release: Paramount Pictures, 1976.)

Blade Runner, dir. Ridley Scott. DVD. Warner Brothers, 1999. [Original theatrical release: Warner Brothers, 1982.]

Bregman, Ahron. *Israel's Wars: A History since 1947.* London: Routledge, 2002.

Canby, Vincent. "Screen: 'Terror over the Super Bowl.'" *New York Times,* 1 April 1977. http://movies2.nytimes.com/mem/movies/review.html?_r=1&title1=&title2=Black+Sunday. Accessed 1 Jan. 2007.

Cooley, John K. *Black September Green March: The Story of the Palestinian Arabs.* London: Frank Cass and Co., 1973.

Harris, Thomas. *Black Sunday.* New York: G.P. Putnam's Sons, 1975.

Iyad, Abu, with Rouleau, Eric. *My Home, My Land: A Narrative of the Palestinian Struggle.* Trans. Linda Butler Koseoglu. New York: Times Books, 1981.

Jacobson, Aileen. "Talk about Cannibalized Stories." *Newsday,* 5 Feb. 2007, B4.

Jonas, George. *Vengeance: The True Story of an Israeli Counter-Terrorist Strike Team.* New York: Simon and Schuster, 2005.

Joshi, S.T. *The Modern Weird Tale.* Jefferson, NC: McFarland and Co., 2001.

Klein, Aaron J. *Striking Back: The 1972 Munich Olympics Massacre and Israel's Deadly Response.* New York: Random House, 2005.

One Day in September, dir. Kevin Macdonald. DVD. Sony Pictures Classics, 1999.

Ostrovsky, Victor. *By Way of Deception: The Making and Unmaking of a Mossad Officer.* New York: St. Martin's Press, 1990.

Reeve, Simon. *One Day in September: The Story of the 1972 Munich Olympics Massacre.* London: Faber and Faber, 2000.

"Significant Terrorist Incidents 1961–2003: A Brief Chronology." *U.S. Department of State: Bureau of Public Affairs, Office of the Historian* (March 2004). http://www.state.gov/r/pa/ho/pubs/fs/5902.htm. Accessed 10 Jan. 2007.

Thomas, Gordon. *Gideon's Spies: The Secret History of the Mossad.* New York: Thomas Dunne/St. Martin's Press, 1999.

Vaeth, J. Gordon. *They Sailed the Skies: U.S. Navy Balloons and the Airship Program.* Annapolis, MD: Naval Institute Press, 2005.

Walker, John (ed.). *Halliwell's Filmgoer's and Video Viewer's Companion.* 11th ed. New York: HarperPerennial, 1995.

Yaari, Ehud. *Strike Terror: The Story of Fatah.* New York: Sabra Books, 1970.

12

Morbidity of the Soul

An Appreciation of Hannibal

BENJAMIN SZUMSKYJ

When first released, six years after its proposed deadline, Thomas Harris's *Hannibal* (1999) was one of the most highly anticipated sequels in twentieth century literature. However, much to the dismay of loyal readers — from book reviewers to Amazon.com customers — *Hannibal* did not live up to their expectations and some critics had no qualms in publicly defaming the novel. However, in reading much of the commentary directed toward the novel, there seems to be little constructive criticism on *Hannibal*. Thankfully, there have been some critics in the sea of verbal abuse, who have rightly stood their ground and highlighted the weaknesses *and* strengths of the novel, of which there are many of the latter, (King 1999, O'Brien 2001, Sexton 2001). While *Hannibal*, like all novels, possessed its flaws — the treatment of Jack Crawford, the actions of Margot Verger, the actual writing of Starling's fascinating transition — it is not, *by far*, the failure many have painted the novel as being. *Hannibal* contains well crafted characterization, an excellent handling of history and psychology, as well as an appropriately realistic — in the sense of not breaching supernaturalism — series of climaxes.

On the writings of Thomas Harris, critic and lecturer Brian Moon comments that the "genre itself can be seen as a response to (or reflection of) the decline of social normativity. Harris' work is interesting in that regard, because it combines elements of traditional modernist detection (with its faith in clues and "the motive") with a more "postmodern" focus on the pathology of everyday life, and the failure of rational detection" (e-mail, June 22, 2006). Though unusual, there are some authors in the sub-genre of "psychological horror," that have consciously crafted their villains — usually serial killers — to appear more than once, in hope to differentiate their work from the countless novels that come out each year, where a hunted villain is confronted and either captured or killed within the space of a few hundred pages. Those authors bold enough to have used their serial killer creations more than once include Bloch's Norman Bates, Highsmith's Tom Ripley and several others from both the realms of cinema and the written word.

The point to be made here is that there seems to have been some dis-approval amongst readers (as attested at Amazon.com) of making Lecter the star of the novel and having him share the spotlight equally with Clarice Starling. This is odd as, Harris assured us that by the end of *The Silence of the Lambs* (1988), we would not be reading any sequel that would again have Lecter imprisoned, for he escaped from custody (which, I am certain, was influenced by Lord Dunsany's "Near the Back of Beyond"). As such, any interaction between Lecter and Starling in *Hannibal* had to be, for the most part, at a distance until the two met and at which point, there would likely be two endings — Starling would die, taking down Lecter in the process, or Lecter would be brought down by Starling. I doubt any-one envisioned an ending to *Hannibal* in which Lecter would be incar-cerated.

It would be exhaustive to cite the many ways in which Harris creates a bridge between history and the present by way of the arts and sciences throughout *Hannibal*, but for the sake of space, I shall address the two strongest recreations of supreme interest; Rinaldo Pazzi and Lecter's genealogic past.

Rinaldo Pazzi is *Hannibal*'s most interesting new creations, a char-acter that draws sympathy from his audience but at the same time, repre-sents an unconscious corruption of actions where intentions are initially good. At the Palazzo Vecchio, Pazzi "looked up at the windows where his own forebear came to grief ... thrown naked with a noose around his neck, to die writhing and spinning against the rough wall" (111). Under the guise of Dr. Fell (face transplants are now a reality as attested by the operation conducted on a 38-year-old French patient from Valenciennes), Lecter notes this merely from a resemblance "from the Della Robbia rondels" in Pazzi's family chapel (126). Whereas the detectives of many authors are often commonplace, Harris interestingly has his chief investigator directly

connected to the history of his city, a manifestation and constant reminder
of the past. He is neither foreign to the land nor an everyday citizen; he
is, through history, apart of its very foundations. That Harris has Lecter
kill Pazzi in a similar manner to his forebear means the author beautifully
repeats — establishing a literary bridge — history, so to enforce its importance in our contemporary world and comment that our actions and fates
are often guided by the past. The scene is worth citing for its visual impact:

> "*Arrivederci, Commendatore.*"
>   Flash of the Harpy up Pazzi's front, another swipe severed his attachment
> to the dolly and he was tilting, tipped over the railing trailing the orange
> cord, ground coming up in a rush, mouth free to scream, and inside the
> salon, the floor polisher rushed across the floor and slammed to a stop
> against the railing, Pazzi jerked head-up, his neck broke and his bowels fell
> out [202–203].

Much has been written about the "Pazzi Conspiracy." Niccolo Machiavelli, in *History of Florence and of the Affairs of Italy*, writes that once
Francesco de Pazzi's involvement in the attempt to assassinate Lorenzo
and Giuliano de' Medici was made public, his bloody fate was sealed:

> In the meantime the whole city was roused to arms, and Lorenzo de'
> Medici, accompanied by a numerous escort, returned to his house. The
> palace was recovered from its assailants, all of whom were either slain or
> made prisoners. The name of the Medici echoed everywhere, and portions
> of dead bodies were seen borne on spears and scattered through the streets;
> while everyone was transported with rage against the Pazzi, and pursued
> them with relentless cruelty. The people took possession of their houses, and
> Francesco [de Pazzi], naked as they found him, was led to the palace
> [Palazzo Vecchio, originally called the Palazzo della Signoria], and hanged
> beside the archbishop [Francesco Salviati] and the rest. He could not be
> induced, by any injurious words or deeds, to utter a syllable, but regarding
> those around with a steady look, he silently sighed [Chapter 52].

It is interesting that some commentators have classified Pazzi as a villain in the novel. While Margot Verger's role as a true villain could be
debated, Pazzi comes across as a flawed hero, trying to redeem a historic
stigma and ensure the welfare of his beloved wife. His methods may not
be seen as ethical, but they are productive and are aligned with the greater
good. The true villain of *Hannibal* is Mason Verger, clearly filling the role
that Francis Dolarhyde and Jame Gumb did in Harris's previous novels.
His upbringing, in which he is sexual abused and as a result reenacts those
same acts of abuse on others (in particular his sister Margot), allows his
character to be paralleled with the aforementioned monsters. However,
while some readers and critics have expressed sympathy toward Dolarhyde

and Gumb, none could be given to Verger who, unlike his counterparts, can psychologically stop himself. Verger continues his sadism because he *wants to.* It's not because of a Blake-induced vision or to make a suit out of women's skins — Verger simply likes being cruel and torturing people for the mere fun of it. He is not wrestling demons, nor seeking redemption. He feels he has been given redemption by Christ and as such, no matter what evil he commits, he will be forgiven.

Genealogically, Lecter is equally as interesting. While there had been subtle insights in *The Silence of the Lambs,* we are told in *Hannibal* that according to fragmentary family records (therefore instantly alluding to incomplete and possibly exaggeratory), that "he was descended from a certain Giuliano Bevisangue, a fearsome twelfth-century figure in Tuscany, and from the Machiavelli as well as Visconti" (136). Historically, Bevisangue (*bevere*—"to drink," *sangue*—"blood") is a cryptic figure, and I am uncertain as to whether Harris meant the warlord Guido Bevisangue, as it is difficult to find any matches for a "Giuliano" and this may be a fictional creation. Later, Lecter "sent catalogs of the most interesting art shows to his cousin, the great painter Balthus, in France" (287). Balthazar Klossowski (1908–2001) was an "anti-modern" artist, whose subject matter was often young exotic women. Whether we are to take this as truth, or rather, an amusing self-belief by Lecter, we may never know.

Most controversial is Lecter's shared history with his sister, Mischa. In "1944 after the Eastern Front collapsed" (255), a six-year-old Lecter watches a group of deserters feasting upon a small deer, little substance during the harsh winter. A few days later, searching for food, they find both Lecter and his sister and choose the latter because she is slightly larger. Though he tried to free her, it proved futile as he later heard the fall of the axe and realized that the deserters had found their much desired meal. According to Sexton, Harris may have been influenced by a story narrated by "Ukrainian murderer Andrei Chikatilo, whose crimes were made public in 1992. Chikatilo claim to have been influenced in his crimes by the fact that his elder brother had been kidnapped and killed by a gang of the cannibals who roamed the Ukraine in the 1930's. However, no proof of this elder brother's existence has been found and Chikatilo was not a witness to trust" (80). Today, there is much debate regarding acts of cannibalism during World War II, determining whether sources — primary and secondary — are true, false, probable, or very rare. A confronting article published by *Anthropology of East Europe Review* (1995) interviewed survivors of the blockade at Leningrad (now St. Petersburg). The privatization of Soviet history has inevitably cast uncertainty over the amount of cannibalistic claims, in some cases, survivors have "adopted" stories told to them as if to ensure they are remembered and instilled as truth. Dickinson notes that "discussion of mental illness and cannibalism served to expand the images of life during the Blockade to include the sordid and the cruel. However, they possess an added narrative shock value, and were usually utilized by survivors in ways which maximized this value. Details of individual encounters with crazy people, or with the evidence of cannibalism, even if reported second-hand, were incorporated into narratives in ways which communicated the shock and fear which the narrator experienced *personally*" (Dickinson). The following two quotes are of passing interest. The first is from a survivor, seven years old at the time, who encountered a partially devoured body. The second, tells the story of a woman recounting a story, only to adopt it as her own as if to instill its authenticity:

> I tripped on something, you know, fell and when I started to get up, I saw what I had tripped on. It was a corpse of a small child and all the meat was cut off him. You know, the soft parts like the cheeks, buttocks, well those parts, you know, the thighs. When I saw that, and understood what it meant, that it wasn't chewed on by rats or dogs, you know it was so horrible. I had such a shock that I even think I didn't even go get bread that day [Dickinson].

In another instance, a woman told me the story of her colleague, who as a boy was lured into an apartment with promises of porridge, only to barely escape alive when he found a room of butchered corpses behind a closed door. In retelling his story, the narrator started with the words: "he said," and then continued the story in the first person, "The man took *me* to an apartment. *I* waited for him to bring the kasha...." She thereby incorporated another's words into her own narrative while maintaining the emotional immediacy and authoritative power of first person discourse" [Dickinson].

The claims of cannibalism have been explored in Harrison E. Salisbury's *The 900 Days: The Siege of Leningrad* (1985), as have the stories of Japanese soldiers who committed cannibalism during World War II. The point to be made here is that several commentators felt that Harris's choice to give Lecter a more definitive history weakened the mystique of the character and was a somewhat superficial explanation as to how this man was *made* evil. Years later, when Harris did write about the childhood in *Hannibal Rising* (2006), it may have not been as fantastical as some may have wanted, but does help to understand both how and why Lecter become a passionate serial killer.

While the approach to developing villains in contemporary literature has been to have the reader both live and understand their villainous nature, few authors competently succeed in constructing an original, or at best, alternative exploration outside the conventional or cliché. In *Hannibal* however, Harris did something very different. He implanted into his character of Hannibal Lecter *ars memoriae*, more specifically, the memory palace. Few authors have applied the art of memory to their fiction. King borrowed the concept from Harris in *Dreamcatcher* (2001), as did Preston and Child in their Dr. Pendergast series, to name a rare few. Similarly, Protosevich's Carl Stargher from *The Cell* is a schizophrenic with Whalen's Infraction, a woman killer who lives in a world he created in his head. That Dr. Lecter has a "memory palace he has maintained since youth" (136), shows the reader Harris's genius in applying a fascinating — and haunting — depth to his serial killer, entrenching Lecter with a psychological depth few characters in literature possess. In *Hannibal* he writes that

> The memory palace was a mnemonic system well known to ancient scholars and much information was preserved in them through the Dark Ages while Vandals burned the books. Like scholars before him, Dr. Lecter stories an enormous amount of information keyed to objects in his thousand rooms, but unlike the ancients, Dr. Lecter has a second purpose for his palace; sometimes he lives there [252].

Harris' research is evident, as he cites that the "palace is built according to the rules discovered by Simonides of Ceos and elaborated by Cicero four hundred years later" (252). Yate's *The Art of Memory* (1966) discusses these philosophers and is cited by Harris in his acknowledgments, as is Spence's *The Memory Palace of Matteo Ricci* (1985). It is from these two works, we can understand what the "memory palace" is. Yates recounts the legendary story of its origins, first narrated by Cicero in *De oratore* and *De partitione oratoria*:

> At a banquet given by a nobleman of Thessaly named Scopas, the poet Simonides of Ceos chanted a lyric poem in honour of his host but including a passage in praise of Castor and Pollux. Scopas meanly told the poet that he would only pay him half the sum agreed upon for the panegyric and that he must obtain the balance from the twin gods to whom he had devoted half the poem. A little later, a message was brought in to Simonides that two young men were waiting outside who wished to see him. He rose from the banquet and went out but could find no one. During his absence the roof of the banqueting hall fell in, crushing Scopas and all the guests to death beneath the ruins; the corpses were so mangled that the relatives who came to take them away for burial were unable to identify them. But Simonides remembered the

places at which they had been sitting at the table and was therefore able to indicate to the relatives which were their dead. The invisible callers, Castor and Pollux, had handsomely paid for their share in the panegyric by drawing Simonides away from the banquet just before the crash. And this experience suggested to the poet the principles of the art of memory of which he is said to have been the inventor. Noting that it was through his memory of the places at which the guests had been sitting that he had been able to identify the bodies, he realised that orderly arrangement is essential for good memory [17].

An additional explanation is supplied by Ricci's biographer, Spence:

> In summarizing this memory system [to the Chinese, Ricci] explained that these palaces, pavilions, divans were mental structures to be kept in one's head, not solid objects to be literally constructed out of "real" materials. Ricci suggested that there were three main options for such memory locations. First, they could be drawn from reality — that is, from buildings that one had been in or from objects that one had seen with one's own eyes and recalled in one's memory. Secondly, they could be totally fictive, products of the imagination conjured up in any shape or size. Or third, they could be half real and half fictive, as in the case of a building one knew well and through the back wall of which one broke an imaginary door as a shortcut to new spaces, or in the middle of which one created a mental staircase that would lead one up to higher floors that had not existed before.
>
> The real purpose of all these mental constructs was to provide storage spaces for the myriad concepts that make up the sum of our human knowledge. To everything that we wish to remember, wrote Ricci, we should give an image; and to every one of these images we should assign a position where it can repose peacefully until we are ready to reclaim it by an act of memory. Since this entire memory system can work only if the images stay in the assigned positions and if we can instantly remember where we stored them, obviously it would seem easiest to rely on real locations which we know so well that we cannot ever forget them. But that would be a mistake, thought Ricci. for it is by expanding the number of locations and the corresponding number of images that can be stored in them that we increase and strengthen our memory. Therefore the Chinese should struggle with the difficult task of creating fictive places, or mixing the fictive with the real, fixing them permanently in their minds by constant practice and review so that at last the fictive spaces become "as if real, and can never be erased" [1–2].

Lecter's memory palace is visited several times throughout the novel and is effectively used as a means to mentally escape annoyance (251) and at one point, torture (404), in addition to being added to ("The sight of Clarice Starling running through the falling leaves on the forest path was well established now in the memory palace" (288). By applying *ars memoriae* to Lecter, Harris empowers the character with a trait rarely seen in serial killers, let alone villains as a whole, so to make him intellectually attractive and in a frightening manner, free of a uncontrollably psychotic nature so to differentiate him from thousands of others killers, real and fictional alike.

Astrophysicist Stephen Hawking's *A Brief History of Time* (1988, rev. 1996) is another fascinating entry into *Hannibal*, as Hawking's work requires a truly mathematical mind to understand his theory of time. In Chapter 73 of *Hannibal*, Harris quotes Hawking's words, as Lecter watches a documentary adapted from the best-selling book (directed by Errol Morris in 1991), contemplating the possibility that his deceased sister "Mischa, eaten, to be whole again" (363) in accordance to Hawking's theory. Hawking states that through the discovery of the speed of light, the theory of relativity destroyed the belief in absolute time. In order to unify gravity with that of quantum physics, "imaginary time" was introduced, interchangeable from directions (with)in space (151). Hawking's commentary, from *A Brief History of Time* entitled "The Arrow of Time," continues the debate:

> The laws of science do not distinguish between the past and the future. More precisely, as explained earlier, the laws of science are unchanged under the combination of operations (or symmetries) known as C, P, and T. (C means changing particles for antiparticles. P means taking the mirror image, so left and right are interchanged. And T means reversing the direction of motion of all particles: in effect, running the motion backward.) The laws of science that govern the behavior of matter under all normal situations are unchanged under the combination of the two operations C and P on their own....
>
> If the laws of science are unchanged by the combination of operations C and P, and also by the combination C, P, and T, they must also be unchanged under the operation T alone. Yet there is a big difference between the forward and backward directions of real time in ordinary life. Imagine a cup of water falling off a table and breaking into pieces on the floor. If you take a film of this, you can easily tell whether it is being run forward or backward. If you run it backward you will see the pieces suddenly gather themselves together off the floor and jump back to form a whole cup on the table. You can tell that the film is being run backward because this kind of behavior is never observed in ordinary life.... [152].

This is because it is prohibited by the second law of thermodynamics. As such, it becomes apparent what Lecter is contemplating, clarified in a discussion with Starling near the novel's end:

> They talked about teacups and time, and the rule of disorder.
> "And so I came to believe," Dr. Lecter was saying, "that there had to be a place in the world for Mischa, a prime place vacated for her, and I came to think, Clarice, that the best place in the world was yours" [476].

Adopting Hawkins's theory of time to dissect *Hannibal,* becomes an interesting excursion. If the laws of science do not distinguish between the past and the future, the transition from Mischa (the past) into Starling (the future), so to place Starling in the past and Mischa in the future, becomes apparent. The forthcoming change Lecter has been preparing from the beginning (C), taking the mirror image (P): "that delicious vision is what you are" (466), and having Lecter reversing the direction of motion (Starling becoming a memory while Mischa becomes the present), is, a rather unique concept within a novel. Whether Lecter will achieve this goal will yet to be seen, but as it is written, "We can only learn so much and live" (484).

Harris's ending for his much loved Clarice Starling, whose role in *The Silence of the Lambs* redefined a genre and influenced a future of female characters, was for many, a betrayal of the character and all that she had stood for. In an almost dreamlike sequence, hypnotized, drugged and semi-willingly to follow her mentor, Starling becomes Lecter's friend, lover, and pending on interpretation, *pseudo*sister. Starling's fall from grace — defined by her inability to truly gain closure from her father's death, her failed loved life with John Brigham, and both her disapproval with the Federal Bureau of Investigation — could easily be mirrored with that of any human being. It is somewhat perplexing that readers would expect Starling to "live happily ever after," as if Harris's work were a fairy tale of some sort. To the well read individual, one could cite numerous heroic figures from literature whose fate — determined by god or human alike — did not forebode well. History is no different, save the occasional grace of dying as a result of old age. Even so, Starling deserved a fate fitting not only to her character but one that her creator could willingly construct. Harris so loved his creation of Clarice Starling, he seemingly was unable to kill her and wanted her to live, though not through a stereotypical ending of defeating Lecter. He worked hard to create a fate where she could both lived *and* go through a metamorphosis, into a new state of being. Harris succeeded.

It is surprising that readers of *Hannibal* were not aware that being an unconsciously Gothic novel (ripe with gothic imagery and influences), the union of Starling and Lecter by the novels end, was an inevitable one. Those well read in the realm of gothic literature, should have expected such a climax. More so, this ending was prophesied as far back at *Red Dragon* (1981) when Dr. Lecter, imprisoned and being interviewed by Will Graham, utters, "The reason you caught me is that we're *just alike*" (67). Almost all the characters who have tried to psychologically understand Lecter — and to some degree, adopt his worldview — have met an untimely death or what could be called, *martyrdom*. As Daniel O'Brien, author of *The Hannibal Files* (2001) has pointed out, when reading *Red Dragon*:

I was surprised how harshly Harris treats Will Graham. We have a burnt-out investigator — with severe physical and mental scars — who risks every-thing — his family, his sanity, his life — to re-enter a dark world and track down a murderer. I'm intrigued by the idea that, far from being redeemed and rewarded for his selfless act, Graham suffers horrible punishment. What is Harris trying to say about the nature of heroism? Why does he not give Graham at least a glimmer of hope? The handful of references in *The Silence of the Lambs* confirms Graham's damnation. When Hannibal Lecter claims that Graham is denying his true nature, is Harris suggesting that Graham damns himself? [E-mail, July 2005].

In both myth and history, heroes often become martyrs. From the myth of Hercules to the historical Jesus, the later whom Starling is meant to be briefly paralleled with — hence the "sacrifice" — heroes don't always win and in some cases, for the greater good.

Regardless, the seed of Starling's fate was sown in *The Silence of the Lambs,* through the interviews conducted by the young FBI agent with Lecter, for she willingly opened herself up to him and in return, allowed the devilish psychiatrist to consciously shape the decisions in her life, pres-ent and future. Starling's fall from grace, not by choice but by forces she could never control, should not be disfavored by the reader. It would be naïve to not only desire the character remain the same, but for her to retain the innocent, wet-behind-the-ears nature that made the character famous in *The Silence of the Lambs.*

Starling's fate is a stroke of genius on the decision of the author. Much has been interpreted that Harris had grown a hate for Clarice, but in reality, Clarice's path was realistic; suffocation within an organiza-tion, unlucky in love, faced with favoritism, nepotism, egotism and illog-ical politics. More so, that Clarice became Lecter's partner, brings her through to a psychological full circle where, for the first time in all her life, she is content and does not have to worry about all that. Though drugged and hypnotized, she may be disorientated, but beneath the sur-face her worldview, her hatreds, and her soul are the same. The world is divided into the civil and the barbaric, one of two natures, but it could be commented that it has come to the point in which the civilized has incorporated, accepted and utilized the nature of the barbaric, while the barbarians have remained true to their nature. Essentially, their natures are eerily comparable. Clarice and Hannibal are far more honest with themselves then readers give them credit for. As Harris discussion of *Han-nibal* in the foreword to *The Hannibal Lecter Omnibus* (2001), "In the end I let them go, as you must let characters go, let Dr. Lecter and Clarice

Starling decided events according to their natures. There is a certain amount of courtesy involved" (x).

Allowing Starling to be one with Lecter, Harris redefines the genre as he did with *Red Dragon* and *The Silence of the Lambs,* by going against-the-grain and initiating a revival of originality. The rhetorical question is this: why must the hero live or sacrifice their life, and why must the villain be incarcerated or be killed? What if, say, both lived *and* both united? Why follow the same tired and old path walked a hundred times before?

Harris's ending, regardless of what critics say, redefines the genre yet again.

Whether *Hannibal* will one day become the masterpiece its predecessors *Red Dragon* and *The Silence of the Lambs* are, remains to be seen. The history of literature has shown us that bestsellers can disappear into oblivion just as easy as an unappreciated novel becoming a classic. Rather then reading *Hannibal* with preconceived notions or superficial expectations, it should be read with the eyes of those expecting a challenging read in which anything is possible. *Hannibal* is rich with fascinating insights into history and psychology, unexpected plotlines and above all, originality. If anything, *Hannibal* shows us that we should never determine the fates of our heroes and villains, for to do so, we rob ourselves of surprise and are likely to be unfulfilled. One would find it hard to locate another novel that was not only waited upon by millions, but delivered an ending *no one* expected. If to read is to be entertained or learn, *Hannibal* succeeded the moment a reader read the final page. One should appreciate what the author crafted for many a year and fairly cit the many successes and strengths the novel harbors. For those who wanted a predictable plot with Hollywood*esque* resolution, direct yourself to the countless novels of mediocre authors who can provide you as such. Thomas Harris is no such author, nor are his written masterpieces.

Works Consulted

Dickson, Jennifer. "Building the Blockade: New Truths in Survival Narratives from Leningrad." *Anthropology of East Europe Review,* vol. 13, no. 2 (Autumn 1995). http://condor.depaul.edu/~rrotenbe/aeer/aeer13_2/Dickenson.html. Accessed 1 Dec. 2007.

Harris, Thomas. *Red Dragon.* London: Corgi, 1983.

_____. *Silence of the Lambs.* London: Mandarin, 1989.

_____. *Hannibal.* London: William Heinemann /Random House, 1999.

_____. "Foreword to a Fatal Interview." *The Hannibal Lecter Omnibus.* London: William Heinemann / Random House, 2001.

_____. *Hannibal Rising*. London: William Heinemann / Random House, 2006.

Hawking, Stephen. *A Brief History of Time: From the Big Bang to Black Holes*. London: Bantam Books, 1988.

King, Stephen. "Hannibal the Cannibal." *New York Times,* 13 June 1999. www.nytimes.com/books/99/06/13/reviews/990613.13kingct.html. Accessed 1 Dec. 2007.

Machiavelli, Niccolo. *History of Florence and of the Affairs of Italy*. In *The Historical, Political, and Diplomatic Writings of Niccolo Machiavelli*, trans. from the Italian by Christian E. Detmold, in 4 vols. Boston: James R. Osgood and Co., 1882. http://oll.libertyfund.org/Texts/Machiavelli0156/Writings/HTMLs/Florence/0076-01_Pt03d_Books7-8.html. Accessed 1 Dec. 2007.

Moon, Brian. Correspondence, 22 June 2006.

O'Brien, Daniel. *The Hannibal Files: The Unauthorised Guide to the Hannibal Lecter Trilogy*. London: Reynolds and Hearn, 2001.

_____. Correspondence, July 2005.

Sexton, David. *The Strange World of Thomas Harris*. London: Short Books, 2001.

Spence, Jonathan D. *The Memory Palace of Matteo Ricci*. New York: Penguin (Non-Classics), 1985.

Yates, Frances A. *The Art of Memory*. London: Penguin, 1969.

Afterword

Mythmaker

CHARLES GRAMLICH

When we think of mythmakers and myths, most of us think of ancient times, of writers like Homer and Gods like Zeus and Apollo. We think of dragons, and the land of Faerie, and stories of Valkyries and Amazons. Yet, myth making didn't stop with the ancients. It continues into the modern age, around Boy Scout campfires and on the silver screens of Hollywood, from the mouths of everyday folk and from the word processors of writers throughout the world.

Most modern mythmakers are really myth "reshapers." They take old stories and archetypes and dress them in new clothing, which is largely what George Lucas did with *Star Wars* (1976). But humans are ever hungry for *new* myths, and new ones do develop, although not with the kind of predictability that the corporate heads in Hollywood would like.

The United States of America is still a fairly young country and we Americans have been eager to develop our own myths. We've done so with flair. Plymouth Rock! The First Thanksgiving! Valley Forge! None of these events appear to have happened quite like we believe, or want to believe, they happened. That doesn't matter. Myths are not literal truths, although they often express an *underlying* truth about an entire society.

One of the most enduring myths that we Americans have created is the myth of the Wild West, and it is one that we have even exported to other countries. I just finished reading part of a series of "westerns" written in England in the 1970s. Karl May (1842–1912), a German author, made good money in his home country from writing westerns, despite the fact that he only visited the United States once and never got further west than New York State. Sergio Leone, one of the most famous directors of movie westerns in history, was Italian.

One particular aspect of the Wild West myth is the way in which gunfighters and outlaws such as Billy the Kid and Jesse and Frank James have been turned into heroes. These men were not victims or freedom fighters. They certainly weren't Robin Hoods. They were criminals who killed and robbed innocent people. But in America such men often become the matrix from which legend develops.

In the past few decades in the United States, a new myth has been building, and it is following the pattern seen with the rehabilitation of outlaws like William Bonney and Jesse James. This is the developing myth of the super predator, the serial killer, and Thomas Harris is one of its major architects with his books about Hannibal Lecter.

Now, I don't mean to imply that there are no serial killers. We know plenty of them — David Berkowitz, Jeffrey Dahmer, John Wayne Gacy, Jr., Henry Lee Lucas. But the "mythic" serial killer that lives and preys in the modern imagination is quite different from these four, and from the other actual serial killers that we find in our prisons and on our death rows. The poster child for the serial killer *myth* is Hannibal Lecter.

Lecter was first introduced in the book *Red Dragon* (1981). He had already been arrested and was in a prison for the criminally insane. Will Graham, the FBI agent who captured Lecter, describes Hannibal as a "monster," as a "sociopath" with no guilt or remorse for the horrible acts he has committed. Graham makes a clear statement that Lecter engaged in sadistic acts against animals when he was a child, a common characteristic of real serial killers, and one that evokes an instinctive revulsion in the rest of us.

We also learn in *Red Dragon* that, while in the asylum, Lecter attacked a nurse who was attending him and tore out her tongue and one of her eyes with scarcely a spike in his pulse rate. We hear from Graham that Lecter is not "crazy," that he is perfectly capable of acting normally, but that he does horrible things simply because he enjoys them. We also see Lecter try to use his intelligence and his training as a psychiatrist to persuade another serial killer, Francis Dolarhyde, to punish Graham for catching Lecter.

These are not endearing descriptions and endearing behaviors. Hannibal Lecter is not a sympathetic character and is not intended to be. He is revoltingly evil, a characterization brought chillingly to life for millions by Anthony Hopkins in the movie *Silence of the Lambs*.

But Thomas Harris was not content to leave Lecter a villain. Or maybe it was the movie-going and reading public that was not content. The core process of mythmaking is the transmutation — perhaps transubstantiation would be a better word in Lecter's case — of one element into another. For Lecter, the revulsion we feel for the character in *Red Dragon* will change gradually into sympathy, and then into empathy. The villain will become the hero. This process began in *Silence of the Lambs* (1988), and although I'm referring mainly to the novel here much the same thing happens with the movie.

When we first meet Lecter in *Lambs* we see him as an educated, sophisticated, and highly intelligent individual. He has style and taste, and never loses his politeness even when confronted with the indignities of his position. We do see a bit of verbal cruelty in his conversational sparring with Clarice Starling, but we also see that he is one who "does not suffer fools lightly." We can respect the strength of his person and his personality.

Later in the book, Lecter's evil surfaces. He slaughters two policemen when he escapes from his cell in Memphis, Tennessee, leaving one of them partially gutted and the other without a face. We know both men as decent human beings, and although we can sympathize with Lecter's need to escape his captivity, we are revolted by his excessive cruelty.

At this point in *Lambs*, Hannibal Lecter has become the prototype for the "mythic" serial killer. He is a white male, highly intelligent, highly disciplined, and with exquisite tastes in art, music, and food. He is also a vicious sadist, but one that is highly creative in expressing his violent tendencies. It is a model followed by such writers as David L. Lindsey (*Mercy*, 1990), Dean Koontz (*Intensity*, 1995), and James Patterson (*Kiss the Girls*, 1995).

Thomas Harris was not content, however, with establishing Lecter as an archetypal villain. The transformation of Lecter had just started. In *Lambs*, we also learn that Hannibal can act for unselfish motives. Early in the book, a prisoner named Miggs throws semen on Clarice Starling when she comes to visit Lecter. Lecter punishes this behavior by driving Miggs into swallowing his own tongue. Lecter takes revenge for Clarice, who is unable to act on her own behalf.

At the end of *Lambs*, Lecter shows that he can even be *considerate* of others. He sends a thank-you note to a man in the asylum who was kind to him, and he also sends a note to Clarice to tell her that she is safe from him. In fact, Lecter's only threat at the end is to Dr. Frederick Chilton, the asylum's director, who is shown throughout as a petty, unscrupulous, and thoroughly unsympathetic character. Thus, the rehabilitation process begins.

It is in the book *Hannibal* (1999), third in the Lecter series, that we begin to see clear signs of Lecter's transformation from villain into hero. Part of the plot of *Hannibal* has Lecter being hunted by one of his previous victims, a man named Mason Verger, who barely survived Lecter's assault. Key, however, is the fact that Verger is a sadistic child molester, a villain far more despicable than Lecter could ever be. Now we see Lecter as an avenging angel, as someone who takes revenge for those who cannot avenge themselves. It is an extension of what he does *to* Miggs and *for* Clarice Starling in *Silence of the Lambs*. Even the death of another policeman in *Hannibal* does not revoke our growing sympathy for the character, because *this* policeman has betrayed his own principles and is seeking to sell Lecter to Verger.

Most importantly for the rehabilitation of Lecter, *Hannibal* reveals glimpses of the killer's childhood. We discover that at age six, with his parents newly dead in World War II Russia, Hannibal had to witness the death of his younger sister, Mischa, who was literally consumed by a band of deserters and criminals. Here is the ultimate appeal for sympathy from the readers. We don't want to see children suffer, but Hannibal has suffered more than we can bear. He loses his parents, his beloved sister, and his prayers to see Mischa again are only answered when he discovers her baby teeth in a stool pit. We learn that since that time, "Lecter had not been bothered by any considerations of deity, other than to recognize how his own modest predations paled beside those of God, who is in irony matchless, and in wanton malice beyond measure." Here is justification for Lecter's murders, provided in almost Biblical language.

And *now* Thomas Harris begins to cloak Hannibal in the robes of the hero. When Hannibal is tortured by Mason Verger's henchmen he bears it without crying out, without begging for mercy. When Clarice Starling is threatened, Hannibal moves to protect her, as if he were her white knight. This is the stuff of heroism in the American mindset. A hero withstands suffering. A hero protects the weak. A hero takes revenge.

It is in the last Lecter book so far, *Hannibal Rising* (2006), that the rehabilitation and transformation of Hannibal Lecter is complete. His early life is revealed to us in great detail. His natural sensitivities and intelligence shine through; his love of his little sister and his protective instincts toward her are revealed. In opposition to what was hinted at in *Red Dragon* about Hannibal, we see that he has *never* mistreated an animal. We see, instead, his kindness toward the family's horse, Cesar. We watch him attack a bully who threatens a young swan, and we learn that he is always a danger to bullies.

When Hannibal experiences the horrors of his childhood we are rooting for him completely. Even when he begins to kill, we root for him. Because the ones he kills are the ones who killed and *ate* his baby sister. In *Hannibal Rising* we again hear the word "monster" used to describe Lecter, but this time it is far from convincing because we have come to know him as a human being who is capable of love and who wants to be loved.

Real serial killers are not very much like Hannibal Lecter. Ted Bundy was said to be fairly intelligent, but most of them are neither highly educated nor very bright. They are not sensitive, urbane gentlemen who enjoy only the finest wines and the most delicate music. The are not often gourmands who delight in truffles and sweetmeats. They are not likely to be lovers of beautiful art, and if they have anything resembling love for beautiful women it's because they want to rape and kill them.

In short, real serial killers are not glamorous. They *are* monsters. They torture and murder for their own pleasure, or because they are insane, not because they are on some kind of search to truly experience life and beauty. They do not protect the weak and the innocent. They prey on them, as beasts. They do not feel sympathy or empathy when others suffer. They are sexually aroused.

A last thing needs to be said about real serial killers. Although some of them indeed have had horrendous childhoods, many of them have not. Many were born to loving parents and were not neglected or abused. And it must be said that many children, indeed *most* children, who *are* abused and neglected do not grow up to be serial killers. It is part of the modern serial killer myth that only an individual twisted early in life by the actions of others could become such a predator. This is not true, as much as we may wish it to *be* true.

Thomas Harris is not the only writer who helped create the myth of the modern serial killer. Such writers as Jonathan Kellerman (*The Butcher's Theater*, 1988) and the previously mentioned David L. Lindsey, Dean Koontz, and James Patterson certainly played a role. But no one has done it as well as Harris, and no serial killer has been so thoroughly transformed into a cultural icon as has Hannibal Lecter. Particularly, no one but Harris has yet dared turn a serial killer into a hero.

Mythmaking lives.

Thomas Harris has shown us the way.

About the Contributors

Scott D. Briggs is a freelance writer, essayist and critic who has been active in the professional, amateur and small press literary fields for over twenty years, specializing in horror, fantasy and SF literature, film, rock and roll, pop, alternative and modern classical music. He has written previous essays for Necronomicon Press and Greenwood Press on the works of William Peter Blatty and Robert Aickman; reviews and essays for *Lovecraft Studies* and *Studies in Weird Fiction*, and various pieces for periodicals such as *The NY Arts Magazine, The Big Takeover* and *www.sequenza21.com*, with a forthcoming critical essay on Robert Bloch for a volume on Bloch to be published by McFarland. He earned a B.F.A. in communication arts and sciences in 1992 from NYIT Old Westbury, N.Y. Mr. Briggs makes his home in Long Island, N.Y., and is also a film devotee, an avid 6- and 12-string guitarist, and enjoys collecting books, music, and films, and, of course, enjoys Italian food, ice cream and playing with cats like one of his all-time idols, H.P. Lovecraft.

John Goodrich has been fascinated by the strange, the grotesque, and man's inhumanity to man, since childhood and consequently decided to teach. He holds a bachelor's degree in English education and a master's in curriculum and instruction, and his shelves groan under the weight of his books on H.P. Lovecraft, necromancy, and World War One. For the past six years, he has been a regular contributor to the *Esoteric Order of Dagon*, an APA of H.P. Lovecraft and weird tales scholars. In the past year, he has sold five short stories, and looks forward to building a career from this start. He recently appeared in *Two-Gun Bob: A Centennial Study of Robert E. Howard* (2006).

Charles Gramlich is professor of psychology at a small university in New Orleans. He is a long-term member of REHupa, the Robert E. Howard

United Press Association, and is assistant editor of *The Dark Man: The Journal of Robert E. Howard Studies*. He is also an author of over seventy short stories, around eighty articles and essays, and about fifty poems. His novel *Cold in the Light* (2003) is still in print and has received excellent reviews.

Phillip A. Ellis has published hundreds of poems in a variety of international magazines, journals, fanzines and e-anthologies and two volumes, *Strange Gardens* (2005) and *21 Sonnets* (2005). He is the editor of *Calenture: A Journal of Studies in Speculative Verse* (http://www.calenture.fcpages.com/) and *Wild Grapes: Australian Poetry* (http://australian-poetry.blogspot.com/). He is also an accomplished critic of poetry who has appeared in *Studies in Weird Fiction, Lost Worlds: The Journal of Clark Ashton Smith Studies* and *Eldritch Dark.com*, to name but a few.

S.T. Joshi is a widely published critic and editor. He is the author of such critical studies as *The Weird Tale* (1990), *H.P. Lovecraft: The Decline of the West* (1990), and *The Modern Weird Tale* (McFarland, 2001). He has edited the standard corrected edition of H. P. Lovecraft's collected fiction, revisions, and miscellaneous writings (1984–95; 5 vols.), as well as *The Ancient Track: Complete Poetical Works* (2001) and *Collected Essays* (2004–6; 5 vols.). He has prepared three annotated editions of Lovecraft's tales (1999–2004). His exhaustive biography, of Lovecraft *H.P. Lovecraft: A Life* (1996), won the British Fantasy Award and the Bram Stoker Award from the Horror Writers Association. He is the founder and editor of *Lovecraft Studies* (1979f.) and *Studies in Weird Fiction* (1986f.). Joshi has done scholarly work on other authors of supernatural fiction. He is the author of a bibliography (1993) and critical study of Lord Dunsany (*Lord Dunsany: Master of the Anglo-Irish Imagination,* 1995), and a critical study of Ramsey Campbell (*Ramsey Campbell and Modern Horror Fiction,* 2001). He has prepared editions of the work of Arthur Machen, Algernon Blackwood, Lord Dunsany, M. R. James, Arthur Quiller-Couch, Donald Wandrei, and other writers. In recent years he has turned his attention to Ambrose Bierce and is the co-editor (with Stefan Dziemianowicz) of *World Supernatural Literature: An Encyclopedia* (2005; 3 vols.).

Ali S. Karim is a freelance journalist and book reviewer living in England. In addition to being the assistant editor of the e-zine *Shots*, he's also a contributing editor at *The Rap Sheet and January Magazine*, writes for *Deadly Pleasures* and *Crimespree* magazines and is an associate member (and literary judge) of both the British Crime Writers Association and The International Thriller Writers Inc. He also helps judge Deadly Pleasures' Barry Awards. Karim is currently working on *Black Operations*, a violent SF-tinged thriller.

Tony Magistrale is professor of English at the University of Vermont. He has taught courses in writing and American literature there since 1983 when he returned to the United States after a Fulbright post-doctoral fellowship at the University of Milan, Italy. He has lectured at many universities in North America and Western Europe, most recently serving as visiting professor of American studies at the University of Augsburg, Germany. He obtained a Ph.D. at the University of Pittsburgh in 1981. Over the past two decades, Magistrale's publications have covered a broad area of interests. He has authored books and essays on the writing process, international study abroad, and his own poetry. But the majority of his books have centered on defining and tracing Anglo-American Gothicism, from its origins in eighteenth-century romanticism to its contemporary manifestations in popular culture, particularly in the work of Stephen King; a dozen of his scholarly books and many published journal articles have illuminated the genre's narrative themes, psychological and social contexts, and historical development. He is frequently cited in scholarly books dealing with the interdisciplinary aspects of American horror art, and has been interviewed on PBS television; ABC Radio, Australia; and by *The New Yorker, Cinescape, The Miami Herald, The Boston Globe, The Baltimore Sun, New York Daily News, The St. Louis Post-Dispatch, The St. Petersburg Times.*

Davide Mana is a paleontologist specializing in statistical analysis of dead populations and the application of new technologies to the study of the past, and he has a few publications to his credit. A long-time reader of fantasy and science-fiction, he has also published essays and short stories in the field and acted as editor and translator for three volumes of the Italian anthology of international fiction *Alia* (2003–2005). Apart from his fossil-related research he is currently reviewing books and maintaining the column "A Natural History of Fantasy Fiction" for the Turin-based literary magazine *LibriNuovi*, taking care of the fourth *Alia* anthology, putting his finishing touches on his first book (about dinosaurs and popular culture) and generally causing more embarrassment among his fellow bone-hunters in academia. He wishes to express his gratitude to Riccardo Valla and Ken Asamatsu for being fellow Leiberians and a timely source of inspiration twenty years apart, to Dr. Giorgio Arduini for long nights spent discussing criminology and for bibliographical support, and to Dr. Silvia Treves for the insight on victim guilt and serial murders in fiction His essay for this volume is dedicated to his parents and three cats, Mousti, Emma and Tubo.

Peter Messent is professor of modern American literature at the University of Nottingham in England. He is the author of *New Readings of the American Novel: Narrative Theory and its Application* (1990), *Ernest Hemingway* (1992), *Mark Twain* (1997) and *The Short Works of Mark Twain: A Critical Study* (2001). He is editor of *Criminal Proceedings: The Contemporary American Crime Novel* (1997) and co-editor of *A Companion to Mark Twain* (2005) and *The Civil War Letters of Joseph Hopkins Twichell* (2006). He has published in many others areas of American Literature and is at present working on a study of Mark Twain, male friendship and Victorian America.

Daniel O'Brien received his BA in film studies and theology in 1988 and his MA in film studies in 1990. A freelance writer with over fifteen years of experience, ranging from encyclopaedia entries and articles to full-length biographies and critical studies, such as *The Hannibal Files* (2001), *World of the Rings* (2002) *Spooky Encounters* (2003) and, most recently, *The BFI Reference Guide to British and Irish Film Directors* (2006).

Philip L. Simpson received his bachelor's and master's degrees in English from Eastern Illinois University in 1986 and 1989, and his doctorate in American literature from Southern Illinois University in 1996. A professor of communications and humanities at the Palm Bay campus of Brevard Community College in Florida for eight years and chair of the Communications and Humanities Department for five years, he is now serving as academic dean of Behavioral/Social Sciences and Humanities at Brevard Community College. He also serves as vice president of the Popular Culture Association and area chair of horror for the Association since 1998. He received the Association's Felicia Campbell Area Chair Award in 2006. He is a book reviewer and was elected Member-at-Large for the Association and a member of the editorial board for the *Journal of Popular Culture*. His book, *Psycho Paths: Tracking the Serial Killer Through Contemporary American Film and Fiction*, was published in 2000. He contributed the foreword to *Dark Parades: The Spectacle of Isolation in Horror Films*, by Carl Royer and Diana Royer (2005). His essays of literary, cultural, and cinematic criticism have also been published in journals such as *Cineaction, Paradoxa, Clues,* and *Notes on Contemporary Literature*; encyclopedias such as *Encyclopedia of the Documentary Film* (2005), *Twenty-First Century British and Irish Novelists* (2003), *Conspiracy Theories in American History* (2003), *The Guide to United States Popular Culture* (2001), *War and American Popular Culture* (1999), and *The Encyclopedia of Novels into Film* (1998); and books such as *Horror Film: Creating and Marketing Film* (2004); *The Terministic Screen: Rhetorical Perspectives on Film* (2003); *Car Crash Culture* (2002); *Jack Nicholson: Movie Top Ten* (2000); and *Mythologies of Violence in Postmodern Media* (1999).

Benjamin Szumskyj is a high school teacher currently teaching at a private Christian high school. He is currently undertaking an external diploma at Tabor Bible College, Western Australia, and was formerly the librarian of that institution. He has written dozens of essays and articles on literary criticism for publications such as *Notes in Contemporary Literature, Wormwood,* www.swordandsorcery.org, and *Calenture: A Journal of Studies in Speculative Verse* and has co-edited books on critical studies such as *Fritz Leiber & H. P.*

Lovecraft: Writers of the Dark (with S.T. Joshi); *Robert E. Howard: Power of the Writing Mind* (with Leo Grin); *Fantasy Commentator # 57/58: Fritz Leiber Theme Issue* (with A. Langley Searles); *Fritz Leiber: Critical Essays* (McFarland); and *Two-Gun Bob: A Centennial Study of Robert E. Howard.*

Robert H. Waugh earned his Ph.D. from Harvard in comparative literature. Besides several poems in little magazines, he has published essays on David Lindsay, Olaf Stapledon, Arthur C. Clarke, Samuel Delany, J.R.R. Tolkien, and H.P. Lovecraft. His literary study of Lovecraft, *The Monster in the Mirror*, was published in 2006. Since 1968 he has taught in the English department of SUNY New Paltz, where he is a professor.

Tony Williams is professor and area head of film studies in the Department of English at Southern Illinois University Carbondale. Author of *Hearths of Darkness: The Family in the American Horror Film* (1996); *Larry Cohen: Radical Allegories of an American Filmmaker* (1997); *The Cinema of George A. Romero: Knight of the Living Dead* (2003) and *Body and Soul: The Cinematic Vision of Robert Aldrich* (2004), he has co-edited *Horror International* (2005) with Steven Jay Schneider and is currently engaged in co-editing an anthology on the political horror film.

Index